1

A World Held Hostage by Cyber

PRESIDENT DONALD JOHN TRUMP was sworn in on January 20, 2017, with Barack Obama's warning on North Korea fresh in his ear, political and legal storm clouds gathering around Russia's role in his election, and little apparent interest in or knowledge about cybersecurity, a key undercurrent of both the Korean and the Russian situations.

Cyber didn't rate a mention in an inaugural speech delivered in the rain and chiefly remembered as a battle cry for supporters and a stark warning for political foes and the various elites he loved to harangue.

That omission was no surprise, but it represented the start of a jolting change from Trump's two immediate predecessors, Obama and George W. Bush, who both grasped the transformational challenges of cybersecurity. Obama would make it a central feature of his administration, though whether his cyber achievements lived up to the impressive rhetoric and high aspirations fueled years of debates.

But cyber was that kind of issue: Failures and flaws could be spectacularly visible to everyone; successes were hard to quantify or brag about.

"Success in our field means nothing happened," said Matthew Scholl, one of the government's cybersecurity gurus. "That can be a tough thing to sell."

Trump, annoyed and threatened by what he claimed was a false narrative about collusion and the Russian hacking of the 2016 election, wanted little to do with cyber. He gave a short nod to the policy needs during the transition: "Within 90 days, we will be coming up with a major report on hacking defense, how do we stop this new phenomena—fairly new phenomena—because the United States is hacked by everybody."

Everybody was hacked by everybody. The hacks wouldn't stop, and the threat was evolving at machine-speed, in directions unforeseen just a few years earlier.

The nature of the cybersecurity threatscape was redefined by Russian-directed hacks and surreptitious social media campaigns aimed at helping elect Trump in 2016, but the classic hacks—including Russian infiltration of America's energy distribution and supply systems—also were moving to another level. In fact, the "traditional" cyber threats were changing every year, from the "big four" nation-state adversaries Russia, China, Iran, and North Korea, as well as from criminal enterprises, political hacktivists, and even terrorists. It was possible that the catch-all Russia "collusion" issue—encompassing allegations of conspiracy between the Trump campaign and Russian operatives and obstruction of justice charges—was taking policymakers' attention away from other emerging problems. Maybe that was the plan, deep in an espionage agency's warrens somewhere across the globe. And maybe it just reflected the chaotic, ultra-high-velocity pace of change in cyberspace. In any case, a dangerous cyber environment was becoming more complex and challenging.

A senior official who worked in administrations of both parties called Trump's fixation on belittling and batting away anything to do with Russia's aggressive cyber activities "a terrible distraction." It absorbed the energies of both the executive and the legislative branches and inhibited the federal government's ability to draw lessons from the 2016 election hacks or to put the necessary thought into crafting a true national cyber strategy. The source, a serious national security policymaker not given to either overstatement or alarmism, asked in an August 2018 email, "WHO IS TAKING CARE OF THE RED BLINKING weapons inside the USA? OMG. It's all really frightening."

A month later, the source replied to a question about Trump's cyber policy: "We have an existential threat to the USA—he has been informed in writing and in voice—and he is doing nothing."

Hacking tools were growing more sophisticated, and bad actors were increasingly willing to use them. The lines between nation-state cyber actors and the criminals of the "dark web" were blurring as all gained access to the same superadvanced cyber weapons. Hospital systems and city governments could be brought to their knees in ransom attacks, while entire nations braced for cyber warfare.

Social media had been weaponized, and Facebook data (surrendered both willingly and unwittingly by users) was used as fuel for any number of malicious cyber campaigns. Donald Trump himself was "click bait," one established security pro noted. Bad actors in cyberspace knew that "Trump" translated into clicks and downloads of links that could be secretly loaded with all kinds of malware to infect computers and devices.

"This presidency has been such an anomaly. People say, 'He said what?!' and click on the Trump stories and inadvertently install malware," Jeremy Batterman of the Chicago-based threat-hunting firm Trustwave observed.

The Trump phenomenon—a Twitter-driven presidency using social media and any other platform to whip up followers and mock foes on the most explosive topics in American politics—was the perfect match for that hacking phenomenon the president-elect noted in December 2016.

Donald Trump didn't create these vulnerabilities in the digital world, he wasn't responsible for hackers hitching a ride on his name, and clearly he didn't intend to reshape the cybersecurity landscape. Cybersecurity and the nuances of the digital economy simply weren't his issues. But that didn't matter, because the forty-fifth president came into office in the middle of a sweeping social and technological revolution that seemed likely to tower over the accomplishments of any single president in the first few decades of the twenty-first century.

Cyber war, espionage, theft, ransomware, and threats still unimagined came hand in hand with the wondrous advances of this digital age.

Vikram Phatak, founder of NSS Labs, an Austin-based tester of cybersecurity products, reached back to the late sixteenth century for the proper analogy for the cyber world during the Trump era.

Foreign powers were using "privateers" or cyber mercenaries to raid America's computer infrastructure, much as the British Crown used sailors of fortune to attack the seemingly superior Spanish fleet over four hundred years ago. In this scenario, the United States risked losing its preeminent place in world affairs, just as Spain did at the hands of the British.

Speaking in the summer of 2018, Phatak said 1.4 percent of global GDP was going to cyber criminals, and that number was rising. "The thing is, some countries are staying afloat because of it—the merging of criminal activity with nation-state activity is alarming." He cited Russia and North Korea as two countries that banked on revenue from cyber theft in the same way other nations counted on sales tax or income tax receipts.

"The last time we saw a spike like this" in state-sponsored theft, Phatak said, "Queen Elizabeth was giving privateers license to steal from Spanish ships, and the Spanish were the ones with the rules-based society."

He said the British government of the late sixteenth century had "plausible deniability" about the plundering taking place out at sea—like China in today's cyberspace, perhaps—and that in the end, "Sir Francis Drake was knighted and the English got themselves deep-water warfighting experience," plus the stolen treasures.

"My concern is that we're the Spanish," Phatak said. "We see the moves by the Russians on the political front—it's all tied together. You can indict them, but so what? I'm very concerned. Cybersecurity needs a national security approach rather than law enforcement."

Director of National Intelligence Dan Coats in early 2019 spelled out the diverse nature of the threats for what seemed the umpteenth time: "We anticipate that financially motivated cyber criminals very likely will expand their targets in the United States in the next few years. Their actions could increasingly disrupt US critical infrastructure in the healthcare, financial, government, and emergency service sectors, based on the patterns of activities against these sectors in the last few years."

Coats said, "Terrorists could obtain and disclose compromising or personally identifiable information through cyber operations, and they may use such disclosures to coerce, extort, or to inspire and enable physical attacks against their victims. Terrorist groups could cause some disruptive effects—defacing websites or executing denial-of-service attacks against poorly protected networks—with little to no warning."

And in this world, a president tweeted and used his mobile device to conduct the nation's most sensitive business, with no apparent concern for security despite anxious efforts of his staff.

In 2017, Trump's first year in power, the hacks and viruses in the cyber headlines included consumer credit-rating agency Equifax; WannaCry; the devastating NotPetya attack that used a stolen National Security Agency tool and struck first in Ukraine before taking down transportation and other systems across the globe; Yahoo!; Uber; and the WikiLeaks revelation of "CIA Vault 7" and "CIA Vault 8," putting some of the most advanced hacking tools out into the public realm.

The next year brought hacks aimed at the Seoul Olympics; ransomware that crippled Atlanta municipal government for days; a major breach at hotelier Marriott; the Facebook hack, compounding that company's cyber problems beyond the well-known misuse of its users' data; many other garden-variety hacks at retailers like Lord & Taylor and Saks Fifth Avenue; and a deeply concerning malware linked to Russia, called VPNFilter, that infected a half million routers in May 2018.

Why the worry among cyber pros about this one? The malware was designed to "actively seek out industrial control traffic and pivot into those networks," Matt Watchinski of Cisco explained. This so-called cyber-physical threat could include the use of malware to infiltrate and disrupt industrial control systems that ran chemical production lines and all kinds of manufacturing processes. As the "Internet of Things" grew and cities became "smart cities" with online interconnections of everything from traffic signals to office building temperatures, the cyber-physical threat was getting more and more dangerous to all citizens.

Back to the hacking hit parade: Nonbrand names with huge impacts on consumers suffered major attacks, including marketing firm Exactis, where a database containing over three hundred million individual records was exposed.

A July 2018 blog by security writer David Bisson found that, in the first half of 2018, "the number of records compromised in Q1 and Q2 2018 [had] already surpassed the total number of breached records for all of 2017, as identified in Identity Theft Resource Center's 2017 Data Breach Industry Summary report." He wrote, "There were plenty of additional data breaches that took place in the first half of 2018, which means the number of compromised records could actually be much higher. Only time will tell whether this is actually the case."

The rest of the year proved it was the case.

"I think 2018 confirms that the diversity of threats we are seeing requires a continued strengthening of collaboration within industry and among industry and government," said Scott Algeier, executive director of the Information Technology Information Sharing and Analysis Center, a body that shared cyber threat data across company lines for the betterment of the entire ecosystem. "The actors are too advanced and diverse for either industry or government to address on their own."

A year-end cyberattack on Tribune Publishing Company affected various newspapers and raised policy concerns.

"Reports on the cyber incidents disrupting newspapers distribution indicate that it was ransomware affecting back-office systems. That in itself is unremarkable," said former Department of Homeland Security (DHS) cyber chief Suzanne Spaulding. "However, there were some indicators linking it to the malware behind WannaCry. There was also at least one report that the message that appeared in place of encrypted files did not specify a ransom amount."

WannaCry was a malware used to take control of computers in order to demand ransom from the device's owner. It "appears to have *originally been discovered by the NSA*, which allegedly kept it on file as a potential tool to use for surveillance or other issues," CNET explained. "We found out about it because a group of hackers, known as Shadow Brokers, in April [2017] released a cache of stolen NSA documents on the internet, including details about the WannaCry vulnerability."

What did that all mean? Well, if true, Spaulding said in an interview with Inside Cybersecurity, "that raises a question of whether it might have been in retaliation for, or designed to deter, negative reporting in Tribune papers that the perpetrator—N. Korea?—didn't like—a la 'The Interview,'" a 2015 movie that allegedly spurred the infamous North Korean–linked attack on Sony

Pictures. That hack ended up costing top Sony executives their jobs when not-so-flattering emails, plus the company's most sensitive internal data, were exposed in retaliation for a movie that mocked Kim Jong-un.

"In any event," Spaulding said, "this latest incident is yet another reminder of the importance of having plans in place to reduce the consequences of such a disruption. We have moved from a world in which theft of personal information was the only cyber risk most companies worried about to one in which business disruption from malware is increasingly common."

This threat environment meant major adjustments for US businesses trying to protect themselves.

Spaulding said, "CEOs and boards need to ensure that they fully understand how business operations can be disrupted by a loss of data confidentiality, access, or integrity, as well as disruptions to operational technology like industrial control systems. And they need to have plans in place to mitigate those disruptions. We've traditionally focused almost entirely on preventing cyber incidents and not nearly enough on planning for how to best operate in the face of a successful cyber incident."

"We live in a world where cyber attack continues to be occurring and individuals and businesses continue to increase security measures," an energy sector source said dryly. "This will continue in 2019." The attacks increased, the security efforts increased, and . . . the attacks increased.

The parade of hacks marched on in 2019. The City of Baltimore was held hostage for weeks in a ransomware attack, with hackers demanding about $100,000 in bitcoin after freezing up many of the city's digital services. ASUS computers were infected with malware—ASUS patched the vulnerability, it said—the Federal Emergency Management Agency and the Oregon Department of Human Services were compromised, college applicants received ransomware notes, a site selling baseball cards was infected, and more, much more.

It wasn't just hacks, explained Mike Echols, a former DHS cyber official who created the International Association of Certified ISAOs, a threat-information sharing group, and later founded a company called MAX Cybersecurity.

"I believe the analysis and scanning that is being done [by infiltrators] is actually worse than specific incidents of hacking," Echols observed. "We all wonder when the big attack is going to occur and to what sector. With the proper insight on slowly resolved vulnerabilities and an understanding of the potential consequences, the adversary is more powerful. It will be possible to deliver a high-consequence blow."

He sketched out a key question for policymakers. "I think the technology opportunities that spark companies and the stock markets expand our reach, but also should make it clear security needs to be a thought at the beginning of the process. . . . Don't engineers/architects have to be certified before they build buildings? So, where is the requirement, when building virtual systems that affect the lives of millions?"

Echols said, "We still haven't learned that the government has a responsibility to lead and protect its citizens. We are letting this thing get so out of hand there will be no putting it back in the box; just victims all around the box. Newly established [DHS] fly-away teams are required, but forcing mechanisms on the network owner can no longer be overlooked. Somebody has to own being the person industry hates and be okay with it."

That was a salute to talented "fly-away" teams of cyber experts from the Department of Homeland Security who would quickly arrive at a company's door in the midst of an attack. They were good, Echols said, and well appreciated in the private sector. But they couldn't be everywhere or respond to every significant hack. So he was also issuing a call for regulation, strict government requirements that companies implement cybersecurity measures. The Obama administration had considered taking a "coercive" regulatory approach toward industry but ultimately shied away, viewing it as politically difficult, if not impossible. The new Trump administration seemed unlikely to consider it.

But the evolving threats demanded new approaches to security. Bad actors were coming up with new methods of attack at around the same speed as defenders were crafting defenses. Data destruction as a means of attackers covering their tracks—akin to burglars burning down the house to get rid of fingerprints—and credential theft for unknown purposes were two fast-growing areas of concern.

The Department of Homeland Security "has stepped up its game in both notifying and protecting American corporations," said Tom Kellermann of the security firm Carbon Black. "That being said, American cyberspace is a free-fire zone with a multiplicity of actors."

He called for high-profile government alerts to the public on the ever-changing tactics of bad actors in cyberspace.

Phatak of NSS Labs said in an email, "There is an ecosystem of 'bad guys'—exploit developers + malware developers + attackers who compromise watering hole websites + fast flux exploit / malware hosting websites + spear phishers that lure people to exploit/malware websites + command and control backend, etc."

It was as bad as it sounded, Phatak said, and "the single biggest problem is the number of infections that are dormant or at least staying hidden under the radar that can be co-opted for an alternate purpose. Just because an employee is infected with a crypto currency mining malware today doesn't mean someone won't purchase access to that employee's computer for a more nefarious purpose tomorrow. . . . Analogy: When you go into the hospital, the first thing they do is stick you with an intravenous injection so that they can give you whatever drugs they want later on."

The bad guys were putting intravenous tubing into systems across the internet, prepping them to receive injections later of . . . anything.

"Having said that," Phatak said, "I think DHS, FBI, and other agencies have a lot of visibility into that ecosystem and who is infected. The challenge becomes competing priorities. Is it worth it to break up a criminal 'crypto-mining' enterprise when they also have ties to terrorists? Or is it better to gain intel? It is a complicated problem that doesn't have an easy answer."

In crypto-mining operations, bad guys surreptitiously used others' computers to create bitcoin. They could take over an office's systems in the evening and use its power to generate crypto currency while no one was around to notice the surge in activity on their network. It was rampant by 2019—and at the lower end of the threat scale. But like so much in cyberspace, it could mask entirely different and much more dangerous activity.

These were the issues, challenges, and threats cyber professionals were considering. A duality of messages permeated gatherings of the cybersecurity community: Security tools were improving, and business and government entities alike were better organizing themselves, and yet the cyber threat environment continued to darken and grow more dangerous.

Part of the reason for that, said Jeff Moss, founder of the annual Las Vegas "hacker" conferences Black Hat and DEF CON, was because offensive actions in cyberspace, such as hacks, were largely a technical matter, while cyber defense involved political questions such as how much to spend and what to prioritize.

"The technology we're creating favors offense . . . on defense, we're stuck with politics," Moss said in an opening speech at Black Hat USA 2018. "We have to build a whole culture around defense."

The audiences at these conferences ranged from vendors of security products to "white hat hackers"—researchers who examine products and the seams of the internet for weaknesses and report their findings—to young people seeking to break into the burgeoning field and law enforcement personnel looking to share insights and pick up new tools.

Google director of engineering Parisa Tabriz, who followed Moss onstage at Black Hat USA 2018, said the key was an "offensive strategy for security."

Google's "Project Zero" was created with that plan in mind, she said, and was showing practical successes such as pushing the shift to "https" and to faster and more useful disclosure of vulnerabilities by software and product vendors.

At events like Black Hat, there was pushback from cyber pros on widely reported threats such as the Russians' alleged newfound ability in 2018 to shut off the lights across the United States. But that didn't mute the underlying theme that nation-states, criminals, and hacktivists alike were wielding cyber powers that threatened every aspect of digital life in the United States.

"The type of threats seen only in the Department of Defense space are showing up all over," Raytheon's Mark Orlando told Inside Cybersecurity. "From a threat/attack perspective, we saw this coming from nation-states a long time ago. But now, those threats are much more commoditized and are showing up in private industry, even from unsophisticated attackers."

A research report unveiled at Black Hat by cybersecurity firm IntSights found tools for sophisticated distributed denial-of-service attacks available on the dark web for less than $800—"bigger than anything I've seen, you can launch a full-scale attack on a government website for very cheap," Itay Kozuch of IntSights said.

State and local government officials appearing at DEF CON explained they were facing sophisticated phishing and scanning operations amid ongoing resource challenges. "It's kind of like Andy in Mayberry being sent to deal with a foreign invasion," said Noah Praetz, then director of elections in Cook County, Illinois.

"Phishing is still the way bad guys get in" to corporate systems as well, Andrew Howard of Kudelski Security told Inside Cybersecurity. He said ransomware, distributed denial-of-service attacks, and general cyber hygiene were increasingly hot topics of discussion around corporate boardrooms.

"The perceived increase in nation-state threats is the number one trend of the year, along with threats to the grid infrastructure," said Tim Erlin of Tripwire, whose firm issued a report at Black Hat USA 2018 on "The State of Cyber Hygiene." "It's not the time to panic but it is time to be concerned," he said.

"Depressing," Phatak responded, when asked to describe the current threat environment.

"They are not really afraid," IntSights's Kozuch commented on the activity of bad actors in the dark spaces of the internet. Companies as well as governments needed to get better at sharing information and "consuming intelligence" to understand the threat, he said.

"Know your enemy," he said, because "not doing anything is very wrong."

Cut-rate prices for powerful cyberattack tools, hacktivist sites with stolen bounty ranging from government personnel files to data from politicians' cell phones, and Chinese sites offering a full gamut of illicit services and products—for yuan, not bitcoin—were among the findings in an IntSights report examining the dark web in Asia.

The report was the culmination of "six months of digging and digging" that went beyond examinations of hacking commonly attributed to Russia, China, and North Korea in order to examine the "dark . . . cyber society" in Asia that posed serious national security threats, according to Kozuch.

Starting with research on the dark web in Japan and "expanding from there" into China, South Korea, Indonesia, Vietnam, and other countries, the research offered a rare look into the criminal underworld operating on the web throughout Asia.

"These websites, nobody really knows them," Kozuch told Inside Cybersecurity. "You need to know the language, the terminology. It takes a lot of time but now we're in good shape."

"We found a lot of things we've never seen before" on sites housed in China, for instance. "We found new malware, tools and techniques, all in Chinese. We found new [criminal] groups. Now we can better understand what's going on in China. The research showed how much we don't know and why Asia is the biggest threat for cyber attacks."

One Chinese site offered distributed denial-of-service attacks powerful enough to "take down a government website" for less than $800. A Japanese-language site was found bartering in prime military, political, scientific, and technological intelligence. A Vietnamese "Anonymous" group "publishes entire stolen databases, going to a different level of crime," Kozuch said.

That hacktivist group's work included the 2016 leak of FBI and DHS employee databases and—in May 2018—a leak from the phone of Andrea Manafort, daughter of Paul Manafort, who was sentenced to a prison term for acts detailed in special prosecutor Robert Mueller's probe of the 2016 election hack.

An Indonesian hacktivist group offered instruction on attack methods and provided malware as a "giveaway," Kozuch said.

And, he said, "this is the tip of the iceberg."

Kozuch said hunters like himself, operating in the dark web, were aware they were being monitored by the bad guys and "sometimes we get caught. But we know what we're doing, how to disappear and how to be a fly on the wall. We provide the best early warnings we can provide."

Finding the proper policy responses to these challenges, however, was "complicated," Kozuch said. Having "a top-notch security system is not enough." He called for better and more meaningful cyber threat information sharing as well as a commitment by corporations and others to "consume intelligence reports in order to understand the risks."

"It's not just technology, it starts with high-level risk assessments," he said.

Info-sharing could be bolstered by "strong regulation" and mandatory reporting with companies required to tell government authorities about cyber incidents, he suggested, while adding, "The Asian dark web is huge and we've just started to understand how big it is. The threat is a lot bigger than we imagined."

Security firm Tripwire found a disturbing assortment of shortcomings in how companies were performing cybersecurity basics, including poor "visibility" into their own systems, inadequate scanning, and other issues.

"A lot of attention is going to artificial intelligence, machine learning—but a lot of companies are still struggling with the basics," Tripwire's Erlin said. "We're hopeful that people see this report as a tool to drive foundational adoption of [basic] controls."

Erlin called himself "a big fan of well-crafted regulation to drive change" in cybersecurity at companies. His firm found that "most organizations implement good basic protections around administrative privileges, but as low-hanging fruit, these controls should be in place at more organizations."

That was basic cybersecurity blocking and tackling, the fundamentals, and it wasn't being done often enough.

About thirty thousand websites were being infected every day, said Darren Guccione, CEO of the Chicago-based Keeper security firm, who cited a statistic bandied about in security circles for several years. Fully 80 percent of breaches were due to poor password security. And 80 percent of Americans reused their credentials across multiple sites and services. Ninety percent of email passwords could be cracked in less than six hours, Guccione said.

In the meantime, cyber as a policy area was immune for a while as Trump romped through official Washington, trampling traditions, customs, manners, and policies. Cyber was nonpartisan, new, and technological, meaning it could be perceived by the new president as an area for specialists. Ordering better log management was someone else's job.

But cyber was about structures and policies as well as about technology, and about people and relationships. That meant it wasn't just a narrow field of experts like surgeons or scientists whom Trump could respect and leave to their work. Rather, it was political, in terms of choices and priorities, as Moss suggested, and it was a problem. Thus, the Trump trampling would come soon enough.

Political turmoil and uncertainty over the president's views and actions toward Russia would be the proximate cause, but his style of thrashing through issues cuts a swath through cyber policy. The cybersecurity ecosystem somehow hangs on and shows its own resilience amid the challenges and contradictions.

Looking at his first term, Trump freed up cyber warriors in the military while his administration launched collaborations with the private sector on big threats like "botnets"—automated attacks using hijacked computers and devices—and promised a moonshot-type crash project to secure the internet within ten years.

However, he put short-term maneuvering on trade issues with China above strategic cyber considerations, regardless of broad consensus within the cyber community on the need for consistent pressure on the Chinese in cyberspace. In the midst of the 2018–2019 federal government shutdown, Trump said he found more "honor" in the Chinese Communist leadership than he could discern in new House Speaker Nancy Pelosi (D-CA) or Senate Democratic leader Charles Schumer of New York, who were sitting across from him at the negotiating table.

"I find China, frankly, in many ways to be far more honorable than Cryin' Chuck and Nancy. I really do. I think that China is actually much easier to deal with than the opposition party."

Trump undermined his own administration's sanctions on Russia for cyber and other violations of international norms and laws by embracing Vladimir Putin's denials of hacking in the 2016 elections. The Trump White House narrative on Russia and cyber was that the new president acted, with the toughest sanctions ever on Moscow—or at least since the Cold War days of the Soviet Union—while the Obama administration dithered. As with many of Donald Trump's sweeping statements, there was a smidgen of truth here.

Ari Schwartz, a cybersecurity director on President Obama's National Security Council, acknowledged the previous administration's hesitancy to act against Russian interference efforts during the 2016 campaign. Officials endlessly pondered the potential ramifications of going public or taking direct action. It was new territory, policywise, and an Obama team that had eagerly taken on cyber issues found itself flat-footed and paralyzed by analysis.

But—and it's a big one—amid disagreements in the Obama years over roles, responsibilities, and priorities, the usual stuff of policy debates, there was general consensus on who the bad actors were in cyberspace. The adversaries were China, Russia, Iran, and North Korea, cyber criminal organizations and lone-wolf cyberattackers acting for profit, political motivations, or perhaps for kicks. The question of who the bad guys were, in the Trump years, was constantly muddied by the president himself. Whether it was Putin, Chinese president Xi Jinping, or North Korea's Kim Jong-un, Trump found things to like about all of them and expressed that odd admiration in ways that tended to negate get-tough steps coming out of his Pentagon, Justice Department, or State Department.

On the domestic front, Trump ruptured US work across a range of cyber areas by triggering the longest government shutdown ever. He downgraded cybersecurity as a policy area at the White House and State Department by axing senior cyber coordinator positions, dismissing them as redundancies.

The president installed a chairman at the Federal Communications Commission who immediately scrapped years of work designed to put the telecom sector at the leading edge of cybersecurity and abandoned efforts to secure—at the start—fifth-generation "5G" wireless networks.

Trump's approach to cyber was entirely transactional and not grounded in any principle, said NSS's Phatak, who was particularly confounded by the president's decision to eliminate the cybersecurity coordinator office in the White House that had been a key point of contact for cyber stakeholders.

Cybersecurity, complex and intriguing, was an area of much consensus across the body politic and the business world as Trump came into office. The "Trump phenomenon" didn't break the cyber community into near-warring camps, as seemed to be happening in civil society at large, but there were deep disagreements over Trump's impact on cybersecurity.

Larry Clinton of the industry-based Internet Security Alliance, while steering clear of the political turmoil of the times, said, "The Trump administration is going in the right direction on many aspects of cybersecurity." Clinton was a security pro's pro, someone who understood the economic, political, and technical challenges, and who had spent decades working to shore up the security of the private sector's computer networks. He cited Trump's 2017 executive order on cyber, a Department of Homeland Security cyber strategy document, and a 2018 strategic botnet report, among other steps, that incorporated a sophisticated risk management approach to cyber.

Ernest McDuffie, who launched the federal government's well-regarded cybersecurity education program and served in the intelligence community, had another take. "For the past two years I have advised my clients to minimize their dependency on federal government resources because of the clear chaos represented by the current administration," McDuffie said in 2018. "In my opinion the clear and present national security threat to the United States of America is the Trump presidency. The sooner it ends the safer we all will be."

Could both sentiments be true?

Perhaps, thanks to the paradoxes that were Donald Trump and to the extraordinary skill and commitment of the cyber community.

In any case, the tests never stopped coming.

Case in point: The Department of Energy on May 1, 2019, circulated a brief notice that a "cyber event" affected electric grid operations in the western United States, but it offered few details.

"DOE received a report about a denial-of-service condition that occurred at an electric utility on March 5, 2019 related to a known vulnerability that required a previously published software update to mitigate," DOE said in a statement.

"The incident did not impact generation, the reliability of the grid or cause any customer outages," DOE said. "DOE continues to work with our industry partners through the ISACs to ensure the dissemination of the appropriate mitigation information to manage their associated risks."

The incident was first publicly reported by E&E News, which stated, "The March 5 incident lasted from 9 a.m. until nearly 7 p.m. but didn't lead to a power outage, based on a brief summary of the electric disturbance report filed by the victim utility."

The news service reported, "If remote hackers interfered with grid networks in California, Utah and Wyoming, as the DOE filing suggests, the event would be unprecedented. A cyberattack is not known to have ever disrupted the flow of electricity anywhere in the United States, though Russian hackers briefly cut off power to parts of Ukraine in 2015 and again in 2016."

That was a taste of the stakes at play in cyberspace.

2

The Promises of 2017

THERE WERE HOPEFUL EARLY SIGNS on cyber policy. Year one in the age of Trump began with the appointment of cyber-savvy former senator Dan Coats as the nation's top intelligence official. Retired Marine Corps general John Kelly would be secretary of Homeland Security. Robert Joyce, an esteemed cyber warrior at the National Security Agency, was named White House cybersecurity coordinator.

Coats, as a GOP senator from Indiana, was a strong backer of the Cybersecurity Act of 2015, voicing particular support for its legal liability protections intended to encourage companies to share what they knew about cyber threats. The law was a modest step against a massive problem, but it stood for years as the most significant congressional action to date on cyber policy. Coats played a role in adding two elements to that legislation. One would ensure the Department of Homeland Security had adequate legal authority to step in and help secure the computer networks at other federal agencies, finally removing a bureaucratic hurdle that had complicated efforts to protect the government's own systems.

In response to a massive hack at the US government's Office of Personnel Management (OPM), Coats and other senators in July 2015 drafted legislation that would give DHS explicit authority for cybersecurity at those other agencies, including the power to shut down insecure systems like the leaky database at OPM.

The measure was crafted to allow DHS to operate cyber intrusion detection and prevention capabilities for all federal agencies and directed the department to assess the risks in systems throughout the .gov domain. Investing one agency—DHS—with the authority to do this seemed pretty obvious. Still, it caused a mild flap with the leaders of the Senate Homeland Security and Governmental Affairs Committee, who were preparing to move their own legislation on securing federal systems.

Such turf fights were the bane of cyber policymaking in Congress, constantly slowing or even killing well-meaning attempts to address cybersecurity vulnerabilities and policy shortcomings. To paraphrase an old Capitol Hill axiom: the hackers were the adversary; the enemy was that other committee stepping on your jurisdiction.

But the dispute was smoothed over, and much of the Coats-backed proposal was added to the Homeland Security and Governmental Affairs Committee's bill—the "Federal Cybersecurity Enhancement Act," which authorized DHS's cybersecurity program for federal agencies and directed the department to speed deployment of "EINSTEIN 3," the pride of its antihacking, continuous diagnostics and mitigation toolkit.

The entire package was eventually added to the Cybersecurity Act and signed into law by President Obama at the end of 2015. The second Coats amendment called for a study of cyber threats to mobile devices that would seem prescient as the dangers of the so-called Internet of Things began to be understood.

So Coats would leave the Senate for the executive branch with strong cyber bona fides—at least for a politician.

General Kelly wasn't a cyber warrior—he'd led the military's Southern Command that concerned itself mostly with border security and drug interdiction. DHS would have a starring role in President Trump's controversial campaign to "build a wall" on the southern border with Mexico, so Kelly's resume made sense for the position.

But he was also seen as having proper appreciation for the cybersecurity issue. Of equal importance, he would bring stature and institutional weight to DHS, a department that battled for respect and authority since its 2002 inception.

Kelly hit the right notes on cybersecurity at his January 10 confirmation hearing, including pledges to ensure DHS's place atop the civilian government's cyber hierarchy, to pursue a collaborative approach to industry, and to respect privacy and civil liberties. Those three issues had become something of a bipartisan, cyber holy trinity on Capitol Hill during the Obama years.

"Working together makes a lot of sense," Kelly said, adding that greater cooperation among the private sector and federal and state governments on cybersecurity would "go a long way."

In some ways Kelly's appearance resembled the 2013 confirmation hearing for Obama's second-term DHS secretary, Jeh Johnson, who had been the

Pentagon's top lawyer before moving to Homeland Security. Johnson would establish particularly strong and bipartisan ties on Capitol Hill; he emphasized at his confirmation hearing the DHS role in securing federal networks, and collaboration—rather than regulatory coercion—with the private sector.

Johnson also demonstrated an appreciation for one of the nuances of the industry-government relationship on cybersecurity, saying it was perfectly valid for the two sides to have "different calculations of risk" as they assessed how best to allocate resources.

That question was at the root of a long-running dialogue—or debate—between the Obama administration and private sector partners. Government had to secure the country—and its cyberspace—against the threats posed today and tomorrow by advanced foreign powers; should a US company have to factor such concerns into its own cybersecurity spending, or was it up to the government to, in a sense, defend these cyber borders too?

General Kelly didn't address that obscure but important policy issue at his hearing. But he did speak positively about reorganizing DHS's cybersecurity functions into a cyber agency—a key priority for lawmakers on the Senate and House Homeland Security committees that would come to pass in 2018, after Kelly moved to the White House and Kirstjen Nielsen assumed the hot seat at DHS.

Kelly discussed "outreach" and collaboration with the private sector—particularly the tech world—and cited work initiated by Obama's defense secretary Ashton Carter as a model. "I also know that . . . three or four or five years ago, we talked about the United States would not have a peer competitor in cyber for 20 years or 25 years," Kelly said. "Now, we know that we have some pretty darn close to peer competitors."

Kelly said, "I was watching something that Secretary Ash Carter started when he first took over at the Defense Department. He started to reach out to the commercial world—Silicon Valley—that kind of thing to engage them as opposed to perhaps, or at least to get, you know, get a report card on how we are doing within the federal government to develop."

He said, "There's unbelievable . . . talent out there in the civilian sector and I think at this point in time, everyone realizes that it's in everyone's interest whether it's personal security or corporate security, certainly U.S. security, everyone realizes I think that working together makes an awful lot of sense."

Kelly highlighted the need to keep privacy concerns front and center as the department fulfilled its cyber functions. A prime reason for giving DHS the lead civilian role on cybersecurity was so that it could provide a uniform approach to protecting privacy and civil liberties as it processed threat data and helped defend government and private sector networks. The general earned high marks for his appearance from Republican and Democratic lawmakers alike.

Rob Joyce wasn't named White House cyber coordinator until March, a time lag that seemed to reflect the Trump administration's ambivalence about a position created by Obama in 2009. In the spring of 2018, a little more than a year after taking the White House job, Joyce would announce his desire to return to the National Security Agency. The Trump team responded by eliminating the coordinator post and handing its duties to a couple of National Security Council deputies.

But as the administration got under way, Joyce was a welcome addition, a solid cybersecurity professional and a serious presence on the White House staff. He'd been a leader on both offense and defense at the NSA, including a stint atop Tailored Access Operations, the NSA's legendary hacking team.

There were questions, plenty of them, as an "outsider" president moved his team into office while expressing disdain for the existing policy apparatus. Former New York City mayor Rudolph Giuliani was hovering around with some kind of cyber portfolio, but no one outside Trump's family circle seemed able to make any sense of it. A ninety-day cybersecurity review was coming, the new president promised, but no one on the outside understood the scope or who would be conducting it.

But there was a sigh of relief in cybersecurity circles: surely the policy veterans like Coats, Kelly, and Joyce would create a stable platform for cyber initiatives, even with a president who seemed to be formulating many policies in a random spray of tweets.

During the campaign, candidate Trump in October 2016 finally provided some specifics on his policy views on cyber. He called for more resources for US Cyber Command to develop offensive cyber weapons as a tool of both deterrence and retaliation. "I will also ask my secretary of Defense and Joint Chiefs to present recommendations for strengthening and augmenting our Cyber Command," Trump said. "As a deterrent against attacks on our critical resources, the United States must possess—and has to—the unquestioned capacity to launch crippling cyber counter attacks. And I mean crippling, crippling."

Trump added, "People don't even know if we have the capability that we're supposed to have when you look at what's going on with other countries."

Congressional critics from both parties frequently called for a more robust US deterrence policy, although the Obama administration argued it had one and was using it. Admiral Michael Rogers, the head of US Cyber Command, testified before the Senate Armed Services Committee in September 2016 that foreign adversaries were well aware of the United States' deadly capabilities in this domain. Cyber Command's arsenal of offensive weapons was generally seen as state of the art.

Perhaps a bit like John F. Kennedy's claims in the 1960 campaign that the Eisenhower administration had allowed a missile gap to emerge with the Soviets, candidate Trump appeared to exaggerate US shortcomings when it came to cyber weaponry. But his criticisms in this case were within the bounds of recognized policy positions, unlike in other areas where Trump seemed to redefine reality to justify his policy prescriptions.

Trump also called for a coordinated law enforcement approach to fighting cyber crime through a joint task force, similar to past campaigns against the Mafia. It was an interesting idea, but nothing new would come from that proposal; perhaps someone mentioned to the new president that the FBI had been running a cyber joint task force since 2008. And he promised a comprehensive, running review of the security of federal computer systems, an idea that actually would be largely incorporated into the government's cyber policy.

But cyber wasn't the candidate's issue. As a businessman, he could have grabbed the subject and injected a private sector view into the policy discussion. After all, his company owned hotels, casinos, office buildings, and aircraft, which all could be prime targets for hacks. In fact, Trump hotels were affected by data breaches targeting guests' credit card information. The company settled one case related to a 2015 incident by paying New York State $50,000 and agreeing to bolster its data-security practices.

According to *Fortune*, "Trump Hotels violated New York law by not providing notice of the breaches to consumers as soon as possible, [state attorney general Eric] Schneiderman said. After learning about malware in 2015, it took some four months for the company to put a notice about it on its website, he said."

Everyone suffered breaches, but not everyone had the megaphone of a presidential campaign. Candidate Trump didn't discuss or offer lessons. So there were just a few promises from the candidate to measure the president's performance against.

In the early days of 2017, the Trump team also signaled continuation of certain Obama-era policy structures that found favor in the business community.

Tom Bossert, the White House's assistant for homeland security and counterterrorism—and a cyber policy pro in his own right—in a March 2017 speech said the new administration's top cybersecurity priorities were securing federal networks, collaborating with the operators of critical infrastructure like telecommunications networks and electric grids to secure against cyber threats, and establishing international cyber norms of behavior and a clear policy of deterrence. Bossert stressed the administration's commitment to voluntary partnerships—as opposed to mandatory rules and regulations. "We cannot achieve this without partnership," Bossert said.

Like Kelly, Bossert was promising consistency on cyber. The new administration, two months old at this point, was not offering such assurances in too many other policy areas.

Trump in May 2017 issued a cybersecurity executive order—Obama delivered his first cyber policy speech at a similar point in his first term—kicking off a series of policy initiatives on threats like botnets and shoring up the government's computer systems.

The Trump team packaged its work as more focused on the most critical cyber threats and on achieving policy goals. The implication was that Trump, unlike Obama, was taking a hardheaded business approach to specific cyber problems rather than a broad, ambling look at cybersecurity and digital life in America. Obama, who was intensely interested in cyber issues, might've chuckled looking over the Team Trump cyber policy list, which offered only modest deviations from the course charted by Team Obama.

In a welcome sign of flexibility, the new administration quickly backpedaled on a draft executive order that showed up in the *Washington Post* just after the inauguration in January, which had suggested major departures from widely accepted policy approaches.

"I would hope this executive order coming down on cyber is done in coordination with this committee," House Homeland Security chairman Michael McCaul (R-TX) told Homeland Security secretary Kelly in the general's first appearance before the House Homeland panel on February 7, 2017.

The leaked draft of the executive order (EO) startled lawmakers and industry stakeholders as it appeared to ignore lines of responsibility crafted in recent years for DHS and other agencies and to give the Pentagon an undefined but expanded role in protecting civilian networks. The issue of allowing the military to operate on domestic turf was a combustible one, and had been for over two hundred years—even as that "turf" morphed into the virtual landscape of cyberspace.

Congressional sources complained about a lack of consultation, and the White House scrapped plans to formally unveil the EO at the end of January. A revised version circulating in early February was stripped of many provisions that triggered alarms. However, industry sources—ever fearful of new regulations, even from a "populist" Republican administration—were still worried over language focused on the communications and electricity sectors and the defense industrial base.

Chairman McCaul noted two major reforms passed by Congress in recent years—on DHS's role in securing federal networks and on cyber information sharing—and suggested he would be vigilant in ensuring the department's position wasn't diminished.

"I'd hate to see any executive order come down that is inconsistent with current law," McCaul said. "I think it would cause a lot of problems and a lot of consternation with the members who have worked so hard to get this done."

That was a pretty clear signal to the cabinet secretary sitting at the witness table, a direct message on structural and policy continuity that even an administration focused on "disruption" would be reluctant to ignore.

Current law had been crafted largely by McCaul's committee—and cyber jurisdiction was jealously guarded in both Congress and the executive branch, a dynamic that often hindered rather than helped efforts to improve cybersecurity. This dynamic wouldn't change. But in the tumultuous Trump era, it would serve in some ways to keep cyber policy from completely going off the rails, as lawmakers exercised more forceful oversight of the new administration in the cyber realm than they did on other issues.

Sitting before the House Homeland panel, Kelly did his best to kick dirt on the earlier version of the EO.

"There was a kind of a draft E.O. that had been leaked some time ago—a week or so ago," Kelly said. "I can tell you that—that the E.O. that's being contemplated is vastly different than that. I don't know whose work that was, but it did send shivers to a lot, my own organization included. So we're working with—we are working with the White House, we will work with the Congress, of course, to make sure that going forward that E.O. says the right thing and gets at the right problems."

Overall, Kelly's interactions with the committee were positive, and he stressed his commitment to working with Congress, other agencies, and the private sector.

"President Trump has ordered a complete top-to-bottom relook on cyber," Kelly testified. "That will include all stakeholders, and hopefully we're going to bring in—and have been I think, successfully in bringing in the private community."

Once released, the May 11, 2017, EO would ease many of the concerns in industry and Congress. The document appeared well in line with cyber policy and priorities that had been evolving over the past decade.

But for the first time, it put the onus directly on the heads of federal agencies and departments to shore up their own cybersecurity and mandated steps, such as using the popular framework of cybersecurity standards, created by the National Institute of Standards and Technology under the Obama administration, across the US government. It called for new steps to protect the most critical of industrial facilities and business operations—where a cyberattack could have "catastrophic consequences." And it launched new initiatives on cyber deterrence and growing threats like "botnets," automated attacks employing thousands or millions of hijacked computers or devices like phones or "smart" appliances.

"We must ensure that our data is secure and our critical infrastructure is not vulnerable to attacks," said Senate Homeland Security and Governmental Affairs chairman Ron Johnson (R-WI). "I'm glad to see the Trump administration is making these issues a priority and I look forward to reviewing the executive order."

Former president Obama's cybersecurity coordinator, Michael Daniel, said the order was consistent with previous work.

"Overall, this E.O. continues the general approach to cybersecurity that started in the Bush Administration and ran through the Obama Administration," Daniel said. "I also strongly support the approach taken to Federal networks, holding agencies accountable while also encouraging the move to shared services. Finally, the focus on finding a solution to the botnet problem, looking at the electrical grid more closely, and further developing a workforce strategy are all smart and important issues to tackle in today's cyber landscape."

There was support on the Hill and in the business community, and it looked like cybersecurity policy might advance on a continuous arc, largely immune from the drama playing out in other parts of Trump's world.

In March, the president and his cyber team would be largely shielded from a "bombshell" WikiLeaks revelation about alleged CIA hacking into the interconnected consumer devices that make up the Internet of Things. The leak quickly spurred comparisons with the Edward Snowden leaks beginning in 2013 that hobbled Obama and congressional cybersecurity policy efforts for years. But this leak landed in a dramatically different environment, particularly with a president who not only had distanced himself from the intelligence community but also seemed at war with it.

There was no allegation that the CIA was using its hacking tools to spy on Americans through their personal devices. Snowden's 2013 revelation that the National Security Agency was pulling in data on Americans' private communications gave that leak an immediate and explosive impact on US policy, and it discredited Obama's claims to be a digital privacy champion in the eyes of online rights groups in the United States and Europe.

The CIA wasn't commenting on the 2017 disclosure, but one high-profile intelligence veteran used an unusual platform to knock down the idea that Americans' TVs and microwave ovens were spying on them. "I can tell you that these tools would not be used against an American," former CIA and NSA director Michael Hayden promised on *The Late Show with Stephen Colbert*.

"But there are people out there that you want us to spy on. You want us to have the ability to actually turn on that listening device inside the TV, to learn that person's intention," Hayden said. "This is a wonderful capability. You give the intelligence community $53 billion a year. You gotta get something for your money."

There were also a multitude of initiatives afoot across the government to address the type of vulnerabilities that the CIA allegedly exploited in consumer devices.

The thousands of documents WikiLeaks posted on March 7, 2017, purported to reveal the tools used by the CIA to get into smartphones, TVs, and other consumer devices. That this would tarnish the CIA's reputation as a sturdy guardian of its own secrets seemed undeniable, although such "permanent" stains came to seem less consequential as the president himself cruised through event after event that would have ended political careers in previous times.

Still, Virginia Tech's Charles Clancy observed, "If the documents are genuine, this is a huge hit to the CIA's covert cyber operations program. Coming on the heels of NSA's Shadow Brokers leaks and lingering impacts of the Snowden disclosures, the consequence is a sustained degradation in the intelligence community's sources and methods for cyber espionage necessitating significant new investment to rebuild capability."

He highlighted a potential kicker for cyber policy: "The natural tendency to combat such leaks is to further restrict access to data on classified cyber capabilities, which could come at the expense of effective collaboration and mission impact across divisions and agencies."

Anything that damaged collaborative efforts potentially would have a huge impact on a fundamental tenet of cyber policy in recent years: that info sharing, tearing down silos, and cooperation among agencies and between the government and private sector were the key ingredients of a successful cyber policy.

There was another potential kicker: The president himself simply might not care whether the CIA's capabilities were damaged. An antagonist—the US intelligence community—had suffered a black eye, Trump may have figured.

Most of the black eyes around the Trump administration in 2017 were self-inflicted, even amid the relative tranquility of cyber policy issues not related to Russia. In fact, it was often the Trump White House that dragged the Russia scandal into other cyber policy spaces, seemingly unable to separate that nettlesome investigation from the daily work of the administration. It was the distraction effect.

Foreign Policy reported in May 2017 that the White House was considering launching a high-profile investigation of the Department of Homeland Security's "Automated Indicator Sharing" (AIS) program for—wait for it—sharing information.

The AIS program, developed in the Obama administration, was and is intended to get cyber threat information to private sector partners and other government entities around the world as part of a common-defense system. According to the report, some in the White House wanted to pin the tail on DHS for leaking classified data, demonstrating an obtuseness so silly that perhaps it had to be deliberate. The White House denied the story amid exasperated eye rolls throughout the cyber and intelligence communities.

Then it got serious: On May 9, 2017, Trump fired FBI director James Comey.

Comey told his story to lawmakers in June at a Senate Intelligence Committee hearing that received saturation media coverage and became a Washington "event," until it was drowned out by the endless series of "media events" the Trump term would produce. In this case, Comey's hugely anticipated testimony shoved aside any cybersecurity narrative that didn't have "Russia probe" in the title. Naturally, the president's legal and political vulnerabilities dominated the media coverage and created an echo chamber that muffled questions of cyber policy and principles. The president loudly denounced the entire matter as "fake news," and the echo chamber was familiar and comfortable turf for him—and it certainly was comfortable territory for cable news. The Russia investigation was raising basic but serious cyber policy questions, such as how the United States "attributes" cyberattacks—identifying perpetrators and in some way calling them out—and the meaning of cyber deterrence. How well was the United States able to link a specific hack back to Russian operatives or any other cyber aggressor? And if the United States knew the identity of the perpetrator in a cyberattack, what should be done about it? There was real cybersecurity policy at play, and the stakes were quite a bit higher than Trump's political fortunes, such as the security of the modern economy and twenty-first-century democracy. But one would need to navigate a political/media circus before getting at those questions.

"There's so many other distractions beyond the [Trump/Russia] probe, I'm not sure the probe is the lone distraction," said one security expert active in the cyber info-sharing community. One potentially positive impact from the controversy was a renewed discussion on attribution of attacks, the source said. This was a critically important issue in cyber circles because, for years, ambiguity about the sources of cyberattacks led to ambiguity in the response by the United States. If they knew definitively who the attacker was, policymakers could choose from a buffet of possible responses. "But my sense is that this [Russia probe] topic is too political to even have a reasoned discussion on attribution," the source said. "Your mind is made up based on what side of the aisle you are on."

Another question was whether the vaunted information-sharing law enacted at the end of 2015 played any role in limiting the damage from Russia's sophisticated intrusions. So far, no one from Intelligence or Homeland Security circles was saying. That was an ongoing issue in evaluating the effectiveness of the Cybersecurity Act of 2015: its successes went largely unreported, out of operational necessity, while cyberattacks against US targets could be portrayed as a sign that the law and related programs weren't working.

At a higher level, there was the eight-hundred-pound gorilla of a question about a foreign power using cyber tools to distort the American political process.

Senate Intelligence Committee Democrats used Comey's appearance to stress strategic and cybersecurity issues and tried to underscore that this wasn't a "gotcha" investigation aimed at delegitimizing Trump's presidency. GOP members agreed key strategic and cyber issues were involved but energetically sought to insulate Trump from potential legal jeopardy related to the investigation.

"We must determine what [the Russian government] did . . . [and take] steps to avoid it happening again," Senate Intelligence ranking member Mark Warner (D-VA) said.

Chairman Richard Burr (R-NC) said the 2016 hacks and other activity "may have been aimed at one party, but in 2018, 2020 and beyond, it could be aimed at anyone."

There was a complete lack of partisan rancor during the session—which seemed less striking at the time than it would later, as events unfolded. But still, Democrats and Republicans clearly had different priorities in their questioning of Comey.

With blanket network and cable TV coverage, and over one hundred reporters in attendance, the panel questioned Comey for nearly three hours on the Russia probe, his firing by Trump, and a slew of related issues.

Russian hacking of the Democratic National Committee and other entities was part of a "massive" cyber-enabled operation that was first detected in the summer of 2015, Comey testified. The Russia campaign had up to a thousand targets in the United States, Comey said. By late 2015, the FBI was notifying victims of Russian "spear-phishing" operations, while the Obama administration began pondering its strategic response in early 2016.

Comey, who said he documented his meetings with Trump because he was concerned the president-elect and then president would "lie" about the encounters, said he wasn't sure of exactly why Trump had fired him the previous month, but "I knew it was because he didn't like something about the Russia investigation."

The Intelligence Committee's Republican members focused on a handful of points in a narrative that began with Comey briefing the president-elect in early January on salacious material contained in an unverified intelligence report, subsequent meetings between the two men in which Trump expressed his hope that a criminal investigation into former national security adviser Michael Flynn could be dropped, and Trump's frustration with the broader Russia election interference probe, and on to Comey's firing in May 2017.

Burr elicited from Comey that neither Trump nor anyone in the administration "ask[ed] you to stop the Russia investigation."

Senator James Risch (R-ID), a dogged and cranky one-time prosecutor, asked Comey to confirm three "truths": that as of Comey's departure from the bureau, there was no evidence of Trump campaign collusion with the Russian government, that the president was not under investigation, and that the president said he "hoped" Comey could "let it go" when it came to the Flynn investigation but did not order him to drop it.

Comey agreed with the first two points. On the third point, Comey said he considered it a directive from the president to end the Flynn probe, an order that he said the FBI would not follow.

Representative Brad Sherman (D-CA)—a stalwart of the House Democrats' liberal wing who sat in the audience during the Senate hearing—called that a "threat" by the president that would form the basis of articles of impeachment that he and Representative Al Green (D-TX) planned to file. They were later dissuaded from doing so by the House Democratic leadership, which was eyeing a big win in the 2018 midterm elections and didn't want impeachment to become a GOP rallying point. (Green would bring a motion to begin impeachment proceedings to the House floor two years later, amid the controversy over Trump's comments aimed at four Democratic congresswomen.)

Beneath those politically explosive issues, deep concerns over ongoing Russian cyber activity and the threat to US institutions and infrastructure ran through the hearing like an electric current that animated members on both sides of the aisle—at least in brief flashes amid the legal and political positioning. The Russian government "interfered in our election" with "purpose . . . sophistication and active measures," Comey said, praising lawmakers for taking a bipartisan approach to sorting out what happened and what should be done about it.

In response to several questions from the committee's Democratic members, Comey testified that Trump never inquired about the broader Russian cyber campaign or about strategic options for responding. It was an unusual lack of curiosity that raised eyebrows on the Democratic side of the dais but not much reaction on the GOP side.

Comey said the Russians' 2016 efforts were part of a "long-term strategy" and warned, "They'll be back."

The Russians were using technology and cyber intrusions "to affect the way we think, the way we vote and the way we act," Comey said. "That is a big deal."

With that in mind, Senator Angus King (I-ME) said, "It's very important that the public understands this is a forward-looking investigation."

Senator Jack Reed (D-RI), also the top Democrat on the Armed Services Committee, suggested the president was "downplaying" the cyber threat from Russia and didn't "appreciate the significance" of that country's activities in 2016 and continuing cyber operations. Warner, at the end of the session, said the committee's probe was going to "get to the bottom" of a number of outstanding questions while also focusing on "the macro issue of what the Russians did and continue to do."

That was going to take a while—more time than the 115th Congress had, as it turned out.

But as Russia-related probes continued through the summer of 2017—and hard as it was to imagine, given the constant state of controversy generated by this administration—cybersecurity veterans said important initiatives were advancing across government and the private sector despite a chaotic national political picture.

This was the unheralded grunt work of cybersecurity: federal agencies' ongoing implementation of the National Institute of Standards and Technology's (NIST) framework of cyber standards under Trump's executive order was one sign the policy wheels were turning in the right direction. Other positive indicators included work on a closely watched, first-ever update to the cyber framework by NIST—in partnership with industry—and outreach efforts to the private sector on cyber initiatives at the Commerce Department and elsewhere.

These were solid nuts-and-bolts cyber activities, clearly in the policy arc begun under George W. Bush and embraced and advanced by Barack Obama.

There was churn on the personnel side, which came to be the norm in a Trump government. DHS Secretary Kelly traded hats to become White House chief of staff at the end of July 2017, for what would end up being an extremely trying seventeen months for the retired Marine. DHS pressed on for a few months with an acting secretary before Kirstjen Nielsen was confirmed as the new DHS secretary in December 2017. Nielsen served as Kelly's top aide at both DHS and the White House, and she started with few personal alliances across the broader government environment or connections on Capitol Hill. She was a recognized cybersecurity professional in the private sector, but her work on cyber at DHS was overshadowed by issues at the US-Mexico border.

Her lack of an independent power base or support structure made her especially vulnerable to the vagaries and temper tantrums of the Trump Oval Office. Nielsen's ability to endure the slings and arrows and keep a focus on cyber objectives could've been the stuff of bureaucratic legend. Unfortunately, pictures of crying children in DHS-managed detention centers defined much of her public legacy.

State Department cyber coordinator Christopher Painter was shuttled out of his job in July 2017. In a stab at normalcy, State quickly reached out to industry on issues such as international collaboration and harmonization on cyber policy, at least in part to offer assurances that its collaborative cyber efforts were continuing even with the departure of the well-liked Painter. State attributed the Painter move to a broader restructuring, but the whispers in the cyber community were that it was about dismantling an Obama-era artifact.

Still, overall, summer 2017 seemed a positive moment in time for the cyber policy world.

"Cyber doesn't seem to be affected by whatever turmoil exists elsewhere," said one business sector source active in multiple cybersecurity efforts. "I don't see any balls being dropped across government. At the implementation level, things are working."

The business source pointed to the executive order itself as an encouraging sign that officials were able to identify and advance cyber priorities even in the midst of controversies that soaked up the Trump administration's energies.

"We waited three or four months for the executive order" after the initial draft was pulled back early in the year, the source said. While that delay caused some consternation, the source said, "When it was released in May, it was comprehensive in addressing the national cybersecurity priorities. It assigned responsibility to the right people at agencies. And it was aggressive in getting feedback on issues like deterrence, international engagement and marketplace transparency."

For years, one of the most-repeated mantras in cyber circles was the need for sustained attention to cybersecurity policy at the highest levels of government. Even Obama, who embraced the issue and spoke on it often, faced grumbling from stakeholders who believed his White House was frequently distracted by other concerns.

But all-consuming distractions were the central feature of the young Trump administration, raising the question of whether cyber policy development was suffering amid a case of not-so-benign neglect.

In the summer of 2017, players at the heart of policy development in recent years—from inside and outside government—were eager to say cybersecurity initiatives marched ahead with a seeming immunity from the nation's day-to-day political drama.

A source with experience on Capitol Hill and within federal agencies pointed to White House Homeland Security adviser Bossert and newly installed Department of Homeland Security cyber official Christopher Krebs as policy veterans who were helping push forward initiatives.

"I think cybersecurity is one area of policy that is being handled by expert professionals—mostly overworked career civil servants at Commerce and DHS, plus a few solid politicals like Bossert and Chris Krebs at DHS—and has not yet been infected with the poisonous turmoil that characterizes so many other areas," the source said.

It remained unclear how General Kelly as chief of staff would organize the White House team, the source said, adding, "I don't know how Kelly's arrival will change or affect that, and don't know his relationship with Bossert, but my guess is on balance it will serve to bolster the forces of expert professionalism."

Kelly was reviewing the roles of White House staff with an eye toward possible reorganization, according to a *Washington Post* article that appeared just before the ouster of presidential adviser Steve Bannon, whose populist instincts ran afoul of the Marine general's desire to create a disciplined internal process.

"Any time a new Chief of Staff comes into the White House, they will review positions, roles, and responsibilities and how the operation is working," said Kiersten Todt, who was executive director of the presidential Commission on Enhancing National Cybersecurity in 2016. She was now managing director of the new Cyber Readiness Institute, a partner at Liberty Group Ventures, and a resident fellow at the University of Pittsburgh Institute for Cyber Law, Policy, and Security, another pro's pro in the cyber world. The report she helped produce in December 2016 became a cyber policy touchstone, and many of its recommendations were folded into the Trump administration's efforts; a few were notably ignored.

"Gen. Kelly's experience at DHS will be an asset and will be constructive and valuable in how it informs his role at the White House on cyber," Todt told Inside Cybersecurity.

Todt noted that Grant Schneider—who already served in one of the government's most important IT roles as chief information security officer at the Office of Management and Budget—was tapped in August 2017 to also serve as senior director of cybersecurity at the National Security Council.

"The dual-hatting of Grant Schneider is an innovative approach—if it works, it will be extremely effective because it will tie together the NSC and OMB on cyber policy, which will create stronger cyber leadership within the executive branch," Todt said. "Grant Schneider and [White House cybersecurity coordinator] Rob Joyce could be an extremely effective team and bring strong senior leadership on cyber to the executive branch. While not the format the commission laid out, it could certainly achieve the same goal of ensuring there is a focus on cyber policy at senior levels in the White House and in the executive branch."

And that, Todt contended, was absolutely essential.

"We can't advance the cyber policy agenda at the working level of government," she said. "Without White House leadership, government won't be able to get anything done—and, we are developing a potentially strong cyber policy apparatus within the White House. NIST did a great job on the framework, but as the senior leaders at NIST will tell you, policy is not their mission. While we commend what we all did to make the framework a success, we need senior leadership at the White House and throughout the interagency to effect enduring change on cyber policy."

In August 2017, Trump fulfilled one of his few pledges on cyber and announced that US Cyber Command was being elevated to full unified combatant command status, a move mostly of bureaucratic importance but one that symbolically imbued the Defense Department's cyber warriors with the same standing as the military's other unified commands, like the ones responsible for the Middle East, Europe, the continental United States, or Strategic Command, which controlled nuclear weapons.

Trump said in a formal statement, "This new Unified Combatant Command will strengthen our cyberspace operations and create more opportunities to improve our Nation's defense. The elevation of United States Cyber Command demonstrates our increased resolve against cyberspace threats and will help reassure our allies and partners and deter our adversaries."

He even tweeted the announcement, though without the usual flourishes.

In September 2017, amid positive reviews of efforts to keep a steady cyber policy approach on track, the sometimes grim realities of cyberspace made themselves felt—in what seemed a true international crisis with North Korea, and closer to home, in an epic hack at a consumer credit rating agency.

Trump was pushing a nuclear confrontation with North Korea's Kim Jong-un into uncharted territory. In the United States, critical infrastructure operators, cyber info-sharing specialists, congressional sources, and others were closely watching unfolding events related to North Korea and other international tensions—acutely aware that any crisis could have major cybersecurity implications that would test tools and policies put in place in recent years.

"I think there is a general awareness that the current geopolitical situation impacts the cyber threat environment," said one source close to industry-government info-sharing activities.

The confrontation over nuclear weapons with North Korea—also a well-known aggressor in cyberspace—put cybersecurity professionals on their toes, while at the same time cybersecurity firm Symantec released a report that fueled anxieties about separate, Russian-linked probing of US energy systems.

Lawmakers were briefed on the Korea situation by administration officials on September 6, 2017.

At the time, government and industry sources declined to discuss specific cybersecurity activities taking place around the North Korea situation, but one source in a critical-infrastructure sector said, "The right people are taking notice [of the current threat environment] and are preparing for it."

In terms of government-industry collaboration, this source said "there definitely is the ability to quickly bring together the right people to engage in a crisis." The source said resources would be marshaled through the Department of Homeland Security's National Cybersecurity and Communications Integration Center and "maybe" even through the Federal Emergency Management Agency, which was being increasingly folded into cyber incident response as recognition grew of the possible physical repercussions of a cyberattack.

However, even as these emergency-response activities geared up, the source said it remained unclear what a full-scale cybersecurity response would look like. "We haven't been through it before," the source acknowledged.

The North Korea standoff raised questions about US cyber deterrence policy, which had yet to be articulated to the satisfaction of critics like then–Senate Armed Services chairman John McCain (R-AZ), who would pass away the next year after battling brain cancer.

"A number of discussions have already been held, but I don't know what the response will be" if North Korea amped up the current tensions by acting out in cyberspace, said the critical infrastructure source. "The government is tight-lipped about what it would do. My understanding is there would be a response if there's a significant [cyber] event. The government is poised to do it when the time comes."

The tensions were also seen as testing the effectiveness of the national cybersecurity threat information sharing system.

The source active in info-sharing noted, "In cyberspace, the key here is understanding the capabilities of the adversary. Studying different attacks they have been involved in will show the actor's methods, tendencies and interests. When I first began this work over 15 years ago, people only wanted indicators—they did not care about the actors. But now people realize that understanding the actor is key to defending networks. Specific actors have specific capabilities, tactics and targets."

The 2015 cyber law tasked the Department of Homeland Security with getting that information into the hands of those in the private sector who defend critical infrastructure. The private sector by 2017 had its own—quite advanced—cyber info-sharing operations in place as well, and was engaging with government in other areas that could be beneficial in a crisis situation.

The critical infrastructure source said of DHS, "When it comes to cyber, they are highly functional." The source also stressed that sectors like finance, oil and gas, electricity, and water were "poised to respond" to hostile actions in cyberspace.

Of course, the 2017 nuclear standoff with Kim Jong-un was ultimately defused, resulting in the oddly happy first summit between Trump and Kim, and months later US intelligence assessments that North Korea had not—as promised to Trump—curtailed nuclear weapons efforts. But in the fall of 2017, cybersecurity pros could examine lessons learned and express some satisfaction with how the national emergency response system worked when it came to cyber (at least in a real-world drill).

It wasn't quite the 1962 "missiles of October," a nuclear showdown between superpowers, but it would suffice as a shaking-out exercise for the new administration and its industry partners.

With the world still gripped by the Korea crisis, yet another hack gave Americans more reason to ask whether their personal information would ever be safe in cyberspace. The consumer credit rating firm Equifax on September 7, 2017, announced a "cybersecurity incident" affecting approximately 143 million US customers' personal data. "Criminals exploited a U.S. website application vulnerability to gain access to certain files," Equifax said in a statement. "Based on the company's investigation, the unauthorized access occurred from mid-May through July 2017. The company has found no evidence of unauthorized activity on Equifax's core consumer or commercial credit reporting databases."

The hacked information included names, Social Security numbers, birthdates, addresses, and some driver's license numbers, Equifax stated. It was one of the largest hacks ever, based on the number of Americans affected and the nature of information stolen. And once discovered, Equifax took over a month to tell people about it.

"If you have a credit history, your information is probably on the dark web," Representative Patrick McHenry (R-NC) would say after the scope of the event came into focus.

Reflecting yet another wrinkle in cyber policy, Equifax held sensitive data on a substantial portion of US households, but it didn't really have relationships with them as customers. The firm collected data on Americans and provided credit reports to other companies. The hack, coming after the company failed to patch known vulnerabilities, and the lack of consumer notification pointed up two big gaps in national cybersecurity policy.

The White House didn't have anything to say about it, and Equifax never starred in a Trump tweet.

The CEO of Equifax wrote an op-ed explaining "why it took six weeks to report the incident to the public," while policymakers on Capitol Hill and at federal agencies began sorting through the implications.

The firm faced intense criticism for the lag between discovering the hack and notifying customers, reviving calls in some quarters for enacting federal breach notification requirements and for further empowering agencies such as the Federal Trade Commission (FTC) to set consumer data security rules.

"Shortly after discovering the intrusion, we engaged a leading cybersecurity firm to conduct an investigation," Richard F. Smith, chairman and CEO of Equifax, wrote in *USA Today*. He called the breach "the most humbling moment in our 118-year history."

"At the time, we thought the intrusion was limited," Smith wrote. "The team, working with Equifax Security personnel, devoted thousands of hours during the following weeks to investigate."

Smith wrote, "Our top priority is doing everything we can to support affected consumers. Our team is focused on this effort, and we are engaged around the clock in responding to millions of inquiries from consumers. Importantly, outside investigators found no evidence of unauthorized activity on our core consumer or commercial credit reporting databases."

Federal Trade Commissioner Terrell McSweeny and Senate Intelligence ranking member Mark Warner (D-VA) were among the first calling on the FTC to launch an investigation. Soon after, the commission did issue a rare public announcement of an investigation. The breach also revived calls for action on legislation setting a federal consumer breach notification standard.

Setting a requirement for telling customers when their data had been illegally accessed was supported across industries and across parties in Congress. But differences over how to write the rules would foil efforts to move legislation beyond the committee level in 2015 and 2016, despite support from the Obama White House, and again in 2017 and 2018 amid sheer indifference from the Trump White House. Trump's Treasury Department eventually endorsed creating a national standard—quietly, in an unrelated report on financial technology—but the White House never weighed in on the Equifax hack and never put any weight behind passing consumer data-notification legislation.

"The Equifax data breach is representative" of the Trump administration's step away from a proactive cyber strategy, said retired rear admiral David Simpson, the former FCC cybersecurity leader.

Simpson called the government response to Equifax, a breach that hit the most sensitive data of half the US population, "an amazing failure and it seems no one in the administration or in the regulatory sphere is acting in the best interests of consumers after these large breaches. [They are] admiring the problem instead of taking affirmative steps or holding companies accountable. I'm concerned that we will see consumers increasingly skittish about online transactions. This will be bad for the future of our e-economy."

Seventeen months after the Equifax hack, CNBC reported that the stolen data "never appeared on any [of] hundreds of underground websites selling stolen information. Security experts haven't seen the data used in any of the ways they'd expect in a theft like this—not for impersonating victims, not for accessing other websites, nothing."

The news report added, "But as the investigations continue, a consensus is starting to emerge to explain why the data has disappeared from sight. Most experts familiar with the case now believe that the thieves were working for a foreign government and are using the information not for financial gain, but to try to identify and recruit spies."

But saying it was about recruiting spies was also too narrow a lens for what was going on. One security expert, Terry Ray, CTO and Imperva fellow, broadened it out, saying in a public statement:

> The way I see it, the fact that the stolen Equifax data hasn't appeared in 18 months is no "great mystery" at all—it's just a likely confirmation that the attacker was a nation-state, which aligns with the current trend in global cyberwarfare. These sophisticated state-sponsored hacker armies are no longer just focusing on attacking government agencies and other traditional targets, but also civilian enterprises and civilian data, largely in an attempt to sow discord and confusion. About three years ago, the U.S. Department of Defense issued a warning that foreign nation-state hackers were targeting not only government contractors with advanced persistent threats but also academic institutions. The FBI reportedly issued a similar warning on the same day, indicating that Chinese hackers were equally interested in compromising sensitive data held by commercial enterprises in the U.S.

Ray said, "It's no surprise this trend has continued. After all, nation-state hackers aren't going after the private sector in the absence of anything better to do. They're doing it because their efforts can pay off big dividends in the long run when it nets them secret and useful economic, military and national-security information down the road."

As for Equifax, in May 2019, Moody's made it the first firm ever to see its rating outlook downgraded due to cyber issues. It was small consolation to millions of Americans who had to worry about their own credit ratings and personal data security because of the Equifax breach.

Amid that threat environment, a few big policy streams were carrying federal cyber efforts as 2017 drew to a close, including an update to the framework of cybersecurity standards, implementation of Trump's cyber executive order, and establishment of new requirements around government IT procurement.

The draft first-time update to NIST's voluntary framework came at the end of the year and was "a significant milestone in the evolution of the framework as it stands to set the projectory for more robust and effective use of the risk management framework both domestically and internationally," said Robert Mayer, senior vice president for cybersecurity at the United States Telecom Association.

Internet Security Alliance president Larry Clinton said, "Since the NIST CSF [cybersecurity framework] was released ISA has consistently called for the development of methods that will enable organizations to not just use, but adapt the Framework to their unique threat picture and business plan in a cost-effective fashion. Without cost-effectiveness measurement, as called for in the [Obama era] EO that gave rise to the Framework, sustained use and development of the Framework is doomed to be limited, notwithstanding unverified testimonials."

But, Clinton added, "Based on our conversations with NIST since the early draft of the 1.1 CSF came out we are anticipating that NIST is moving toward metrics in a realistic fashion that will be consistent with the voluntary nature of the NIST Framework."

Important next steps under Trump's May executive order would come quickly in the new year, including a January 5, 2018, draft Commerce Department–Homeland Security Department report on botnets that kicked off the next major industry-government collaboration modeled on the process that produced the cyber framework in 2014.

"We *need* a process similar to the one used for the NIST framework," an industry source stressed. This worried stakeholder called for a series of workshops, regular industry-government engagement, and strong encouragement from the White House to craft a comprehensive security strategy that could effectively confront the botnet challenge. The stakes were enormous, as was spelled out by Todt's commission in 2016: botnets threatened to disrupt the emergence of the Internet of Things, which was nothing less than the world's next great technological evolution.

A third major policy stream was on information technology—IT—procurement, ensuring that government was purchasing cyber-safe equipment and services. "Procurement" and "supply chain" were becoming buzzwords in cyber policy circles.

Some of the renewed focus on IT security came out of the defense domain—NIST issued guidelines for defense contractors on complying with new Pentagon cybersecurity rules that went into effect December 31, 2017. And implementation began immediately on the 2018 National Defense Authorization Act, which included government IT modernization requirements extending to all federal agencies.

"There is a real awareness of the need to create efficiencies on procurement," said Todt. The commission's recommendations were reflected across the Trump White House's work on cyber, including its procurement, botnet, and cyber workforce language.

There was also increased pressure to assess the effectiveness of these initiatives. "Comparatively speaking, the executive order, the framework, procurement are big work streams," ISA's Clinton said. "But they're not big enough."

Clinton frequently cited the need to comprehensively address the economics of cybersecurity and development of effective incentives for industry. "We can make incremental progress but we're still not getting at the real problems," Clinton asserted. "We can't just 'do the basics.'"

He was seeing progress in a greater recognition of cyber economics, but as 2017 closed, Clinton was still worried. "I don't think the key policy makers get that," he said of the need for a comprehensive, economic-based approach.

Other industry voices said there were plenty of policy debates going on, but at least the right questions were being asked and the right subjects were being tackled, both within and outside government. Todt, Clinton, and others pointed out that the private sector was moving ahead with initiatives on info sharing, international engagement, bolstering the cybersecurity of small and mid-sized organizations, and improving the cyber workforce.

"Everyone is engaged on not losing momentum," Todt said.

3

Coordinators? Who Needs Coordinators?

AMID PROMISING EARLY SIGNS that the Trump administration was serious about cybersecurity, it was pulling apart the wiring of an effective cyber approach. The spring 2018 decision to eliminate the White House cybersecurity coordinator position would be a case in point and a moment when the history of cyber and the Trump administration appeared to pivot.

What was needed, in the face of the complexities and cross-cutting nature of the cybersecurity challenge, was coordination. And that's the one thing Trump decided to do without. The disruptor presidency wasn't going to simply allow cyber policy to evolve in a political vacuum, after all.

Cyber in the age of Trump, year two, began with the head of US Cyber Command and the National Security Agency trekking up to the Hill in February 2018 to testify before the Senate Armed Services Committee. Admiral Michael Rogers managed to roil the political waters by saying he hadn't been directed to counter Russian activities aimed at US elections in the aftermath of 2016. In fact, Rogers said there was no order from the president related to Russia's ongoing offensive in cyberspace.

Democrats reacted with outrage and a call to act on their election security bill; the White House and some congressional Republicans fired back, charging the opposition with ginning up a phony controversy.

Despite the important cyber policy streams that began flowing through the executive branch in 2017, lawmakers were prone to get antsy for tangible signs of progress on cybersecurity. That was a tough demand in the best of times. In this administration, the president never spoke about cyber, an issue publicly overshadowed by the Russia affair. Meanwhile, DHS's cyber work was publicly overshadowed by the immigration debate; the extremely talented White House cyber coordinator was not the high-profile evangelical type; and there was no piece of cyber legislation—like the info-sharing bill during the Obama years—to crystallize cyber issues and galvanize action by lawmakers and the executive branch alike.

This was also an exceptionally insular White House, and its decisions were made in a tight circle. Business sources had once complained about the Obama White House deciding policy without enough input from stakeholders; by 2018 they realized the Trump White House aspired to be a sealed fortress. The Trump team's collaboration on the 2017 executive order with industry and Obama veterans appeared to be a one-off.

The Trump administration's reluctance to forcefully and publicly spell out its cyber positions and moves only provoked criticism on Capitol Hill. In early 2018, there were positive things happening within the bureaucracy, but in many cases the "good news" wasn't being shared effectively with congressional overseers or private sector partners. The "one-team, one-fight" mantra first articulated for cyber during the George W. Bush years didn't work when the partners were holed up in their own castles.

In early March 2018, Director of National Intelligence (DNI) Coats acknowledged, during his own appearance before the Senate Armed Services Committee, that extensive work on cyber remained to be done.

Coats assured the senators that White House officials were engaged on cybersecurity issues—a point that reflected ongoing congressional concerns about the administration's commitment to cyber. The longtime senator from Indiana knew what his former colleagues wanted to hear, and he agreed with the lawmakers that the federal government had yet to develop an effective strategy for deterring and responding to cyberattacks by foreign adversaries. Progress on a whole-of-government strategic and deterrence policy for cyber wasn't coming quickly enough, Coats conceded. "It's a dicey issue."

Coats faced close questioning from senators of both parties on whether the Trump administration was doing enough to secure the 2018 midterm elections from Russian cyber aggression, or to articulate a cyber deterrence strategy. "A plan to take action seems to be missing," said Armed Services ranking member Reed.

Armed Services Cyber Subcommittee chairman Mike Rounds (R-SD) asked directly whether "we have a clear policy on cyber warfare."

"No," Coats responded, saying that putting together such a plan "needs to be a whole-of-government" exercise, while also highlighting the cyber threat facing the private sector. "We still haven't defined how we'll support" critical infrastructure operators, he said. Electric grids, the telecom system, and financial institutions were all prime targets for cyber criminals as well as nation-state adversaries. "Responses" to attacks on these targets "need to be discussed," Coats said. "I've been an advocate of playing offense as well as defense."

Coats said White House Homeland Security adviser Bossert and Cyber Coordinator Joyce were working closely with defense and civilian agencies on how to best defend against, respond to, and prevent cyber aggression. Coats mentioned "working with state election officials" as an ongoing effort by federal agencies to fend off cyberattacks aimed at the midterms.

He also cited "ongoing discussions" within the administration on putting together a deterrence plan, but he agreed there still wasn't "formulation of a lead agency" to drive that effort.

But "ongoing discussions" just weren't going to cut it; lawmakers had already made up their minds that something was missing in the administration's approach. Rounds said he and cyber subcommittee ranking member Bill Nelson (D-FL) "have come to the conclusion . . . that we don't have the appropriate policy in place. . . . Our defensive capabilities won't match the offensive capabilities of our adversaries . . . deterrence has to be a part of this."

Senator Mazie Hirono's (D-Hawaii) critique was more pointed, saying her "conclusion is this is not a priority for the president."

"It starts at the top if we're going to get anything done" on deterrence and securing elections from foreign interference, Senator Reed commented.

A few days later, Senator Rounds and a bipartisan group of senators wrote to Trump and Joyce, saying, "The lack of decisive and clearly articulated consequences to cyber-attacks against our country has served as an open invitation to foreign adversaries and malicious cyber actors to continue attacking the United States."

It would still take a couple of months, but amid the concerns about a drifting policy, cybersecurity reports began flying out of the Trump administration that spring. The White House staff seemed determined to produce black-and-white evidence—for the president, as well as for those congressional audiences—that cyber was under control.

The reports came too late to headline a once-planned-then-scrapped event to mark the May 11 first anniversary of the president's cybersecurity executive order, but it finally provided a good indication of the Trump government's cyber focus and priorities. The one-year anniversary of Obama's first cyber executive order, in February 2014, had included a major White House event featuring some of the most prominent CEOs in the country. In early 2018, the new president's team seemed determined to one-up that event. They didn't manage to pull it off.

The Trump-ordered reports covered botnets, identified by the administration as one of the worst cyber threats facing the internet and digital economy; deterrence and global partnerships; protecting the most critical facilities, like financial and telecom systems, from attack; security of the electricity grid; the cyber workforce; and—a big one—the Department of Homeland Security's "Cyber Strategy."

Reactions were mixed. The botnet report was crafted in close consultation with industry and set off a major new collaborative process on a strong positive footing. With all of the private sector input and interest, this report attracted the most reaction following its release.

The focus was understandable: "Bad bots . . . accounted for one-fifth of all internet traffic in 2018," Politico would report later, citing a study by Distil Networks. "The leading sector for that traffic is the financial industry at 42 percent given the theft motive, compared with 30 percent of the traffic in the government sector, where the bots enable attacks on voter registration accounts and business registration listings, Distil found. More than half of the bad bot traffic originates from the U.S., according to the company."

The deterrence report—or what was publicly released—received mixed reviews, with critics charging that it mostly restated the problem, and it garnered little reaction on Capitol Hill despite the intense interest among lawmakers in the deterrence issue. The congressional audience was still awaiting a big and bold policy declaration on deterrence and global engagement, and this document came across as rather skimpy.

And the DHS "Cyber Strategy" was something of a Rorschach test, with some seeing productive patterns and others seeing policy holes.

Each of these reports might have spurred immediate, extensive feedback in years past. That they received such a low-key response was a sign of the extraordinary times; important government policy papers came and went with little notice as immigration and other controversies, largely generated by the president himself, intensified.

May 11, 2018, was significant for another reason: It was Rob Joyce's last day on the job as White House cybersecurity coordinator.

Joyce had been tapped one month earlier to replace his boss, Tom Bossert, as White House Homeland Security adviser, at least on an acting basis. The gesture toward continuity was appreciated by industry groups amid the White House turnover accompanying the appointment of conservative stalwart and political bomb thrower John Bolton as national security adviser. Bolton was a Fox News commentator and, a decade earlier under George W. Bush, a brawling ambassador to the United Nations. Trump named him national security adviser in April 2018, and Bossert was gone shortly thereafter. (Bolton himself would depart a little more than a year later, amid acrimony with the president.)

"Bolton is a more traditional security official," said one source from the national security establishment. "He sees cyber as a piece of broader issues. He doesn't see cybersecurity as different or special."

"It's a good sign that Joyce is taking over, it means we don't have to start all over on the reports," said a former high-ranking government cyber official. The reports, at least, were in good shape.

"But it is surprising—Bossert was a hawk on cyber issues," the source said, adding that Bossert's approach fit neatly with the worldview of both Trump and Bolton. Bossert's departure drew a relatively muted reaction from industry sources, who said he rarely engaged with private sector groups, and, in any case, the well-respected Rob Joyce would be there. Just days later, Joyce announced he was leaving the White House and returning to the National Security Agency.

"Rob Joyce, a career federal employee detailed to the National Security Council, has conveyed his intent to return to his home agency, the National Security Agency," White House Press Secretary Sarah Sanders said in a statement. "However, he has agreed to stay on as needed to provide continuity and facilitate the transition with his replacement. We are all grateful for Rob's continued service to the nation."

Just a routine civil service reassignment, nothing to be seen here.

Once, it looked like a high-profile White House event would be held on May 11, with Joyce presenting a recap of administration cyber efforts as something of a going-away present from an accomplished cybersecurity professional.

Instead, the event was quietly dropped, and hints emerged from the White House that it was killed as a message: that the cyber coordinator position itself was in the trash can. The move probably wasn't that clever; it was more likely that the White House staff simply couldn't pull off the event.

Joyce announced that he wanted to return to his longtime billet at the National Security Agency, but it was clear that he didn't want anything to do with Bolton. The new national security adviser had just forced out Bossert, and though Joyce himself wasn't forced out—officially, at least—Trump's people within the National Security Council could barely conceal their satisfaction over his departure.

The Trump White House confirmed shortly after Joyce left that it would not fill the cyber coordinator position, a portentous decision. Two "senior directors" on the National Security Council staff would pick up the portfolio. "Moving forward, these Senior Directors will coordinate cyber matters and policy. As they sit six feet apart from one another, they will be able to coordinate in real time," an NSC spokesman said in a statement.

That proximity would help in shuffling papers between the two staffers, but it missed the points of the coordinator role. First, the very position itself was a signal to the rest of government and the public that cybersecurity was a paramount issue; the coordinator, as the role was defined by Joyce's

Obama-era predecessor Michael Daniel, was a national and international evangelist on cyber.

Second, it addressed the cross-cutting, jurisdiction-hopping nature of cyber and created a space for figuring out whether and how activities at one department meshed with others. Third, it ensured that one high-level official and government office was focused on cyber and nothing else, particularly relevant given the conflicting demands that always pulled at the DHS secretary and other cabinet leaders.

There were other reasons for having a cyber coordinator—plenty of them—but the position apparently was an annoyance to Bolton, and it was gone.

Kiersten Todt noted that the Obama cyber commission called for investing the coordinator with even more authority in order to "ensure the individual responsible for cybersecurity has direct reporting to the president, given the importance of the issue to the national and economic security of our country."

"Every administration comes in and tries to organize as they think will be most effective," Todt said. "But I don't see a structure and organization in place to respond to the cybersecurity threats as we are seeing them."

The problem predated the departures of Joyce and Bossert, she said, because Trump gave both officials extensive duties beyond cyber. They were working on hurricane preparedness, for instance, an important but hugely time-consuming responsibility placed on top of their cyber roles.

In fact, federal authorities in the fall of 2017 were dealing with severe hurricanes and a mass shooting in Las Vegas as the historic hack at Equifax came to light and unfolded, Todt recalled. "Equifax was put on the back burner, but there should've been a team of people working on that," she said.

"When Howard Schmidt, Michael Daniel, or Rob Joyce spoke on cyber issues, the world paid attention," retired Air Force brigadier general Gregory Touhill said in a statement after the decision was announced to kill off the cyber coordinator role.

Touhill, the former US chief information security officer and senior Department of Homeland Security official, now with Cyxtera Federal Group, was referring to the three men who held the position since 2009: Joyce had just resigned; Schmidt, who died in 2017, was Obama's first cyber coordinator; and Daniel held the post in Obama's second term.

The remaining Trump White House security team brushed off concerns. But Touhill elaborated on the purpose and value of the cyber coordinator position, noting that it was created with an eye toward extensive engagement across government as well as internationally, and with the private sector and other entities.

"The cybersecurity coordinator position was created in 2009, culminating efforts launched during the Clinton and Bush administrations to address growing cyber threats to critical infrastructure, which could potentially jeopardize national security and national prosperity," Touhill said.

"The position was created to coordinate interagency cybersecurity policy development and implementation and to coordinate engagement with federal, state, local, international and private sector cybersecurity partners," he added. "The position also became a critical and invaluable cybersecurity leadership position inside and outside of the U.S. government."

Touhill explained, "The White House cybersecurity coordinator did more than just coordinating development of national cyber policy, representing the U.S. at national and multilateral discussions about cybersecurity, chairing the Vulnerability Equities Process (which governs whether and how 'zero day' vulnerabilities discovered by the U.S. government are disclosed) as well as the Unified Coordination Group and Cyber Response Group processes as spelled out in the National Cyber Incident Response Plan and PPD-41."

He concluded, "How these vital duties will be executed now is unclear—and troubling."

For her part, Todt added that, overall, "we're lacking a White House strategy on cybersecurity—not a PowerPoint, a strategy. The White House has to endorse and drive the strategy."

House Homeland Security ranking member Bennie Thompson (D-MS) said, "A lot has changed since the last time John Bolton served in the White House, but after just a month in the Trump White House he is already wreaking havoc on the National Security Council."

Thompson added, "With cyber threats ever-changing and growing more sophisticated by the day, there is no logical reason to eliminate this senior position and reduce the already degraded level of cyber expertise at the White House. Without an experienced cybersecurity coordinator to drive and advance high-level, sound federal cybersecurity policy, the Trump Administration will be less able to keep cyberspace—and critical infrastructure like our voting systems—secure from malevolent influence."

The decision also landed with a thud with industry groups active on cyber issues.

"A cohesive and comprehensive cybersecurity strategy across all agencies within the federal government can only be accomplished when there is one office specifically tasked with coordination. We hope that the Administration re-considers its decision to eliminate the White House cybersecurity coordinator role," said Elizabeth Hyman, executive vice president of advocacy for IT industry trade association CompTIA.

The cyber coordinator had become a key point of contact for security professionals, business groups, and myriad stakeholders and, among other things, was seen as an honest broker in policy discussions.

Senator James Lankford (R-OK), a leader on cyber issues on the Homeland Security and Intelligence committees, on May 16 issued what his office characterized as the first statement from a Republican "to challenge the White House on this."

"It is absolutely critical that we have a clear cyber doctrine and strategy to defend ourselves against the numerous international and domestic threats—especially those that target our infrastructure and the foundations of our democracy," Lankford said. "There are a multitude of government organizations working in cyber and I encourage the Administration to clearly define who is leading the mission of coordinating the cyber landscape full-time before our adversaries are allowed the opportunity to exploit our cyber vulnerabilities."

Said one well-placed business source, "It is hard to comprehend why the White House would retreat from having a visible role in articulating administration policy and coordinating the activities of multiple agencies. We are at a point in time when strong leadership is required to signal our determination to our adversaries and this sends a message to agencies and to industry that you are on your own."

In mid-May 2018, the widespread, sharply negative reaction to elimination of the White House cybersecurity coordinator position suggested that move was the low point in what became a week of cyber policy miscues. The fumbles included a scrapped plan to release the botnet report that would launch that critical new government-industry collaboration on cyber, as well as Trump's curious maneuvers in the case of Chinese telecom company ZTE.

The botnet report had cleared Commerce Department review and was awaiting final signoff at the Department of Homeland Security, but all of that bureaucratic procedural minutiae should've been cleared up in time for a May 11 release. It was to be the centerpiece of events—including industry-planned gatherings—marking the one-year anniversary of Trump's cyber executive order. "That was mostly a dog-and-pony show to package together reports that were already out, but it was pulled at the last minute," commented one source privy to the internal machinations.

Meanwhile, Trump's tweets on ZTE appeared to kick aside significant policy undertakings aimed at a potential cybersecurity threat to the US supply chain in exchange for possible gains in trade negotiations with China. ZTE was in lawmakers' crosshairs over cyber issues, but it had been sanctioned for violating a prohibition on selling technology to Iran. The sanctions prevented US tech companies from selling components to ZTE, which crippled the Chinese firm's operations.

From the president's Twitter account on May 13, 2018, two days after cyber adviser Joyce decamped for the seemingly calmer environs of the National Security Agency: "President Xi of China, and I, are working together to give massive Chinese phone company, ZTE, a way to get back into business, fast. Too many jobs in China lost. Commerce Department has been instructed to get it done!"

The next day: "ZTE, the large Chinese phone company, buys a big percentage of individual parts from U.S. companies. This is also reflective of the larger trade deal we are negotiating with China and my personal relationship with President Xi."

It marked the first time in the relatively short history of cyber policy that an identified cybersecurity risk was blatantly disregarded in exchange for achieving an unrelated policy goal. Congressional Democrats demanded more information on the ZTE risk. Representative Mike Conaway (R-TX) gamely argued that the Trump tweets didn't undermine legislation he and prominent colleagues had introduced to ban ZTE and fellow Chinese telecom Huawei from the federal supply chain.

The botnet report delay and the confusion over ZTE suggested why George W. Bush and Barack Obama both saw a need for an empowered, high-level cybersecurity coordinator with a direct line to the Oval Office.

Obama named the first coordinator, the late Howard Schmidt, a former Microsoft executive, but the idea germinated under Bush's cyber policy adviser Melissa Hathaway. Her seminal work on developing first-time policy structures around cyber was so well received that Obama asked her to stay on into his administration.

Fast forward to 2018, when, with the departure of Rob Joyce from the coordinator role, Bolton decided that the position amounted to redundant bureaucracy.

"The National Security Council's cyber office already has two very capable Senior Directors," an NSC spokesman said in a statement. "Moving forward, these Senior Directors will coordinate cyber matters and policy. As they sit six feet apart from one another, they will be able to coordinate in real time. Yesterday's actions continue an effort to empower National Security Council Senior Directors. Streamlining management will improve efficiency, reduce bureaucracy and increase accountability."

A year later, there was a small but telling episode that demonstrated how something had been lost by scrapping the White House coordinator role. One of the NSC deputies wanted to piggyback a "White House event" onto the annual RSA Security Conference in San Francisco, one of the premier cyber events of the year. The White House wasn't commenting, but the deputy made the rounds suggesting he would headline a session at the

Hoover Institution at Stanford University, about thirty-five miles down the road from San Francisco.

"The problem is it's right in the middle of RSA and he just isn't a big draw," said one source familiar with the discussions around the event. "Maybe if it were Bolton . . ."

Or if it were Rob Joyce or Michael Daniel—or even that deputy, if he had the White House coordinator title.

The White House declined to comment on any aspect of the proposed event. But it didn't come off.

Key players were well aware of an emerging vacuum on cyber leadership. "Maybe Bolton thinks DHS has the role," said one cyber policy expert. "But if that's his position, he needs to put it in writing and formally give DHS that endorsement."

Maybe the assurance came in a private communication, but, in any case, one newly confirmed senior DHS official was ready to state the case that his department was in charge when it came to cyber. Christopher Krebs was sharp, he was quick, and he didn't need anything in writing; he was a walking, talking cyber embodiment of the maxim "Go big or go home."

"There is a nasty rumor in town that there is no cybersecurity leadership," Krebs, now the top cyber official at the Department of Homeland Security, said at a June 2018 industry conference. On the contrary, he said, punching the air for emphasis, "There is a plan . . . there is a strategy."

It was an assertion applauded by some and drawing smirks from others in the US cybersecurity community—a loose group that didn't carry membership cards, but one in which the members recognized one another. It was not a body given to partisan or political divisions, but nonetheless it was challenged, like every other aspect of American society, by a "disruptor" president with little regard for convention or precedent.

Krebs was well known in cybersecurity circles, a youthful former Microsoft executive with respected organizational skills and policy chops. He was part of the group of private sector advisers who helped NIST shape its framework of cybersecurity standards in 2013 and 2014, and he had been close to the action since the early days of cyber policy development. He came aboard at DHS early in 2017 as an adviser to the new secretary, General Kelly, and then was named to successively higher posts at the bureaucratic forerunner to the department's cyber agency. After a long delay in the Senate for reasons entirely unrelated to his qualifications for the post, Krebs was sworn in as undersecretary for the cyber-focused but poorly named National Protection and Programs Directorate on June 15, 2018.

Now, with a chance to lead a team into battle, he would strive relentlessly to drum up excitement within his department, with industry partners and overseers on Capitol Hill. And Krebs would steadfastly ignore the existence of any barriers to achieving a set of cyber policy goals.

But he was up against a policy environment created by an impetuous and unpredictable president. Saying there was a strategy just didn't make it so.

Hathaway, veteran of the George W. Bush and Obama White Houses, in the spring of 2018 cited a disconnect between the batch of Trump executive order–inspired strategic documents and the scale of the cyber threat. She also flagged a government report finding that seventy-one of ninety-six federal agencies were "either at risk or high risk" of cyberattack.

"I do not believe that there is a strategy and I am really disturbed with the risk report . . . [showing] that 74 percent of the USG institutions are either at risk or high risk," Hathaway said. "When coupled with the announcement that Russia is deliberately targeting our critical infrastructures—I have to conclude that we are not serious—and the complacency regarding what I believe to be an existential threat, is remarkable."

She pulled out a quote that Bush liked to use: "We need, what my old boss would say, [is a] '2x4 shampoo' and get some honest leaders dedicated to the situation."

To the contrary, said Larry Clinton of the industry-based Internet Security Alliance. There were still shortcomings, Clinton said, but the real progress was in framing the way the government saw its engagement with industry and its growing embrace of a forward-looking risk management model both for its own networks and in collaborating with the private sector.

"I see prioritization" in the DHS strategy, the botnet report, the recent update to the National Institute of Standards and Technology's framework of cybersecurity standards, and in the underlying Trump executive order, Clinton said.

"DHS is reaching out to the private sector," Clinton said, adding that "substantive policy discussions are underway."

Clinton concluded that "a lot of this is carried over from the Obama administration—and that's very powerful, it's an enhancement of the consensus approach to cybersecurity."

But that consensus was strained—by unforced errors at the White House such as eliminating the cyber coordinator spot; dropping the State Department's top cyber position; and the decision by Trump's Federal Communications Commission to abolish "net neutrality" and a related cybersecurity package, as well as canceling an FCC initiative aimed at securing the next generation of wireless telecom services known as "5G."

It was strained by the president's awkward dance with China and seeming willingness, on the one hand, to sell out security concerns in the quest for trade deals and, on the other, to ignore international partners whenever the administration decided to escalate its trade wars.

The passel of reports issued by federal departments offered steps toward a cybersecurity strategy, policy veterans said, but actually forging a national plan of action was yet to be accomplished—and would be hindered by the lack of a cyber coordinator at the White House or any other overarching authority on cybersecurity.

"I agree that we have seen some progress and though we welcomed the DHS cybersecurity strategy and the [Department of Energy] cyber strategy, I still don't believe that adds up to a comprehensive, national strategy," commented Ann Beauchesne, director of the Aspen Institute's Cybersecurity and Technology Institute.

Beauchesne emphasized that "cybersecurity is a cross-cutting issue and it is essential that there is coordination between the federal agencies and the private sector." With that in mind, she said, "It is beyond puzzling to me that amid the growing cyber threats we face we have no national cybersecurity strategy nor do we have a White House cyber coordinator."

And the cyber consensus was strained by the Trump administration's aversion to confronting certain cybersecurity questions, perhaps from fear that the very issue tended to bleed into questions of Russia's role in electing a US president.

The cyber world was grappling with major hacks like the one at Equifax that affected nearly half of all Americans and the exploding scandal over Facebook's uses of personal data. But the Trump administration had little to say about either.

"If people aren't dying, it's not a priority," acidly noted a cybersecurity policy veteran of the previous administration.

The question remained: Did the Trump administration actually have a cybersecurity strategy, or was it hell-bent on dismantling years of consensus building on how the nation should respond to an existential threat to its digital life blood? And why the curious shortcomings? Was Russia, as a cloud around the Trump brand name, inhibiting administration efforts to craft a true cyber strategy?

Beneath it all, the question lurked on what was to come out of special counsel Robert Mueller's Russia investigation. Mueller had been named to the independent investigator post by Deputy Attorney General Rod Rosenstein on May 17, 2017, a week and a day after Trump fired Comey at the FBI. Mueller himself was a ramrod-straight former director of the FBI, who inspired confidence on both sides of the aisle. He was a highly decorated combat Marine officer in Vietnam, and he was a Republican.

Rosenstein made the appointment because then–attorney general Jeff Sessions recused himself from the probe into Russian interference in the

2016 elections after acknowledging previously unreported meetings with the Russian ambassador to the United States. Trump never forgave Sessions for recusing himself, and he wasn't very forgiving toward Rosenstein either. Ironically enough, Rosenstein's own—voluntary—departure from government would be accompanied by Trump-like blasts at the media as news emerged of his efforts to reassure the president about the likely outcome of the Mueller probe.

Meanwhile, that nagging Russia question was at the heart of what former House Speaker Newt Gingrich (R-GA)—a Trump ally—called the worst mistake of his presidency: the disastrous July 16, 2018, press conference following Trump's summit with Russian president Vladimir Putin.

4

A Fiasco in Helsinki

In July 2018, as President Trump prepared for a trip to Brussels to meet with NATO leaders and then to Helsinki for an anxiously awaited summit with Russian president Vladimir Putin, the Department of Justice announced the indictment of twelve Russian military intelligence officers for hacking activities aimed at the 2016 US elections—a case developed under Special Counsel Mueller's investigation.

The White House was briefed that the indictment was coming, according to published reports. Democrats swiftly issued statements ranging from a call to cancel the Putin summit—from Senate Minority Leader Charles Schumer (D-NY)—to Senator Warner's remarkable warning that Trump shouldn't be allowed to meet alone with Putin.

"Today's indictment of a dozen Russian military intelligence officials confirms that hacking of Democrats during the 2016 campaign was conducted by Russia's intelligence services, a campaign that the U.S. intelligence community has already assessed was directed by Vladimir Putin," said Senator Dianne Feinstein (D-CA), a longtime leader on cyber issues. "Given the serious allegations in this indictment, I support Senator Schumer's call for President Trump to cancel his meeting with Vladimir Putin until Russia takes meaningful steps to prove it won't interfere in future elections."

Feinstein added, "The indictment of these 12 Russians provides further evidence that Special Counsel Mueller's investigation is following the facts and producing tangible results. One allegation in today's indictment that we need to know more about is that Russians communicated with at least one

American who 'was in regular contact with senior members of the presidential campaign of Donald J. Trump' about the release of stolen documents."

The Democratic statements were surely to be expected, but the president's approach to Russia stirred bipartisan concern on Capitol Hill that wasn't tempered by news of indictments.

Senator Ben Sasse (R-NE), an emerging voice on cyber, said, "The U.S. intelligence community knows that the Russian government attacked the U.S. This is not a Republican or a Democrat view—it is simply the reality. All patriotic Americans should understand that Putin is not America's friend, and he is not the President's buddy. We should stand united against Putin's past and planned future attacks against us."

It sounded like something a GOP senator might've said about Jimmy Carter or Barack Obama, not about a fellow Republican in the White House.

Reflecting the ongoing political sensitivity around anything involving Russia, the White House released a statement on the indictment, saying, "As Deputy Attorney General Rod Rosenstein said today: 'There is no allegation in this indictment that Americans knew that they were corresponding with Russians. There is no allegation in this indictment that any American citizen committed a crime. There is no allegation that the conspiracy changed the vote count or affected any election result.'"

The White House statement stressed, "Today's charges include no allegations of knowing involvement by anyone on the campaign and no allegations that the alleged hacking affected the election result. This is consistent with what we have been saying all along."

There was also an interesting cyber tidbit in the indictment that David Corn and Dan Friedman would later note in *Mother Jones*:

> And then there is this nugget: In Mueller's indictment of 12 Russian military intelligence officers for hacking and leaking Democratic emails, he noted that "on or about July 27, 2016, the Conspirators attempted after hours to spearphish for the first time email accounts at a domain hosted by a third-party provider and used by Clinton's personal office. At or around the same time, they also targeted seventy-six email addresses at the domain for the Clinton Campaign." Earlier that day, Trump had exclaimed at a rally, "Russia, if you're listening, I hope you're able to find the 30,000 emails that are missing." Nowadays, Trump claims he was merely joking. But this is another question Mueller's investigation has prompted: Was it anything but a coincidence that hours after Trump made this request, Russian hackers for the first time attacked Clinton's personal office and also went after email addresses at the Clinton campaign?

Neither the president himself nor the White House issued a statement of condemnation regarding the Russian hacking actions targeted in the indictment. There was no presidential voice framing the issue, explaining its importance to American voters, friends, and adversaries abroad, and, of course, to the Russians. As usual, there was an unmistakable sense that Trump was allowing certain steps to be taken by the DOJ because, well, because it was expected and perhaps unavoidable. But his own buy-in was minimal or nonexistent.

"On election interference, they still haven't issued a clear statement saying this is unacceptable," said former State Department cybersecurity coordinator Christopher Painter. "They still need to say something clear and definitive on past [Russian] conduct."

That wasn't in the works. But still, just before the July 11–12 NATO summit that would precede Helsinki, Painter commented that the alliance was working well together on cybersecurity at the operational level amid larger political tensions and a general scaling back of US initiatives.

"The U.S. has continued to work closely with its allies on cybersecurity issues," Painter said from Brussels that week. But he said the United States "is not playing as energetic a role" either within NATO or on the international stage in general, since deciding a year earlier to eliminate the coordinator position at the State Department.

"I don't think our European partners think we're abandoning them on cyber, that hasn't been an area of concern," Painter said. "But there is a question about the U.S. commitment to providing high-level leadership."

Major news outlets, including the *Washington Post*, ran extensive pieces on European leaders' gloomy views on the state of the alliance, though cyber generally didn't feature in these articles. Painter said it wasn't hard to detect concerns from the Europeans on the issue of Russia and cyber deterrence.

"There have to be consequences [for cyberattacks] and this applies to Russia too," Painter said. "We've sent mixed messages—we need high-level messaging that we're going to do something about this," he said of Russia-linked hacks aimed at US and European elections.

"We need a firm, consistent message, and the message has been mixed," Painter said. "The U.S. and the NATO allies are still on the same page on cyber, although U.S. leadership has fallen off some. The coordinator position was key on this."

Ann Beauchesne of the Aspen Institute noted, "In addition to eliminating the State Department cyber coordinator, getting rid of the White House cyber coordinator doesn't help either. I suspect and hope that cooperation continues on cybersecurity with our NATO partners behind the scenes. Chris is right, the structures are in place." With the allies, at least.

But she was willing to say bluntly and on the record things that other policy pros only whispered: "I don't expect President Trump will ever be a leader on cybersecurity with NATO or in general," she said. "And given his refusal to accept the findings of the entire U.S. intelligence community that Russia interfered with the 2016 elections and his upcoming one-on-one meeting with Putin in Helsinki I don't see this changing anytime soon. And DHS has been spending more time on the 'illegal immigration crisis on the southern border' rather than an actual real crisis that is our nation's cybersecurity."

The indictment, plus a surprisingly strong NATO declaration that sharply targeted Russian cyber aggression, would form the backdrop for the July 16 summit between Trump and Putin, which had the potential to shape cyber relations between the two countries for years to come.

"I hope the two leaders have an honest conversation about security in cyberspace," Bruce McConnell, vice president of the EastWest Institute and formerly the top cyber official at the Department of Homeland Security, said in advance of the summit. "These two major cyber powers should be cooperating to reduce the chances of large-scale cyber conflicts, not attacking each other under the table."

After weeks of Trump haranguing NATO and questioning whether the organization was even necessary, the US president and the alliance's other leaders ultimately agreed to a communique in Brussels that explicitly called out Russian aggression in cyberspace. There were audible sounds of relief amid the fears that Trump, in a running dispute with allies over defense spending and other issues, might refuse to sign a tough statement targeting Russia. Trump's high-decibel rhetoric toward the European defense partners before and during the summit had ratcheted up concerns that he might cause irreparable damage to the alliance on the eve of his Putin summit.

The president displayed "a destructive attitude during the NATO summit that could undermine his position going into the Putin summit," commented Painter. "But the communique had strong language on cybersecurity and cyber threats. That was all very good." Painter added, "The communique communicated a position of strength. The question is, how much of that will Trump communicate to Russia?"

Maybe Trump's tough language toward NATO allies actually strengthened his hand in dealing with Putin, a US business source suggested, because the Europeans did recommit to more defense spending. But there was one caveat, this source said: "Trump still hasn't addressed the reality of them hacking our elections."

The summit in Helsinki provided an opening to address that criticism, and the NATO declaration and the Department of Justice indictment of Russians gave the president fresh ammunition to use in his talks with Putin, if he chose to do so.

The "Brussels summit declaration" stated, "We face a dangerous, unpredictable, and fluid security environment, with enduring challenges and threats from all strategic directions; from state and non-state actors; from military forces; and from terrorist, cyber, and hybrid attacks. Russia's aggressive actions, including the threat and use of force to attain political goals, challenge the Alliance and are undermining Euro-Atlantic security and the rules-based international order. . . . We face hybrid challenges, including disinformation campaigns and malicious cyber activities. . . . In light of all this, our unity and solidarity are stronger than ever; we will take all necessary steps to ensure our collective defence."

The seventy-nine bullet points in the communique included extensive discussion of cyber issues. The document read, "Cyber threats to the security of the Alliance are becoming more frequent, complex, destructive, and coercive. NATO will continue to adapt to the evolving cyber threat landscape, which is affected by both state and non-state actors, including state-sponsored. Cyber defence is part of NATO's core task of collective defence."

But many of the points, on cyber and other issues like the Crimea annexation, directly and forcefully addressed Russia challenges.

Coming out of a meeting in London with British prime minister Theresa May, Trump said he didn't have high expectations for the Putin summit but that he would warn the Russian not to interfere with US elections. At the Trump-May joint press conference, Trump described "a tremendous meeting that we had with NATO. . . . And we left that meeting, I think, probably more unified and wealthier as a group than ever before. So we go in strong" to the meeting with Putin.

"I know you'll ask will we be talking about meddling," Trump said to reporters. "And I will absolutely bring that up. I don't think you'll have any 'Gee, I did it. I did it. You got me.' There won't be a Perry Mason here, I don't think. But you never know what happens, right? But I will absolutely firmly ask the question."

In order to begin getting past the domestic political turmoil over cyber policy toward Russia, Painter suggested that Trump needed to "raise it and raise it strongly" in his meeting with Putin. "And I hope he goes beyond just raising it," Painter said. "There's a difference between raising the issue and consistently pressing it at a high level."

Painter said the NATO communique "was the kind of message you wanted," but "whether the president follows up remains to be seen."

The Trump-Putin summit in Helsinki, if this was even imaginable, turned out worse than the pessimists were predicting.

On July 14, the president went on Twitter to say, "I have arrived in Scotland and will be at Trump Turnberry for two days of meetings, calls and hopefully, some golf—my primary form of exercise! The weather is beautiful, and this place is incredible! Tomorrow I go to Helsinki for a Monday meeting with Vladimir Putin."

On July 15, Trump tweeted, "Heading to Helsinki, Finland—looking forward to meeting with President Putin tomorrow. Unfortunately, no matter how well I do at the Summit, if I was given the great city of Moscow as retribution for all of the sins and evils committed by Russia . . ."

At his breakfast with Finnish president Sauli Niinisto prior to the Putin meeting, Trump said, "NATO has, I think, never been stronger. It was a little bit tough at the beginning, but it turned out to be love. . . . NATO has never been more together. People are now agreeing to pay. We were having a lot of problems with a lot people not paying, as the president will tell you. . . . They're paying more rapidly." President Niinisto politely didn't comment on the fact that Finland is a partner but not a dues-paying member of NATO, but no matter.

Asked about his message to Putin, Trump said, "We'll see him a little while. . . . We'll do just fine."

Trump blasted the Mueller probe in a round of tweets before heading over to the Putin meeting.

The tweets drew this response from former House Intelligence chairman Mike Rogers, a Michigan Republican, on Russia's behavior: "Waged continuous & increasingly aggressive cyberattacks against us, Interfered in our 2016 elections, Annexed Crimea, Shot down a civilian airliner, Supports Assad in Syria, Invaded our ally Georgia, Murdered opponents in London, Should I continue?"

Putin's late arrival pushed the start of the summit back by nearly an hour, but the one-on-one session lasted for two hours. Planners had allotted an hour and a half for the private meeting. Standing by for the broader talks were Secretary of State Mike Pompeo; Chief of Staff Kelly; National Security Adviser Bolton; Fiona Hill, senior director for Europe and Russia on the National Security Council; and US ambassador to Russia Jon Huntsman. Pentagon and intelligence community leaders weren't in the waiting room, but a very senior and hardheaded bunch was on hand to buttress the president on whatever demands he was going to put before Putin.

When the two presidents finally emerged, Trump said he directly raised the issue of Russian interference in US elections in his one-on-one meeting with Putin, while remarkably casting doubt on the US intelligence community's conclusions and stressing that prospects for wide-ranging cooperation between the two countries were enhanced by the summit in Helsinki.

Putin, during the leaders' joint press conference, categorically rejected accusations about a Russian government role in the 2016 election hacking and offered to allow Special Counsel Mueller's team to participate in questioning of the twelve Russian military intelligence officers indicted by the United States. But Putin said Russian officials should be allowed to interview US intelligence officers in other cases.

Trump called that "an interesting idea," causing jaws to drop throughout the US intelligence community. He cited Putin's "strong and powerful" denial of a Russian role in election meddling. He noted that DNI Coats "came to me" and said Russia played a role in the hacking. But standing next to Putin he added, "I don't see any reason why it would be" Russia behind the hacks.

Trump raised questions about how the US investigation into 2016 election hacks had been conducted while stating repeatedly that there was no collusion between his campaign and Russian entities. He called the Mueller investigation "a disaster for our country, it's kept us apart."

Putin called the collusion claims "nonsense." He said he did want Trump to win the election because the Republican "talked about normalizing relations," but he ignored a reporter's question about whether Russia played an active role in ensuring that outcome.

The two presidents both said bilateral cooperation between the countries would improve on cybersecurity and other issues, but they didn't announce any specific steps. Putin said cybersecurity could now be discussed in "an atmosphere of cooperation," and that hacking allegations could be addressed through a US-Russia cybersecurity working group.

Trump called his meeting with Putin "deeply productive" and said he would take the political risk of seeking peace between the nations. The two leaders agreed to meet again "often" in the future, Trump said, and would "hopefully resolve every one of the problems."

There was no calling Russia to account for its cyber aggression against the United States—or against American allies or the liberated former Soviet states, for that matter.

Back home, the reactions came quickly from both parties, the intense negativity taking Trump by surprise, according to numerous accounts.

Senator Sasse issued a statement condemning Trump's assertion that both countries are to blame for deteriorating relations. "This is bizarre and flat-out wrong," Sasse said. "The United States is not to blame. America wants a good relationship with the Russian people but Vladimir Putin and his thugs are responsible for Soviet-style aggression. When the President plays these moral equivalence games, he gives Putin a propaganda win he desperately needs."

Trump's remark that "I don't see any reason why it would be" Russia behind the hacks on US elections systems in 2016 was "outrageous," Senator Warner said.

"This is the defining day for the Trump presidency, and I think the president came out on the wrong side," Warner said, telling reporters that "if some of my colleagues' heads aren't spinning after this press conference, well, time will tell . . . in light of some of the president's comments today, I think there are times in the Senate where people have to stand up and take a side, and this is one of those times."

Senator Marco Rubio (R-FL) said Trump's remarks were "not accurate," citing the "unparalleled amount of evidence in regards to" Russian interference in the 2016 elections.

Rubio also warned of the dangers of Russia, or other foreign adversaries, interfering in other critical infrastructure sectors, saying that having control over such sectors could be a "powerful tool in times of conflict."

"It could include our banking sector . . . it could involve all sorts of critical infrastructure, which used to be vulnerable to nuclear attack or conventional attack, now are a few clicks away from being used by a potential adversary," Rubio said.

"To think that Russians are just trying to penetrate just election infrastructure is wrong, they are trying to penetrate all of our systems, we are looking at protections of our judicial systems, in our power grid system, the vulnerabilities we have in the cyber domain," Warner added.

The fallout seemed likely to endure, though in many ways it would become another outrageous episode in the running reality show that was the Trump presidency.

Reports would gradually emerge alleging Trump destroyed his interpreter's notes from the Putin meeting, and a *New York Times* blockbuster months later stated that the FBI was investigating whether the Russians had something on the president.

But in the immediate aftermath of Helsinki, there was only bewilderment and outrage.

The day after, amid growing bipartisan criticism, Trump expressed "faith" in the US intelligence community's conclusions about Russia's meddling in the 2016 election and said efforts were under way to prevent interference in the 2018 midterms.

"I have full faith in our intelligence agencies," Trump told reporters prior to a White House meeting with House members on tax issues. "I accept our intelligence community conclusion that Russia's meddling in the 2016 election took place." The president wasn't unequivocal, adding, "Could be other people also; there's a lot of people out there."

Trump stressed again on July 17 that there was "no collusion" between his 2016 campaign and Russian agents, and said, "We are doing everything in our power to prevent Russian interference in 2018."

Trump offered a clarification of one comment at the joint press conference with Putin: "I actually went out and reviewed a clip of an answer that I gave, and I realized that there is need for some clarification. It should have been obvious—I thought it would be obvious—but I would like to clarify, just in case it wasn't."

Trump said, "In a key sentence in my remarks, I said the word 'would' instead of 'wouldn't.' The sentence should have been: I don't see any reason why I wouldn't—or why it wouldn't be Russia. So just to repeat it, I said the word 'would' instead of 'wouldn't.' And the sentence should have been—and I thought it would be maybe a little bit unclear on the transcript or unclear on the actual video—the sentence should have been: I don't see any reason why it wouldn't be Russia. Sort of a double negative. So you can put that in, and I think that probably clarifies things pretty good by itself."

The president took a shot at his predecessor, saying, "President Obama was given information just prior to the election, last election 2016, and they decided to not do anything about it. The reason they decided not to do that was pretty obvious because they thought Hillary Clinton was going to win the election."

The Obama administration "buried" information on Russian meddling, Trump said.

Obama administration cybersecurity officials offered extensive insights into their internal deliberations on how to handle evidence of Russian hacking in 2016, and they did communicate with congressional intelligence leaders on what they were seeing. The former president said he was concerned that publicizing what US intelligence was learning about Russian activities would be seen as politicizing the information in order to benefit Democratic nominee Clinton.

Meanwhile, congressional Democrats and even some Republicans took steps to subpoena Trump's interpreter to find out what was said in the president's one-on-one session with Putin.

Senators Jeff Flake (R-AZ) and Chris Coons (D-DE) offered a sense of the Senate resolution calling for information on the meeting and other steps, while the top Republican in the Senate—Majority Leader Mitch McConnell of Kentucky—quickly directed the Banking and Foreign Relations panels to examine possible additional sanctions as a way to influence Russia's behavior. It was also a way for Senate Republicans to subtly distance themselves from the president with a transparent message on getting tough with Russia.

Representative Adam Schiff of California, the top Democrat on the House Intelligence Committee, told Inside Cybersecurity that "Congress is going to have to be far more interventionist on policy because we cannot count on our president." He said Trump's actions at the summit would have a "lasting impact" and "broke through the confusion of the [ongoing Mueller] investigation."

Collusion charges were up to Mueller, Schiff said, but "for whatever reason, the president cannot stand up to Russia."

Walking toward the Capitol on a sunny July morning, Schiff made clear his belief that the Russians, somehow, for some reason, were manipulating the president and that collusion was in the air.

The former White House cyber adviser Ari Schwartz said, "The Helsinki meeting was so outside the realm of anything that has ever come before that it is impossible to know what the long-term implication is. Also, the president's own advisers don't seem to know exactly what was agreed upon which makes it even harder to judge."

The president's seeming embrace of—and then reversal on—Putin's denials of hacking was followed by word out of the White House that Bolton had invited Putin to a second summit in the fall in Washington, DC. The White House appeared to be trying to frame Helsinki as just a step in a process for compelling Russia to change its behavior.

"That's going to be special," DNI Coats quipped at an Aspen Institute event, obviously surprised and taken aback by the news. That second summit ultimately did not come to pass, to the relief of everyone with the possible exception of Trump, Bolton, and Putin. However, Coats's sarcastic crack would get back to the president and start the slow but inexorable process of pushing the intelligence chief out of the circle of trust. Coats would leave the administration a year later.

Secretary of State Pompeo, who worked hard to keep his membership in that circle, came to Capitol Hill on July 25 for the first congressional appearance by a senior Trump official since the summit, drawing a media swarm and a panel of senators obviously ready for a turn in the spotlight.

Senator Cory Booker (D-NJ), a presidential contender for 2020, said the administration was unconvincing in saying that Trump didn't discuss relaxing sanctions with Putin. "I really don't believe you know what happened in the president's two-hour meeting with Putin," Booker charged.

"I've been here almost three hours and you're making a political soliloquy," a combative Pompeo responded.

In an intense exchange with Senate Foreign Relations ranking member Robert Menendez (D-NJ), Pompeo finally said he would work with Congress on additional sanctions aimed at Russia, while stressing that Trump emphasized to Putin that the United States would not relax existing sanctions on that country.

Trump's reluctance to publicly call out Putin spurred bipartisan criticism, but Pompeo said the president made clear that the United States would impose "severe consequences" if Russia repeated such actions in the 2018 elections.

Senate Foreign Relations Chairman Bob Corker (R-TN) expressed "serious doubts" about Trump's conduct of foreign policy, saying that "Russia [is] the most troubling example of this reality." Corker said Congress must know "what our president is agreeing to" in his private conversations with Putin.

"Convince us they know what they're doing" at the White House, Corker urged Pompeo. Corker said groups of lawmakers would go to the White House for meetings on foreign policy, but "none have left with the sense there is a coherent strategy."

He said the White House's "ready, fire, aim," approach was exemplified by its approach to Russia.

Pompeo was having none of this. He said Trump made the point to the Russian president that the United States would use the "toughest tools" to counter cyber and other aggression, but said progress was impossible "if we don't talk." He said Trump had a "complete understanding" of what Russia did in 2016 and did have faith in the US intelligence community, despite repeatedly questioning its conclusions about the cyber-enabled campaign aimed at the election system in support of candidate Trump.

In response to a question from Rubio, Pompeo spoke favorably of the proposed "Deter Act" that would require a report within thirty days of an election on whether there was foreign interference and apply automatic sanctions if there was. The Trump team could live with that, Pompeo suggested, and with that green light, Senate Majority Leader McConnell also would signal interest in the Deter Act, a bipartisan measure sponsored by Rubio and Senator Chris Van Hollen (D-MD).

The underlying theme of the Senate Foreign Relations hearing with Pompeo—on the GOP side of the dais—was that good deterrence policies were being implemented on cyber and other threats, regardless of controversies over Trump's equivocal statements over Russia.

Corker, Flake, and to some extent Rubio challenged Pompeo on the impact of Trump's public musings about his own intelligence services and Putin, and other aspects of Trump's approach. But even Corker saluted the administration's policy work on deterrence. It was a stark example of the delicate line walked by congressional Republicans—and of the seeming paradoxes in the Trump administration's cyber approaches: solid work down in the policy trenches, while a circus up top raised endless questions about what the president was doing and wanted in cyberspace.

"They are putting in place strong policies," Corker said in response to a question from Inside Cybersecurity. "The things [Pompeo] said about policy are true. It's the confusion at the top" that's worrisome.

"Really it's the confusion that comes from the White House," Corker told reporters at another point. "These statements from the White House matter."

Corker engaged in an occasionally tense back and forth with Pompeo. "In many ways the policies being put in place are stronger than ever, I agree with you," Corker told Pompeo during the hearing. "It's the president that causes concern."

He said Trump "purposely caused the American people to doubt" NATO, among other examples, adding, "Why does he do those things? Is there some strategy in creating doubt in the minds of U.S. senators?"

Pompeo pushed back, citing "the toughest sanctions" ever on Russia and a massive US military buildup as directly hurting Putin, while also noting that the Trump administration blacklisted tech products from Russia-based Kaspersky Lab and expelled numerous Russian "diplomats."

"I notice you are not responding to what I'm saying," Corker said. "It is the president's statements that create concern."

Corker told reporters afterward that Pompeo "acquitted himself well," although he said there was little new insight into what was said between Trump and Putin at their private meeting on July 16.

But most other committee Republicans dutifully saluted the administration's approach to a wide range of foreign policy issues, and most followed Pompeo's lead in praising the president himself as the one who demanded and shaped these policies.

There were similarities to another high-profile hearing on Capitol Hill: former FBI Director Comey's June 2017 appearance before the Senate Intelligence Committee. In that case, most committee Republicans hammered on one point: that there was no allegation of legal transgressions by the president. Likewise, two years later, House Judiciary and Intelligence committee Republicans would be united around one key point in their hearings with Special Counsel Mueller—namely, that his investigation didn't recommend any criminal charges against the president.

The GOP point this time was a little less dramatic but still highly significant: the Trump administration was on the right track with its deterrence policy and should be supported in Congress.

It was left to committee Democrats to press Pompeo for details on the Trump-Putin Helsinki meeting, to minimal effect. Pompeo stressed that Trump made clear there would be serious consequences for continuing to interfere in US elections and that sanctions would remain in place.

Pompeo's combativeness, and the litany of policy moves recited by the secretary, seemed to be exactly what most of the Senate Republicans were hoping for from this important congressional engagement with a top Trump official: nothing was being conceded to the Democrats, and the secretary of state was giving them evidence they could cite of tangible get-tough policies.

Chairman Corker framed the July 25 hearing as a first step in determining the need for additional actions—such as more sanctions—aimed at curbing Russia's aggressive behavior in cyberspace and in the physical world. But obviously, it was also a first step in giving Republicans political cover after what many in both parties saw as the president's disastrous performance in Helsinki.

Trump's seeming acquiescence to Putin's cyber provocations in the 2016 election, before a global audience, came just three days after Mueller generated the indictment of a dozen Russian military officers for hacking Democrats during the election. It came days after Trump signed onto a NATO statement that condemned Russian cyber aggression and had the makings of a principled and well-articulated stand on cybersecurity.

In one press conference, Trump obliterated those gains and potentially undermined and alienated his own intelligence community. Well-connected sources said Trump's comments reverberated through cybersecurity circles. DNI Coats put out an extraordinary statement defending the work of US intelligence agencies against their own president.

"The [intelligence] community is pretty unhappy," said one source who served in Republican and Democratic administrations. "No silver lining either. . . . It's all bad. Morale is truly affected."

But it wasn't a one-off: Trump's entire approach to cybersecurity was antithetical to good cyber policy.

Retired admiral David Simpson, who ran cybersecurity at the Federal Communications Commission during the Obama administration, said the trouble with Russia went well beyond the Helsinki disaster.

"Russia, while called out with regards to elections, is still getting 'kid-glove' treatment," Simpson said. "The administration has not called their government to task for the continued Russian support and safe harbor provided to cybercriminals, who know that as long as they don't undermine Russia's goals, they'll continue to be given wide latitude to hone their skills in western economies and governments. It is encouraging that there have been a few public attributions and indictments, but these are not enough to counter the continued malicious role Russia plays in the digital ecosystem."

And this, the admiral said, "applies to both cybersecurity and information influence operations that have greatly damaged the concept of 'the public square' for democracy-loving countries. Continued administration attacks on U.S. media have greatly undermined our counter-narrative around the world, which for over a century had been 'the gold standard' for free, fair and open press. This administration has given authoritarian governments 'top cover' for asserting strong state control of messaging without a respected alternative voice."

These were facts that neither tough rhetoric and indictments aimed at Russia nor Trump's extended hand of friendship to Putin were changing.

5

You Want "Tough"? OK, We'll Be Cyber Tough

THE DUALITY OF MESSAGES coming from the administration could be dizzying.

In July 2018, the president claimed the mantle of peacemaker in Helsinki and brushed aside the most serious allegations of Russian cyber war on the United States. In August, the White House let it be known that it was making it easier for the military to launch offensive operations against cyber aggressors, presumably including Russia.

The juxtaposition caused plenty of double takes, but there were also serious policy issues to consider. Some industry sources and Obama administration veterans expressed concerns about the decision to scrap Presidential Policy Directive-20 (PPD-20)—a not-so-secret secret document that guided how decisions were made on using the military's cyber weapons—while other sources said it simply removed bureaucratic hurdles that undermined cyber deterrence policy.

The *Wall Street Journal* posted an exclusive story August 15, saying, "President Trump has reversed an Obama-era memorandum dictating how and when the U.S. government can deploy cyberweapons against its adversaries, in an effort to loosen restrictions on such operations, according to people familiar with the action."

The White House didn't publicly acknowledge the policy change, and a National Security Council spokesman said there would be "no statement." That was standard operating procedure with classified policy documents. But the policy issues were well known.

Under PPD-20, offensive actions by US Cyber Command were subject to both presidential authorization and an interagency review process, the latter an additional step that other military commands didn't have to go through. "This makes Cyber Command like the other commands, and that's a good thing," James Lewis of the Center for Strategic and International Studies said of reversing PPD-20. "I'm not sure they needed to do this [through a presidential order] but the Pentagon wanted clarity and they had a legitimate complaint" about the PPD-20 process.

Lewis blamed Obama administration "indecisiveness" about cyber actions for creating a problem in the first place and said that now, apparently, "it will work like every other presidential military authorization: A commander at the four-star level will develop and execute an operational plan without having to go through an inter-agency review."

The previous approach "slowed everything down by weeks or months," Lewis said. He observed that there would be deterrence value in publicly articulating at least some of the administration's new approach. Asked whether such a statement was likely from the White House, Lewis said, "My bet would be no."

The Foundation for the Defense of Democracies (FDD), a think tank that favored taking a proactive, aggressive approach to cyber defense, in an early 2019 "midterm" report noted, "The Trump administration inherited a cyber policy based on Presidential Policy Directive 20 (PPD-20) of January 2013. An unclassified White House summary of the directive explained, 'It is our policy that we shall undertake the least action necessary to mitigate threats and that we will prioritize network defense and law enforcement as preferred courses of action.'"

The FDD stated, "During President Trump's tenure, senior U.S. officials have issued blunt assessments of the previous administration's approach. General Joseph Votel, commander of U.S. Central Command, noted that at the operational level, the approval process can be 'so cumbersome that these capabilities are narrowly irrelevant.'"

The report continued: "The Trump administration appears to have taken these critiques and recommendations to heart. In May 2017, the president signed an executive order requiring departments to work with the private sector to support critical infrastructure security. Seven months later, in its first National Security Strategy, the administration pledged to impose 'swift and costly consequences' on malicious cyber actors, and explicitly noted the danger of adversarial cyber-enabled economic warfare."

A change to PPD-20 was anticipated for months, although sources on Capitol Hill and in cyber policy circles said that, once again, they weren't brought into the policy discussion by the White House.

An industry source who long pushed for a more aggressive national deterrence policy said, "The implications of the apparent policy change are unclear. What's needed is a dialogue between key officials and the private sector. While assertive cyber actions against U.S. adversaries would be welcome in many cases, the rippling effects—blowback, for example—need to be jointly considered. Engagement, discussions are crucial."

Added Ari Schwartz, the NSC director of cybersecurity under Obama, "I don't see any deterrent in leaking that they are removing a process and not publicly describing what they are replacing it with. I don't have an understanding of what is replacing PPD-20. There has to be some process by which decisions are made. PPD-20 replaced an older policy. Until we see that, it is difficult to gauge implications."

He added, "When we replaced the old policy with PPD-20, we made sure that we met with many stakeholders and provided them with as much unclassified detail as possible. I think this was the right step to both bring clarity and create a greater deterrent effect. It showed we were serious about having a deterrence plan. The lack of information suggests the opposite."

A few months after the PPD-20 decision leaked out, the libertarian CATO Institute released a report suggesting "offensive cyber warfare has not been a particularly effective tool for securing foreign policy goals. There have been 272 documented cyber operations between rival states throughout the period of the years 2000–2016, but only 11 of these operations produced even temporary political concessions. These successful operations were also coupled with activities such as diplomatic negotiation, sanctions, and military threats."

The report was written by instructors at the Marine Corps University and said, "Cyberspace to date has been a domain of political warfare and coercive diplomacy. An offensively postured cyber policy is dangerous, counterproductive, and undermines norms in cyberspace."

It was an interesting message of restraint from teachers affiliated with a Marine Corps institution, written in the context of this White House.

Loosening up the rules of military engagement for cyber had a good ring to it; it was action oriented and "tough," all appealing to Trump. But like walls at the Mexican border, the simple answer wasn't necessarily an effective answer in a complex world.

In a more public action aimed at Russia, the Department of Justice on October 4, 2018, announced another indictment, this against seven officers of the Russian military intelligence service GRU for computer hacking, "aggravated identity theft," and other charges related to what officials framed as a cyber-enabled retaliatory campaign aimed at antidoping international athletics organizations, chemical weapons investigators, and the Pittsburgh-based Westinghouse. The indictment was filed in the US District Court for the Western District of Pennsylvania in Pittsburgh, the corporate home of Westinghouse.

This indictment did not flow from Mueller's probe into Russian interference in the 2016 elections, officials said, though there was some "overlap" in the individuals involved. The new indictment offered more information and context on Russia's overall social media and influence campaigns aimed at the West, the officials said.

"The 'how' of this operation is fascinating," Assistant Attorney General for National Security John Demers said at a press conference. He noted the use of distributed denial-of-service attacks, spearfishing, malware, spoof domains, and creation of "a false profile"—"Fancy Bear"—to disguise attribution of the attacks.

In the case of Westinghouse, according to DOJ:

> On December 10, 2014, [the conspirators] registered a fake domain and website, "https://webmail.westinqhousenuclear.com" to mimic a legitimate WEC domain. Spearphishing emails were sent to at least five WEC employees, designed to appear as routine emails from the Westinghouse.com Microsoft Exchange Server. Upon clicking an enclosed link, users were directed to the spoofed domain where their login credentials were stolen and saved. Once stolen credentials were determined to be authentic by the conspirators, victims were then re-routed to the original, legitimate WEC network so that they were unaware that the theft of their passwords had occurred.

Further, it said,

> Following the targeting of WEC corporate accounts, on December 24, 2014, January 15, 2015, January 17, 2015 and November 18, 2015, using Bit.ly accounts, [the conspirators] sent spearphishing emails to the personal email accounts of four WEC employees who resided near Pittsburgh, Pennsylvania. The users of two of the accounts clicked on the malicious link which would have enabled the theft of the login credentials to their personal email accounts. These employees worked in the nuclear energy field and were involved in advanced nuclear reactor development and new reactor technology.

The indictment followed a British-Dutch intelligence operation that "caught red-handed" some of the same GRU officers trying to hack The Hague, according to Demers. FBI Deputy Assistant Director for Cyber Eric Welling called the case "a victory of international cooperation and information sharing," praising officials in the United Kingdom, Canada, the Netherlands, and Switzerland for their efforts.

"We fully identified these conspirators, we can show who they are" and their affiliation with the Russian government, Welling said. He added, "There is deterrence value even if we can't lay hands on the defendants at this time."

Welling cited the 2014 indictment of five Chinese military intelligence officers on hacking charges as a law enforcement action that led to policy changes by the Chinese government. The cause and effect—and effectiveness—have been debated ever since, but presidents Obama and Xi Jinping in 2015 signed an agreement stating that neither side would use cyber espionage as a way to advance the commercial interests of their domestic companies. The Trump administration, as its conflict intensified with Beijing over global trade rules, eventually would assert that China had grossly violated that agreement, which some cyber analysts called a misrepresentation of what was happening tailored to support Trump's trade objectives.

In the fall of 2018, the Trump administration also produced that long-awaited national cyber strategy.

National Security Adviser Bolton took the podium himself to announce what he called the first updated national cybersecurity strategy in fifteen years, with a strong emphasis on deterrence, interagency coordination, and protecting critical infrastructure. In an off-camera appearance with reporters at the White House, Bolton said Trump had signed a new strategy based on "four pillars," including protecting the "American way of life" in part by ensuring the security of federal networks and critical infrastructure, and "improv[ing] incident reporting."

"Peace through strength"—including an explicit commitment to identifying, deterring, and countering cyber aggression, along with a commitment to creating international norms of behavior—was another pillar, along with preserving a "vibrant digital economy" and advancing US influence in the cyber domain.

Bolton said the strategy included a classified annex that addressed the White House move in August to repeal PPD-20 in order to give the military more flexibility to use offensive cyber weapons. "For any nation" that takes cyber actions against the United States, Bolton said, "we will respond offensively as well as defensively."

The strategy created "a structure of deterrence," he said, so the "costs to adversaries are higher than they want to bear." He said cyber strategy overall was a "continuous process" and would be updated.

The national security adviser said no single agency was in charge of the strategy, but that its implementation would be overseen by the National Security Council. The strategy allowed for a "comprehensive approach [and] each agency knows its lane," Bolton said. He noted a "huge role" for the Department of Homeland Security as well as for Treasury and others.

Bolton again downplayed the impact of eliminating the White House cyber coordinator position, saying the previous structure was "duplicative and overlapping." Cybersecurity has "two senior directors" within the NSC whose "job is to coordinate policy," Bolton said, and "the whole thing works."

Bolton's announcement came two days after the Pentagon unveiled its updated cyber strategy, which included a sharper focus on protecting private sector critical infrastructure from cyberattacks. Bolton said the Defense Department strategy "is covered" by the president's directive.

The Trump team's new national strategy included an enhanced role for DHS in securing federal systems, more attention to supply-chain risks, and a commitment to global norms of behavior backed by the willingness to take offensive action in cyberspace spearheaded by the military.

Trump said in a statement, "As I have made clear since my election as President, my Administration will use all available means to keep America safe from cyber threats. The National Cyber Strategy that I have released today is an important step in keeping that promise."

Trump continued, "We cannot ignore the costs of malicious cyber activity—economic or otherwise—directed at America's Government, businesses, and private individuals. Guided by this National Cyber Strategy, the Federal Government will be better equipped to protect the American people, the American homeland, and the American way of life."

The strategy featured elements promoting "communications infrastructure and Internet connectivity that is open, interoperable, reliable, and secure," and protecting and promoting "internet freedom" globally. It delved into wide-ranging issues such as protecting intellectual property, free flow of data across borders, and building the cyber workforce.

Bolton also stressed that the strategy would not have a negative impact on privacy protections, saying it was hacks like the one affecting the Office of Personnel Management that violated citizens' privacy—and, he said, were carried out without consequence for the aggressor.

Bolton said, "we will respond offensively as well as defensively" to cyberattacks, adding, "Our hands are not tied like they were in the Obama administration."

Policy veterans of the Obama administration took issue with the characterization.

"In general, I think that there is new tone in the policy but not much new policy other than the revocation of PPD-20, which had already been announced," said Ari Schwartz.

"In my experience it has not been deterrence policies that held back response, but the inability of agencies to execute," Schwartz said. "Oversight was often a convenient excuse for not getting the job done. I guess we will see what happens if this strategy really leads to less oversight, but a lack of oversight will likely lead to a lot of confusing finger-pointing in the wake of any failure."

Another former high-ranking cyber official called the new strategy a "disappointment" and said it signaled a lack of urgency within the Trump administration.

The source said the PPD-20 elements included "no thought on escalation/de-escalation," and the policy change "presents an even bigger problem when you look at it in context of all the mixed messages with Russia, North Korea and China."

The new strategy document did cite the value of international coalitions on cybersecurity, saying,

> The imposition of consequences will be more impactful and send a stronger message if it is carried out in concert with a broader coalition of like-minded states. The United States will launch an international Cyber Deterrence Initiative to build such a coalition and develop tailored strategies to ensure adversaries understand the consequences of their malicious cyber behavior. The United States will work with like-minded states to coordinate and support each other's responses to significant malicious cyber incidents, including through intelligence sharing, buttressing of attribution claims, public statements of support for responsive actions taken, and joint imposition of consequences against malign actors.

At the Pentagon, Lieutenant Colonel Dave Eastburn said in a statement, "The National Cyber Strategy highlights the critical and growing threat that malicious cyber actors pose to U.S. national security. The Department of Defense [DOD] stands ready, as part of the synchronized whole-of-government approach articulated in the National Cyber Strategy, to preserve peace through strength by identifying, countering, disrupting, degrading, and deterring behavior in cyberspace that is destabilizing and contrary to U.S. national interests."

Eastburn added, "DOD's focus is on preserving U.S. superiority in cyberspace and defending forward to disrupt the activities of malicious cyber actors before they reach U.S. networks. DOD is also strengthening its defensive posture through network hardening, improved cybersecurity, and working with our international allies and partners and our Defense Industrial Base and Defense Critical Infrastructure partners to secure critical information and infrastructure."

The immediate responses were limited and didn't necessarily break down along party lines. Republicans were quicker to express satisfaction with the document and the progress it suggested in formulating a national plan on cyber, while the critiques from Democrats were a little sharper.

House Homeland Security chairman McCaul issued a statement saying, "I commend the Administration for taking yet another step to protect the cybersecurity of our nation. This strategy will help better combat malicious cyber acts from foreign adversaries like Russia, China, Iran, and North Korea. I have consistently said we must call out our enemies, send a strong message that we will respond when attacked, and ensure there are real consequences if we are."

He added, "As Americans have become more reliant on computer networks, everyone is now a potential victim of hacking by cybercriminals, nation states, and others. That is why over the course of my Chairmanship, I have made strengthening the DHS' cybersecurity mission and capabilities one of the Committee's top priorities."

Former Obama cybersecurity coordinator Daniel, now president and CEO of the Cyber Threat Alliance, also praised the strategy, saying,

> [R]elease of the U.S. National Cyber Strategy builds on work over the last 12 years to improve our country's cybersecurity. It charts a solid path forward to strengthen and protect users who rely on the Internet and the digital ecosystem. It strikes a good balance between defensive actions and seeking to impose consequences on malicious actors. Further, it's clear that this strategy was informed by reports tasked out of last year's Presidential Executive Order on cybersecurity, and is a reflection of a strong policy development process across administrations.

Daniel concluded, "The resulting product is an example of what a national strategy should look like on an issue that truly is nonpartisan. This strategy protects end-users, disrupts malicious actions, and elevates overall security for everyone. I commend the U.S. government for issuing such a strong document." Another former high-ranking official said the document failed to inject the sense of urgency needed to organize a whole-of-government response to an "existential threat," while key congressional Democrats offered compliments along with suggestions of an element of unfinished business.

Representative James Langevin of Rhode Island, top Democrat on a cyber-focused Armed Services subcommittee and cofounder of the Congressional Cybersecurity Caucus, said the "four pillars" that set the foundation of the strategy were on the mark, but just a first step.

"In each of the four pillars, the document lays out important steps that need to be taken," Langevin said in a statement. "For example, we do need more clarity on the roles and responsibilities of federal agencies with respect to critical infrastructure."

He added:

> However, the document often fails to provide the strategic guidance regarding what tradeoffs we should expect to make between regulating, supporting, and responding to the needs of critical infrastructure owners and operators. Ironically, the very position best able to address these tradeoffs at a national

> level—the Cyber Coordinator—was eliminated earlier this year. Without strong executive leadership from the White House, I am concerned that agencies will approach their priority actions under this strategy in an ad hoc manner that does not translate into a decisive national policy.

Langevin said that

> Bolton described the strategy in starkly offensive terms. I agree that our adversaries need to know that we can—and will—challenge them in cyberspace. But as the country with the most innovative economy in the world, we must also acknowledge the abiding interest of the United States in encouraging stability in this domain. It is incontrovertible that we must respond to malicious activity violating well-established norms of responsible behavior, but that response must be whole-of-government and need not always include a cyber component. Public attribution, indictments of foreign government agents, and sanctions are all important tools that this Administration has made good use of.

He said, "I am intrigued by the proposal to establish an international Cyber Deterrence Initiative to advance such responses in coordination with our allies in a manner that avoids escalating conflicts. I also strongly support further centralization of authorities for federal civilian cybersecurity at DHS in order to better deter competitors by denying their ability to strike at our networks."

The strategy "does not break much new ground," Langevin said, but "I hope it will lead to an increased focus on this vital topic. I share the goals of the strategy, and I look forward to working with the Administration to help protect American interests in cyberspace."

There wasn't much visible progress on the Cyber Deterrence Initiative in the months that followed, though Robert Strayer of the State Department in March 2019 offered some insight into a process under way.

Politico's Tim Starks reported:

> The State Department sees four core pillars to its new Cyber Deterrence Initiative and is "increasingly bringing [U.S. allies] in to have further discussions" about the program, according to Strayer. The first element of the initiative is deciding what types of malicious cyber activity the U.S. hopes to deter, he said at a CYBERSEC conference. . . . The second element involves honing the ability to do joint attribution announcements. "We learned how to work very closely" in response to Moscow's poisoning of Sergei and Yulia Skripal in the U.K., Strayer said. "We need to demystify cyber in the same way, so that the decision-making that needs to occur very quickly can occur without resistance in the internal system."
>
> The third element focuses on how to impose consequences on bad actors. U.S. officials frequently cite their "all-tools" approach. Strayer said governments

need to develop "a broader range of tools that we can bring to bear to change the calculus of the adversaries." The fourth element involves warning about consequences in advance of provocations so that the provocateurs think twice.

In the fall of 2018, the Trump administration probably didn't care about Democrats' in-the-weeds policy criticism, but it did seem eager to show the "get-tough" aspects of its cyber strategy in action.

On the eve of the midterm congressional elections, the administration let out word of a US cyber operation aimed at disrupting Russian plans for meddling once again with the democratic process. In the absence of details, the move at first was widely seen as more of a "message" to bad actors than actual offensive strikes against the Russians.

But even that would mark a significant new step in cybersecurity policy.

"We're short of details, but the message seems to be, 'We know it's you, we're watching you,'" Painter, formerly of the State Department, told Inside Cybersecurity.

"It sounds like they're 'outing' the Russians—that in itself is a significant break from before, when the policy was one of holding things very close to the vest," Painter said.

Historically, the US government was reluctant to tip off adversaries that it was aware of their cyber activities, due to considerations ranging from fear of unintended consequences to protecting intelligence-gathering sources and methods. But observers and insiders alike said this reluctance contributed to the slow and ineffectual response to Russia's 2016 election interference.

"The question is how much difference does it make," Painter noted. "It puts the Russians on guard, but will it stop their activism? They may look for other means to be more stealthy."

Painter was quick to add, "I'm not minimizing the importance of letting them know we're watching, but alone that's not enough. We need to impose costs if we want to deter them."

As the midterm elections approached, the administration pulled back the curtains a bit more on its offensive action. A "first of its kind" operation was launched by US Cyber Command, as ABC News put it, "targeting individual Russian operatives to deny them the ability to carry out malign activities related to the election. . . . That includes denying them access to resources, information and cyber tools that might be used in meddling operations, [an] official said."

It was a splashy story dished up for the media.

CSIS's Lewis told Inside Cybersecurity the US action had its roots in Russian moves aimed at critical infrastructure beyond elections.

"The discovery of the Russians in the power grid was the signal—they knew this was coming," he said. "I think retaliation is a good idea, if they've thought through how to manage escalation, messaging, and working with allies."

Lewis added, "I know they started working on the necessary pieces some months ago, so maybe they have this in place, I'm assuming that."

Industry sources said they didn't see any Russian countermoves targeting critical infrastructure since Defense officials let it be known that they had taken steps against Russian entities.

"I've seen the government reporting," said one source in a critical-infrastructure sector. "What I've seen is pretty generic," in terms of current Russian cyber activity, but "industry continues to implement security measures to counteract cyber threats."

When election day 2018 finally arrived, the Department of Homeland Security was able to report that it was "not aware of any cybersecurity related compromises of election infrastructure" but would, in Chris Krebs's words, "foot stomp" the technical results to see whether anything popped out.

It was a good result for DHS, which had received reports of "scanning" of elections systems—none successful and none tied to nation-states, including Russia.

In an after-action report to the president, DHS secretary Kirstjen Nielsen and acting attorney general Matthew Whitaker determined that neither the Russians nor any other hostile actor had managed to hack the midterms.

"Although the specific conclusions within the joint report must remain classified, the Departments have concluded there is no evidence to date that any identified activities of a foreign government or foreign agent had a material impact on the integrity or security of election infrastructure or political/campaign infrastructure used in the 2018 midterm elections for the United States Congress," DHS and DOJ said in a joint February 5, 2019, statement.

The security pros apparently had a good day. Trump's political allies didn't fare quite as well: Republicans lost control of the House for the first time since 2010, though they expanded their lead in the Senate. A Democratic House meant closer scrutiny, and deeper skepticism, of the Trump administration's cyber efforts on Capitol Hill.

The Helsinki fiasco hadn't been forgotten or entirely brushed aside as the year ended. But as with many things related to Trump, a whirlwind of other statements, events, and controversies swept it out of view and diluted, at least momentarily, what might be the seminal question of the Trump administration: Did Russia have something on the president that provoked such bizarre behavior from a US president?

The *New York Times* in early January 2019 sent media outlets around the world chasing a possibility unimaginable in anything but a political satire or thriller: Was the president of the United States a Russian asset?

"I never worked for Russia and you know that answer better than anybody. I never worked for Russia. Not only did I never work for Russia, I think it's a disgrace that you even asked that question because it's a whole big fat hoax. It's just a hoax," Trump told reporters as he boarded Marine One for a trip to New Orleans on January 14, 2019.

Asked whether he would release the interpreter's notes from his meetings with Putin, Trump said,

> I just don't know anything about it. I read it this morning. It's a lot of fake news. That was a very good meeting. It was actually a very successful meeting and I have those meetings with everything. I just know nothing about it. . . . It was a very, very successful meeting. We talked about Israel, we talked about the pipeline that Germany is paying Russia a lot of money—I don't think it's appropriate. We talked about that. We talked about many subjects, but I have those meetings one-on-one with all leaders including the president of China, including prime minister of Japan, Abe. We have those meetings all the time. No big deal.

But the president was on a roll, clearly agitated by the story:

> The people that started that investigation are [former FBI official Andrew] McCabe, who's a proven liar and was fired from the FBI, are Lisa Page, who was forced to leave the FBI, and her lover, Peter Strzok, who we got their text messages. And what they said in those text messages was shocking when you talk about bias. And also Comey and I guess they started it because I fired Comey, which was a great thing I did for our country. So, the people doing that investigation were people that have been caught that are known scoundrels. They're . . . I guess you could say they're dirty cops. And I'll tell you what, it is so unfair what's happened to the FBI in terms of the men and women working in the rank and file of the FBI. I know many of them, these are great people and they are so embarrassed by their leadership. You've never seen—I have never seen a turnaround in a bureau or agency like I have with the FBI. They are so embarrassed. I think twelve people now have been terminated and others. If you look at what's happening others are going to go. What happened at the FBI. So, when you say, did I have confidence in the FBI or intelligence agencies when I see [unintelligible] and I see all of these people. When I see Lisa, and her lover, and their notes, and their texts get captured and you see what they said about me having nothing to do with investigation.

Trump told the reporters:

> Let me tell you something. When people see that, you have an angry country because the whole thing is a hoax. It's a big hoax and it's very bad for our coun-

> try. So what happened with the FBI, I have done a great service for our country when I fired James Comey because he was a bad cop, and he was a dirty cop, and he lied. He really lied. All you have to do—wait a minute—all you have to do is take a look at the Crooked Hillary Clinton investigation where they brought her on July 4th weekend, July 4th. They didn't swear her in. They didn't do a tape. They didn't do anything. They just let her go and she usually said—mostly said, "I don't know." She didn't know anything, just like James Comey a week ago. He was interviewed by Congress and, you know, unfortunately people didn't see it because the Republicans with Paul Ryan, unfortunately they didn't put him out there. But what he said was either he's a bad liar or he's grossly incompetent. . . . You can read the transcript.

Meanwhile, *Washington Post* writer Max Boot that same morning offered eighteen reasons why the spectacular allegation could be true, including a half dozen with cyber-related angles. These included Russian hacking and cyber-enabled offensive actions designed to bolster Trump's vote and hold down turnout among Democratic constituencies by spreading exquisitely targeted falsehoods regarding Democratic nominee Hillary Clinton. Boot left unsaid that Trump, wittingly or not, had been a vessel for redefining cybersecurity itself, which going forward would now include the kind of social media manipulation that exploded across the 2016 election.

Boot, an erstwhile Republican and senior foreign policy adviser to presidential candidates John McCain and Mitt Romney, cited Trump's "Russia, if you're listening" call—facetious or not—to hack Clinton's emails; the refusal "to consistently acknowledge" Russian interference; the firings of Comey and Attorney General Sessions; public attacks on the Justice Department and FBI; conflicts with Europe and NATO; and acting "utterly supine" in meetings with Putin, including the political horror show in Helsinki.

The *Post* writer also listed "sowing chaos in government," which would have the most perilous impact, in a cybersecurity context, on the Department of Homeland Security.

With that thought in the air, in February 2019 the *Washington Post* offered more details on that mysterious first-of-its-kind offensive action by US Cyber Command. The *Post* reported that the "infamous" Internet Research Agency located in St. Petersburg, Russia, was knocked off-line before the US elections, in a strike by Cyber Command intended to decisively curtail that entity's hacking abilities.

"The U.S. military blocked Internet access to an infamous Russian entity seeking to sow discord among Americans during the 2018 midterms, several U.S. officials said, a warning that the Kremlin's operations against the United States are not cost-free," the *Post*'s highly regarded intelligence reporter Ellen Nakashima wrote.

From her February 26, 2019, report:

> The strike on the Internet Research Agency in St. Petersburg, a company underwritten by an oligarch close to President Vladimir Putin, was part of the first offensive cyber campaign against Russia designed to thwart attempts to interfere with a U.S. election, the officials said. "They basically took the IRA offline," according to one individual familiar with the matter who, like others, spoke on the condition of anonymity to discuss classified information. "They shut 'em down." The operation marked the first muscle-flexing by U.S. Cyber Command, with intelligence from the National Security Agency, under new authorities it was granted by President Trump and Congress last year to bolster offensive capabilities.

"This was the most significant development of the past two years," former Department of Homeland Security official Paul Rosenzweig, now of the moderate Republican R Street Institute think tank, commented at a public event.

"The idea that the U.S. will say military assets will be deployed is a sea change, a Rubicon moment," he said. "I'm not sure I like it . . . but now we are actively engaged in use of military assets to effect consequences on people in Russia. That may be enough to influence their behavior. It may not."

"Let the games begin, we're engaged," said CSIS's Lewis.

6

DHS and a Chance for a Refresh

On July 31, 2018, Vice President Pence traveled to New York City for a "DHS Cyber Summit," organized by the ever-embattled secretary Kirstjen Nielsen. It was a chance for a refresh, a way for DHS to exert its authority as the government's leading voice on cyber, with a seal of approval from the White House.

A standing-room-only crowd topping four hundred packed the auditorium at the Alexander Hamilton US Custom House in Lower Manhattan for an event that began with Nielsen leading a panel discussion with senior administration officials and CEOs, and wrapped up with the appearance by Pence.

After a full day of sessions with government and industry leaders focused on nitty-gritty cyber issues like supply chains, risk management, national critical functions, and the cyber workforce, the vice president launched into a campaign-style speech in which he cited a litany of cyber shortcomings by the Obama administration.

"We inherited a cybersecurity mess . . . they ignored cybersecurity threats," Pence proclaimed.

This represented one of the most forceful attempts to date to recast the Trump administration as a proactive cyber policy initiator that had to largely pick up the undone business of its predecessor. An audience that included plenty of cyber officials from the Obama years—and industry representatives who worked with them—sat quietly during Pence's campaign-style applause lines.

"But sadly, previous administrations have let the American people down when it came to cyber defense," Pence said. "At the outset of this administration, it became clear from early on: In a very real sense, we inherited a cyber crisis. The last administration all but neglected cybersecurity, even though the digital threats were growing more numerous and more dangerous by the day."

He continued: "In 2014, a foreign government actually hacked into the White House network itself, and yet, in the face of constant attacks like that, the last administration too often chose silence and paralysis over strength and action."

Pence declared, "But make no mistake about it: Those days are over."

At Trump's direction, the vice president said, "Our administration has taken decisive action to fortify America's cybersecurity capabilities. We're also forging new partnerships, evidenced by this conference today, all across our society and also with state and local governments and with great corporations so well represented here."

The Trump administration, he said, strengthened state and local partnerships, requested "a record" $15 billion for cybersecurity from congressional appropriators, banned potential supply-chain risks like Russian cyber firm Kaspersky Lab from federal contracts, and was "putting the finishing touches on a national cybersecurity strategy," the document Bolton would unveil in September.

Pence offered strong support for the new national risk management center that Nielsen announced at the summit and other cybersecurity initiatives, while defending the Trump administration's efforts to secure elections from foreign interference. Pence formally acknowledged Russian interference in the 2016 election and urged "every state to take renewed action" to defend their election systems and to "take advantage" of tools offered by DHS. "We've already done more than any administration in history to protect the ballot box, and we've barely just begun," he declared.

And Pence urged the Senate to finally pass a measure creating a Cybersecurity and Infrastructure Security Agency at DHS, saying "cybersecurity needs a hub" and calling it "an idea whose time has come." That—amid the partisan shots Pence was firing—was an important message of bipartisanship. It also spoke to the most conservative wing of the Republican Party, Pence's base: it's OK, in the case of cybersecurity, to actually create a new government agency.

Cybersecurity professionals, even Obama veterans, would choose to move past the partisanship of the speech. The charges were inaccurate, and they clearly rankled. But Pence wasn't really directing his message to this crowd of cyber experts sitting before him in the Custom House; it was directed toward the president. Pence was recasting cybersecurity, the issue, in a way that Trump could understand: the outsider president had to ride in and save the day, and save the country, from the misguided, soft-headed actions of the previous occupant of the Oval Office.

Still, a speech castigating the Obama administration's cyber efforts wasn't calibrated to encourage new industry involvement: many Obama-era policy veterans were active in the business community's cyber initiatives, and many business leaders worked closely with the Obama team.

"I was sitting there just steaming," said David Turetsky, a former Federal Communications Commission security chief, corporate lawyer, and now a professor of cybersecurity at Albany University in New York. "After what was such a good day, it was shocking. Someone at the White House wrote that with a political bent and it was very inappropriate to the day and to what DHS was trying to do in bringing everyone into a common effort."

Turetsky said it fit into "a tale of two approaches" to cyber in the Trump administration. "The people in the trenches are doing pretty decent work," he said admiringly. "I say to students, let's move away from Russia and the elections for a minute, and they're doing a lot on securing supply chains, a lot on sharing threat information through the National Cybersecurity and Communications Integration Center. NCCIC sends out alerts that specifically cite what the Russians are doing. They aren't pulling any punches regardless of what's going on in the political arena."

But Pence, taking a rare turn in the cybersecurity spotlight, delivered a "horrible" speech that was "totally inappropriate," Turetsky said. "I felt sorry for the DHS people sitting there."

"Overall our folks give very high marks to DHS on execution," an industry source said of the summit. On Pence's speech: "I don't think it was helpful [but] folks are pretty sophisticated about separating political talking points from government action or inaction," the source suggested.

Others were more critical.

"The vice president was an important component of the meeting," commented Mike Echols, a former senior official at DHS who now ran a firm called MAX Cybersecurity.

"Again, stakeholders want to see signs of leadership," Echols said. "I think he sullied a great beginning by making it so political. The bottom line is credit will come from success, even if only limited. The need to say things like nothing was done by the past administration to protect our cyberspace is shortsighted, given everyone in the room has been working this issue for the last 10 years." At a practical level, the summit had the earmarks of a success story for Nielsen—and one achieved in the president's hometown.

It was Nielsen's brainchild and was seen internally at DHS as a way to showcase the department's strength on cyber policy and a platform for illustrating its vision and goals. Nielsen and her senior deputies were making clear that collaboration and industry leadership were key components to the department's strategy and would be a focus of the summit.

Nielsen had worked in the large shadow of General John Kelly from the time he ran DHS at the beginning of the Trump administration through the first months of his tenure as White House chief of staff, until she was confirmed as secretary in December 2017. She helped write Trump's cybersecurity executive order and had an extensive private sector background in cyber. Nielsen had degrees from the Georgetown University School of Foreign Service and the University of Virginia Law School.

She had also been a Homeland Security adviser to George W. Bush, a history that some Democrats clicked on to recall the botched preparation and response to Hurricane Katrina, which caused historic devastation along the Gulf Coast in 2005 and was a low point, domestically, of Bush's two terms.

"On Aug 27, 2005, two days before Hurricane Katrina made landfall, officials at the American Red Cross wrote to a top homeland security adviser at the White House, warning that the storm was likely to slam New Orleans as a major hurricane," the *Washington Post* wrote upon Nielsen's October 2017 nomination to lead DHS.

"The message was sent to Kirstjen Nielsen, whose title was special assistant to the president for prevention, preparedness and response. She was 33 years old," the *Post* noted ominously.

"It was the first of many alarming emails Nielsen would receive over the following days as water poured into New Orleans and the city was deluged. And in the storm of blame that followed the costliest natural disaster in American history, Nielsen's team was widely criticized for its passive and clumsy response."

"'Despite the clear warnings before landfall that Katrina would be catastrophic, the President and the White House staff were not sufficiently engaged and failed to initiate a sufficiently strong and proactive response,'" the *Post* quoted Democratic senators from a report on Katrina. "Nielsen's team was singled out for failing to properly manage the flow of urgent on-the-ground reports sent to the White House."

The *Post* also found plenty of sources who defended Nielsen's efforts at the time.

Over a decade later, at DHS she was immediately thrust into the partisan tensions surrounding immigration and Trump's demand for a wall at the Mexico border. She was publicly harangued by the president, and her job seemed to hang by a thread for months.

Fast forward to July 31, 2018, and the old Custom House in New York bustled with tech sector leaders of the "new economy" and cyber pros at the vanguard of security efforts. The departments of Defense, Treasury, and Energy participated, along with the FBI and NSA, and leaders from "sectors including telecom, financial, and energy" were on hand "to lay out a vision for a collective defense model to protect our nation's critical infrastructure," according to a DHS statement at the time.

Nielsen's job didn't seem any more secure (publicly, at least), but she gamely rang in the summit with the announcement of the National Risk Management Center and a commitment to a whole-of-government campaign against cyber threats to be coordinated by her department.

DHS will "contextualize" the threat, plan against it, and help take action, Nielsen told reporters after a closed session with government and corporate leaders. Noting that the cyber threat was coming from nation-states and didn't recognize boundaries around sectors or between the government and industry, Nielsen said to the gathered CEOs, "What you see here is our offer to bring together all that we have in government."

What was this National Risk Management Center that Nielsen was so eager to launch? It was designed to "create a cross-cutting risk management approach" between the government and private sector and to "identify, assess, and prioritize efforts to reduce risks to national critical functions," according to DHS.

The center would provide "a simple and single point of access to the full range of government activities to mitigate a range of risks, including cyber, across sectors," DHS said in a release.

DHS officials engaged in extensive policy discussions with the private sector leading up to the summit. Internet Security Alliance president Larry Clinton characterized the engagement as part of a renewed DHS commitment to partnership with the private sector, founded on risk management principles. "That provides the basis for a much more productive partnership," Clinton said.

Robert Mayer of USTelecom said DHS was "making a tremendous effort to make sure the event is successful" and called it "an impressive undertaking to bring together multiple agencies, sectors and CEOs to have an important conversation on cross-sector interdependencies."

He noted that the telecom sector was already engaging with the electricity and financial sectors on cyber initiatives and pointed to USTelecom's work with the information technology sector through a new group they'd christened the Council to Secure the Digital Economy.

"This is not going to be a one-shot wonder, it'll set forth a journey of co-operation that's essential to addressing rapidly evolving systemic risk," Mayer said of the DHS summit.

ISA's Clinton said that "leading up to the summit, there have been serious, productive conversations with industry on partnerships, cybersecurity spending, incentives, law enforcement and other issues. There have been ongoing weekly meetings, sometimes twice weekly. The policy work has been far more intensive and serious than I've experienced before with DHS." Clinton said, "The policy leadership has been much more in-depth. I chalk it up to the leadership" of Krebs and then–assistant secretary for the Office of Cybersecurity and Communications Jeanette Manfra, under the overall leadership of Nielsen.

"Manfra has a wealth of experience and contacts," Clinton said, "and has always been eager to engage with the private sector. Krebs and I were on the [Information Technology Coordinating Council] together when he was at Microsoft and he has a lot of background and contacts." The DHS leaders "have done a good job of listening, and industry has come forward and been even more assertive on what needs to be done."

Part of that, Clinton said, was related to the evolution of the cyber threat and part was due to an evolution in government thinking.

"Previously," he said, "some people were looking for quick fixes, but we need a comprehensive approach, we need proper incentives. This is more of a maturation process, we're evolving away from the 'blame-the-victim' model. That took a long time."

Clinton, in years past, praised Obama for collaborative initiatives such as developing the NIST framework of cybersecurity standards, but he complained that the previous administration's work often neglected the economic side of cybersecurity—an assertion that the Obama White House was always quick to dispute.

Now, Krebs "is being very articulate about the differences between the public and private sector, that there is a gap in how we address the issue [of cyber risk]," Clinton said. "For many years there was an assumption that it was the same—that if only industry would spend more the problem would be solved."

Clinton noted, "But appropriate spending for industry is different from what it is for government—companies have to make money and government has national security, privacy and other concerns that are different."

These differences, Clinton said, "are realities and legitimate. But that is just now being appreciated on the government side."

"It took some time for DHS to establish its bona fides on cybersecurity," observed Suzanne Spaulding, the former undersecretary in charge of cyber programs. "There's a growing understanding in Congress and elsewhere of how far DHS has come. I do see this as a significant event."

Throughout the day, corporate CEOs and trade association leaders, along with Nielsen, Energy Secretary Rick Perry, and other senior federal officials, discussed ongoing and new cross-sector and industry-government collaborations. DHS announced an "ICT Supply Chain Task Force" that, in coordination with the tech and communications industries, would be "a key element of the newly established" risk management center.

Nielsen said the new risk center "allows us to move beyond routine information sharing" and would produce "policies, plans and playbooks." She directed Krebs to embark on a national tour to meet with cybersecurity experts as part of building up the center.

USTelecom president Jonathan Spalter and Information Technology Industry Council president Dean Garfield—whose groups were working together closely on the supply chain and a separate botnet initiative—both said this DHS project could provide a model for other industry-government efforts.

The risk management center will be "incubating best practices," Garfield said, and will "create an institutional framework for that."

"This can be a model for working together," Spalter said.

If so, it could be an important step forward in forging collaborative ties between industry and government and cementing the partnership approach that the business community desperately wanted as an alternative to regulatory commands from government. DHS wanted to be the hub for this effort, and it was very much in industry's interest to help the department accomplish its goal.

Overall, former DHS official Echols said, "I heard a lot of things we would have heard a few years ago. This signals the slow progress. However, I was encouraged because I believe the number one issue has been a lack of visible leadership. Companies look for signs of government policy direction and a united vision towards accomplishing our mutual cybersecurity goals. Those goals have rarely been stated and silos have prevented a united front across industry and government."

The need for visible leadership and articulated goals was something Krebs recognized and was tapping into—he was going to provide it, if no one else could or would. The statements that quickly shot out from industry groups suggested a ready and willing audience, and the realities of a symbiotic relationship between DHS and industry: business groups wanted to understand government's goals, they would be partners in a clearly defined mission—and they wanted their own issues addressed in the bargain.

This was how government worked, when it worked. Encouraging statements from industry groups were important because they translated into commitments and buy-in from organizations representing huge parts of the US economy. There was real uncertainty among the business leaders about whether there would be enough follow-through, but they were all-in with the vocal support that DHS needed.

DHS was always in need of a fresh gust of wind at its back, as it always faced complaints related to immigration or airport security, among its wide-ranging responsibilities, and cyber was the area where Nielsen—and her predecessors—often looked for victories. But there was always work to do here too, at the big strategic level as well as nuts-and-bolts matters. Cyber, as noted, was that kind of issue. The department's premier and much-ballyhooed cyber information sharing function—exchanging so-called threat indicators, or tell-tales of cyberattacks—was still experiencing growth pains, or, more accurately, pains due to a lack of growth. Some kind of incentives were needed to persuade more private companies to participate in the information-sharing system, according to former DHS attorney Allison Bender. She said "very few organizations [were] sharing into" DHS's Automated Indicator Sharing (AIS) program even as sharing expanded among private entities.

As a result, she said, the privacy protection regime included in the Cybersecurity Act of 2015 was largely untested. The department wasn't dealing with much personally identifiable information through its info-sharing systems because it wasn't receiving very much data from private groups that might include personally identifiable information.

In the aftermath of Edward Snowden's leaks, much of the long-running congressional debate leading up to the 2015 law revolved around creating adequate safeguards at DHS for personal information that could be swept up inadvertently in data shared between the private sector and government. But in practice, the private sector was slow to share with DHS, she said.

For one thing, Bender said, "it's still a pain to get signed up and configured" to participate in AIS. For another, she said, "there is still concern" among businesses about potential legal and regulatory liability that could arise if they shared certain data with the government. The 2015 law granted liability protection for sharing within certain guidelines.

"The 2015 act was the smallest thing on which the security and privacy communities could agree," Bender said. But "to make info-sharing more attractive," she said, the government "needs to explain the benefits. We're seeing more sharing in the private sector but companies are watching to see how different agencies get on the same page. That's why the population is so small."

The private sector had moved ahead with its own services to share threat indicators, but many in the industry believed this was still an area where DHS was most suited to play a positive role. The department promised more progress to come, with senior officials Krebs and Bob Kolasky and top corporate leaders pledging that creation of a top-tier info-sharing service was a high priority. They would take steps to simplify the paperwork and make it easier for the appropriate people on the industry side to see sensitive information, but getting it right was a long, tedious process.

Echols's group and others like the Cyber Threat Alliance run by former White House cyber coordinator Daniel, as well as private firms, were already offering robust cyber info-sharing services, but the government had access to intelligence unavailable elsewhere, plus the reach and ability—in theory—to connect the dots and create a comprehensive view of the threatscape. Getting it right on the government side would still be important even as the private sector applied its energies and talents to the info-sharing challenge.

In another area where DHS was anxious to demonstrate strength, the government-wide cybersecurity tool known as the continuous diagnostics and mitigation system, run by the department to secure the entire federal enterprise, was entering a new phase. The individual leaders running each federal agency were now directly accountable for cybersecurity under the Trump cyber executive order and needed all the help they could get. When DHS officials showed up at the door at various agencies, they were welcomed—eagerly.

"The responsibility has always been there but the [2017] executive order added the word 'accountability,'" said Bill Rucker, president of Trustwave Government Solutions. "Some government executives said, 'we've been doing this all along, we'll repackage it and present it'" under the mandate of the executive order, Rucker said. "But some needed the push." A DHS official explained that "data out of CDM [would be used] to create a scoring system that will help agencies address their worst problems first." That scoring system was intended to translate into accountability, as agency leaders would see their cyber efforts rated in black and white. Managers throughout the federal departments expressed trepidation about rating their work this way, but the availability of such metrics was an emerging tool that couldn't be ignored in either the public or the private sectors.

DHS was knocked around incessantly by the president, lawmakers, and multiple other critics, particularly over intensely controversial border and immigration issues. But the department was steadily building credibility in the cyber domain. Amid Nielsen's political perils in late 2018, the department was poised for a major victory: creation of the Cybersecurity and Infrastructure Security Agency (CISA), the federal government's first standalone cyber agency. After years of pushing for such a designation, DHS was finally rewarded on November 16, 2018, when Trump signed into law a measure creating CISA. DHS's Krebs would become its first director, gleefully shedding the clumsy title of undersecretary for the National Protection and Programs Directorate (NPPD).

Representative McCaul had crafted the legislation and pushed it for years when no one was listening, it seemed, to his detailed case for consolidating and elevating cyber functions at DHS. The department's leaders—from the

Obama era into the Trump years—all wanted this bill to become law. But it languished, sometimes a hostage to unrelated issues like border security and sometimes amid lawmakers' sheer indifference.

Constantly prodded by McCaul, Senate Homeland Security chairman Johnson engaged in some adroit maneuvering to get it on the Senate floor just before lawmakers broke for the 2018 election, where it was approved by unanimous consent. There weren't any real substantive objections; Johnson just had to get his leaders' attention and make sure none of his colleagues wanted to raise a fuss, about anything, before the bill could be waved through. It was the usual Senate operating procedure—lengthy, frustrating, and sometimes futile—but in this case it worked. As soon as Congress returned following election day, McCaul secured House passage of the final version, and the measure went to the president.

Naturally, the House's final action on the bill came at the end of a day, November 12, 2018, when news reports swirled that Secretary Nielsen would be fired by the president over her handling of immigration issues.

If that really happened this time, said an industry source who worked frequently with DHS, Nielsen's departure would take a toll on the multiple partnerships being run out of her department, "but it's hard to know how significant a toll. It could be anything from a wrecking ball to a mild hiccup."

The source doubted that a leadership change—DHS would be getting its fourth secretary, including an acting secretary, during Trump's first two years—would make industry less willing to work with the department on cyber. "We have a strong interest in keeping DHS at the center of critical infrastructure risk management and presumably the key [senior cyber officials] would remain," the source said.

But, the source added, "I actually think she has done some important stuff at DHS and has put competent people in charge."

The reports of the president's impending move to replace Nielsen also came as the secretary prepared to formally announce the "formation and chartering of the nation's first Information and Communications Technology Supply Chain Risk Management Task Force, a public-private partnership to examine and develop consensus recommendations to identify and manage risk to the global ICT supply chain."

It was way down in the weeds of the way industries worked, but it was where the cybersecurity war was being fought, and DHS had managed to secure participation from leading industry groups for this initiative.

And on yet another cyber front, Nielsen had just announced that use of the global positioning system, or GPS, would be one of the first "systemic risks" to be addressed by the new National Risk Management Center. Cybersecurity as an issue often existed on an amorphous plane that was hard for the public to visualize, Nielsen and others believed, and the GPS effort could resonate as something that mattered to every citizen. Further still, DHS and the Commerce Department were poised to put out a "roadmap" to guide the government's efforts to combat botnets, under the Trump executive order. DHS was also playing a lead role in the administration's "moonshot" effort.

It was up to the president to set priorities for his administration, including emphasizing border issues over cybersecurity in the DHS secretary's portfolio. But raising the prospect of a Nielsen firing or forced resignation inevitably affected cyber policy, and it would take a while to see whether this would be a hiccup or a more ominous setback to the work that numerous DHS officials were doing.

On Capitol Hill, lawmakers were well aware that Nielsen and all of her top cyber deputies had been campaigning vigorously for final passage of the Cybersecurity and Infrastructure Security Agency Act. Sources close to McCaul and other lawmakers declined to comment on whether the quick action was a message to the president not to fire the secretary. But they pointedly didn't deny it.

In any case, reports of Nielsen's political demise were premature, once more, and the old NPPD, a Soviet-sounding bureaucratic construction, was now CISA.

The drama was far from over for DHS, of course. Just over a month after the celebrations of CISA's creation, half of its staff was furloughed by a partial government shutdown that would go on to become the longest in US history.

DHS said operational security activities would continue during the shutdown, including at the National Cybersecurity and Communications Integration Center, but that numerous other efforts were halted by the lapse in funding that began on December 21 and ran until January 26. A source with close ties to CISA said the number of employees furloughed was "much higher" than 50 percent.

"They aren't doing risk and vulnerability assessments [for individual companies], they have no chemical inspectors [on duty], and no risk management with the private sector," a congressional source said. Further, the source said, "With about 50 percent of CISA furloughed, we don't know what they have prioritized and what they have stopped working on."

DHS and the Commerce Department were both affected by the shutdown—and both played key roles in ongoing cyber collaborations. Discussions planned between industry representatives and Commerce Department officials on botnets and other initiatives were postponed. Months after the shutdown ended, industry sources said stakeholders were still struggling to make up for lost time in the botnet effort.

Amid the complexities, uncertainties, and anxieties of a government shutdown that sent home hundreds of thousands of federal workers and halted projects, Trump injected another disturbing note, raising the idea of declaring a national emergency in order to get his wall built without Congress's explicit approval.

"It is a huge mess," commented an industry source, who added that if Trump declared a "national emergency" related to the US-Mexico border, the political dynamics around the shutdown would be upended in possibly dramatic ways. "Then it's a whole new ballgame," the source said.

"I would expect that if the president makes such a declaration, we have a full-blown constitutional crisis and that would throw a wrench in all the gears of government," the source said.

"I'm changing my view, somewhat, from last week," another industry source said in week three, after suggesting the previous week that a short shutdown wouldn't seriously impact collaborative activities.

"The shutdown is beginning to have an impact on DHS's ability to convene public-private functions," the source said. "This situation will only become more challenging. Key stakeholders want confidence that the department's ability to respond to a significant physical or cyber incident, including coordination with other agencies and industry, is not degraded."

"Anxiety seems to be high," noted a former White House official on January 8.

New House Homeland Security chairman Bennie Thompson, on January 8—day eighteen of the shutdown—released a list of ten questions for the Trump administration on impacts, including two on cyber issues: "Is the Cybersecurity and Infrastructure Security Agency (CISA) still inspecting high-risk chemical facilities urging the shutdown?" And, "Is CISA able to perform cybersecurity risk and vulnerability assessments for the Federal government, critical infrastructure owners and operators, and state election agencies?"

Congressional sources said neither of those functions—chemical inspections or risk assessments—were being performed. "We have pinged CISA and they are not doing these things," a congressional source said.

"Trump's needless shutdown could soon become the longest shutdown in our nation's history, with consequences still unknown," Thompson said in a statement. "Almost three weeks into this calculated crisis and we still do not know what DHS is doing to ensure the safety and security of the American people while it is operating without funds. With each passing day, the effective functioning of key homeland security operations are imperiled. The President must put the country first and put his ego aside. It's time he reopen the government."

The White House declined to comment on cyber implications, saying—off the record—"please contact DHS." DHS didn't respond to repeated requests for comment. Its spokespeople were furloughed; so-called essential personnel were obviously short-handed and under increasing stress.

A former top cybersecurity official at DHS warned in January 2019 that the shutdown had substantial impacts on the government's cyber workforce, ranging from sinking morale to new openings for the private sector to lure away trained federal workers.

"In the short and mid-term there will be significant impacts and they will grow over time," said Phil Reitinger, president and CEO of the Global Cyber Alliance and a former cyber chief at DHS under Obama.

"Your DHS cybersecurity people are there, but they're not getting paid," Reitinger said. "Collaboration [with industry] has pretty much stopped. The pain is already there and it's going to get worse every day."

Further, he said, "Something bad happening"—like a successful major cyberattack—"is more likely." The operational people at DHS "who are there working are giving everything they've got, but over time you're going to see a declining ability to meet the needs."

Reitinger also cited potentially severe impacts on the federal cyber workforce, saying the shutdown damaged morale of current cyber professionals within government and crimped the government's ability to "onboard" and train new employees.

"In six months," he said, "the federal cybersecurity workforce is not going to be in better shape. [Cyber] training stops, you can't replace workers who retire, and 'on-boarding' stops because you can't do security checks for new employees," said Reitinger. "There will be a ripple effect for a long time."

Employees classified as essential—including many at the DHS National Cybersecurity and Communications Integration Center—worked without pay, "which is not really saying we value your service like we ought to," Reitinger said.

He commented, "The long-term effects will be much greater on the workforce. They make less money and get less benefits than they would in the private sector, they work more hours—because they believe in the mission. All they ask is 'let us do our jobs.'"

And he pointed to Twitter traffic urging current federal cyber workers to apply for private sector cyber jobs, tapping into the uncertainty surrounding the shutdown to make a pitch. "People are recruiting federal employees right now," Reitinger said.

The shutdown is "a disincentive to working for the government," he said.

There were about 350,000 cybersecurity job openings in the United States at the time of the shutdown, according to CyberSeek, a project supported by the government's National Initiative for Cybersecurity Education. The government was in intense competition for cyber workers, a long-running concern for federal authorities that was only being exacerbated.

Gary Hayslip, chief information security officer (CISO) at the security firm Webroot and the former CISO for the City of San Diego, raised a similar point: "What should be worrying the federal government is that they already said they are in a crunch to try and hire enough cybersecurity personnel," he said. "With this ongoing shutdown, you have to wonder how many of their current cybersecurity personnel aren't looking over the fence at private industry and thinking maybe it's time for a change?"

DHS, Commerce, Judiciary, and Transportation were among the departments affected by the shutdown, and all had extensive cybersecurity portfolios. The shutdown hurt cyber efforts at all of them.

"The Justice Department's cybercrime attorneys can work on cases and support the FBI's hacking investigations during the partial government shutdown, but they must keep strict records about how much time they spend working and cannot do any other work, according to a DOJ employee," Politico reported on January 9, 2019. "Like many DOJ offices, the Computer Crime and Intellectual Property Section does prosecution and investigation work that cannot cease due to a shutdown, but until that work pops up in their email, CCIPS attorneys are essentially furloughed along with many other government workers."

Work on the cybersecurity of self-driving cars halted at the Department of Transportation. Commerce Department cyber activities came to a full stop.

But DHS was both at the center of the budget dispute between Trump and Democrats over "the wall" at the US-Mexico border and the chief victim of the resulting funding cutoff when it came to the federal government's cybersecurity activities.

By week four, the warnings were getting louder and louder.

The US Chamber of Commerce sent a letter urging lawmakers and the Trump administration "to restore full operation of the federal government. The shutdown is harming the American people, the business community, and the economy. The Chamber strongly urges Congress and the administration to resolve this impasse and reopen the government."

The Chamber noted that "federal rulemakings are halted, and hundreds of thousands of federal employees and contractors go without pay. With each passing day, the situation will only get worse."

Federal workers were sharing stories of the extraordinary financial hardships hitting civil servants. A celebrity chef, José Andrés, tweeted, "Big news! We will open a kitchen on Pennsylvania Ave this week to join private sector effort to feed federal employees during the shutdown. It's only fair to feed Americans in need!"

The political system was a spectacle in the theater of the absurd. This was serious business for furloughed workers trying to pay bills, and it was serious business for cybersecurity.

"From past experience both inside the intelligence community and private sector operations I'm more than certain there is negative significant impact on all operations due to the government shutdown," said Ernest McDuffie of the cyber consulting firm Global McDuffie Group. McDuffie was a former NIST computer scientist and led the federal government's National Initiative for Cybersecurity Education, or NICE.

The partial government shutdown was having a cascading negative impact on federal cyber personnel, partnerships with industry, and ultimately the overall state of US cybersecurity, insiders said. "The shutdown is a major distraction for the entire cybersecurity ecosystem," said Andrew Howard, global chief technology officer at Kudelski Security.

"Fundamentally, the private sector does not need the government for cybersecurity, but the government does play an important role," Howard said. "Agencies like DHS, the Secret Service, and the FBI are actively involved in cybercrime investigations that impact, and benefit, the private sector. Shutdowns distract from these important activities."

The distractions were broad and substantial, said Daniel, the former White House cybersecurity coordinator. He said serious impacts would be seen in areas ranging from cyber personnel to policy development.

"The personnel performing vital cybersecurity functions such as defending networks, working with the private sector to investigate intrusions, or projecting power through cyberspace, are usually deemed 'exempt,' so that work will continue," Daniel said. "However, like so many areas across the government, over time a shutdown will steadily erode the federal government's cybersecurity readiness."

He cited a variety of impacts to watch for, saying, "Government shutdowns tend to affect support activities disproportionately, such as hiring or letting contracts; thus, over time personnel slots will go unfilled and contracts will expire, making it difficult to sustain the workforce or upgrade equipment."

Daniel added, "Recruiting new cyber employees is always hard for the government, due to the pay differential; the shutdown certainly deters some people from even considering working for the government. And even when it's done, the spectre of the shutdown will linger as a deterrent for people considering whether to take a government cybersecurity position."

On top of that, he said, "New policy work is essentially frozen, so needed changes or updates to existing policies will not occur, nor will the government develop policies to address new areas. Agencies will have a harder time keeping up with patching and routine cyber hygiene activities, due to the limited number of exempt employees."

Kudelski's Howard added, "Without question, the shutdown will have an impact on the federal government's cybersecurity posture."

Howard explained: "The government depends heavily on contract labor for the day-to-day cybersecurity hygiene tasks, such as patching and auditing. During a shutdown, these contractors are typically sent home and their critical cybersecurity responsibilities fall to the remaining government employees, who are already overloaded. You can imagine scenarios where hundreds of systems, managed by tens of contractors, are now the responsibility of a handful of government employees."

Jamie Brown, the director of government affairs at Tenable, said "in terms of essential employees, the government is well prepared to respond to cyber incidents," but the "pain" from the shutdown was being felt in delays to collaborative processes between government and industry.

"The momentum since the July 31 [DHS cyber summit] could be lost as the shutdown goes on," Brown said. "These are areas where we're trying to be proactive, to prevent attacks. We're not at a tipping point yet," he added.

Out among private company security officers in the field, Brown said the limited engagement from government during the shutdown wasn't "preventing CISOs from doing their jobs, but guidance from the National Risk Management Center and the tri-sector [cybersecurity initiative managed by DHS] is being delayed. Those are things that help them be better prepared to prevent attacks. Best practices won't be filtered out as quickly."

Compared to years past, Brown said, "there's a much greater understanding in industry that cyber risk management is very important," meaning the businesses were more likely to have taken steps to secure themselves regardless of whether the government was fully functioning.

The problem, though, he said, "is the threat is getting more dangerous too."

The longest shutdown in US history finally was resolved on Friday, January 25, 2019, after exactly five weeks and as airport operations began shutting down too, with unpaid air traffic controllers and other workers simply unable to show up to work for free.

"Finally, President Trump has come to his senses and has agreed to end his ridiculous shutdown," House Homeland Security chair Thompson said. "The fact that he allowed our frontline workers at the Department of Homeland Security to be unpaid for over a month still defies comprehension. The damage his shutdown inflicted on the country will take months—if not years—to recover from. This is a permanent mark of shame for Trump and his Administration."

Government officials and their industry partners said they reengaged on cyber within hours and that collaborative efforts on supply chains, cybersecurity in critical industries, botnets, and other cyber issues were being pursued once again at full tilt. It was another example of the cyber professionals in the trenches and policy leaders taking responsibility and acting, even amid the greatest uncertainty at the top of government and a seeming lack of appreciation for their efforts.

"It's apparent there was a lot of thought given to the re-entry strategy by both government and industry," said USTelecom's Mayer, who cochaired the government-industry supply chain task force.

"We started discussions with DHS two hours after the president signed the legislation" reopening the government, Mayer said. "Absent another disruption, like another shutdown, our plans and expectations are intact." Mayer said he was "optimistic that collaborations [would] soon be back on track."

An official with the Cybersecurity and Infrastructure Security Agency said, "We are happy to be back at it, and look forward to getting the full force of CISA back up to speed. Even during the shutdown, CISA maintained critical operations and thanks to our dedicated team we issued CISA's first-ever Emergency Directive, requiring federal civilian agencies take a series of immediate actions in response to a global Domain Name System hijacking campaign. As we move back into a fully operational posture, working with agencies on implementing the directive will continue to be a major focus."

As for next steps, the DHS official said, "We're focused on getting our employees paid as soon as possible and re-energizing critical partnerships and priorities—like our election security work, pipeline security assessments, supply chain task force, soft target security engagement, and helping organizations counter Chinese hacking."

The official added, "Thanks to our partners for their patience and understanding, and we look forward to re-engaging and working through their requirements and needs. Special thanks to our valued team who have already sacrificed so much, we are confident in our ability to move forward efficiently and effectively."

On the essential information and communications technology supply-chain effort, Mayer said, "There is an understanding of what the next steps will be. The goal is to avoid drinking water out of a fire hose, but on the other hand, re-establish the momentum we had before the shutdown." Mayer said supply-chain task force leaders met quickly to put together a "punch list" of to-do's on "meetings, deliverables and establishing milestones."

"We're doing the best we can to make up as much time as quickly as possible," Mayer said. "We will work with DHS to set high-level expectations around schedules."

Mayer said the industry-government partnership's goal of beginning to show results in the first half of 2019 "still stands," and "the expectation is we'll show progress at regular intervals."

A separate "trisector" cyber initiative including the telecom, energy, and financial sectors also revved up again, and discussions resumed on the government-industry botnets initiative, according to Mayer, which was still expected to produce a report to the president by the end of 2019.

"We will find ways so that deadline is met," Mayer said. "We've moved forward and now we'll coordinate with our government partners so that it comes together in anticipation of the botnet report."

That was the positive to come out of the shutdown: after years of effort, stumbles, and distractions, DHS had also built relationships with critical infrastructure operators durable enough to come through a period when the overall government was at its worst and couldn't even open its doors.

But there were plenty of negatives, which lawmakers quickly pointed out.

"I am very concerned about CISA's ability to carry out that mission over the past month, in light of a statement by the agency's spokesman that, due to the shutdown, it had 'ceased a variety of critical cybersecurity and infrastructure protection capabilities,'" Senator Warner wrote to Secretary Nielsen days after the shutdown ended. "The same spokesman indicated that an estimated 43 percent of the agency's employees had been sent home during the shutdown. Certainly, for employees who continued to work without pay, the shutdown inevitably had a negative effect on morale."

"Guidance issued by CISA directed agencies to confront the 'significant and imminent risks' to information systems by taking a series of actions, urgent enough that they must be completed within 10 business days," Warner said in the letter. "Left unmentioned was how federal agencies, already understaffed as a result of this reckless shutdown, could successfully accomplish this task while managing a range of other essential functions."

Senator Amy Klobuchar (D-MN), about to announce her presidential candidacy, also wrote to DHS with a group of Democratic senators including Cory Booker of New Jersey, yet another lawmaker with Oval Office dreams.

"We write to express concern about the recent government shutdown's effect on the security of our cyber-networks," the senators wrote. "Reports indicate that government cybersecurity teams, such as the Department of Homeland Security's Cybersecurity and Infrastructure Security Agency, were operating with less than half staff during the shutdown. To make matters worse, many government websites were rendered either insecure or inaccessible because the websites' security certificates expired. Experts have warned that our reduced capacity for cybersecurity during shutdowns provides an opportunity for adversaries and cybercriminals."

These senators wanted a report on "suspicious activity" detected while DHS was operating at half staff.

And, as usual in the Trump era, other issues intruded on DHS's abilities across all domains, including cyber. Three weeks after the shutdown ended and final spending legislation for DHS and other agencies was signed into law, the president declared his national emergency along the border. It wasn't cyber, but it would strain DHS's relationships with key leaders on Capitol Hill.

"Far worse than one of his usual temper tantrums, the President is bypassing Congress and the rule of law to try to do what he pleases to fulfill his partisan campaign promises," Bennie Thompson said in a statement. "This clearly violates the law. It must be repeated that there is no emergency to declare. The American people will not be fooled by this menacing and authoritarian action, and I hope both parties in Congress come together to quickly stop it. We must not allow the President to continue his incessant malice to distract from his failed leadership and failed border security policies."

It didn't bode well for any DHS official who would be summoned to appear before the Homeland Security Committee. The emergency declaration gobbled up both the House and the Senate Homeland Security committees' time and energy, and it would be months into 2019 before either panel held a cyber-focused public hearing, much later than in previous years.

When Thompson's panel finally met to consider DHS's budget and priorities in May 2019, it was a remarkably toxic and partisan affair punctuated by tense exchanges over border policy and the new chairman's assertion that immigration politics was pulling the department away from its cyber mission.

At the same time, the DHS cyber leadership had undergone something of a metamorphosis and didn't intend to spend much time rocked back on its heels by criticism or bad breaks. Once again, Chris Krebs was the face of the assertive, confident new cyber agency at DHS.

Krebs on March 5, 2019, made his first appearance as head of CISA at the huge annual RSA cybersecurity conference in San Francisco; the previous year he had appeared at the packed Moscone Center event as acting head of the old NPPD. Now, after years of joking about the Soviet-sounding connotations of the earlier name, Krebs said his agency's handle finally reflected what it actually did for a living. That made everything from recruitment to interagency relations so much easier, he said.

And, Krebs confided, he'd done a little research and discovered there was a "Soviet connection" to NPPD: "NPPD was a chemical marker that the Soviets used to track people in the USSR," he said, offering yet another good reason for losing that name.

Getting down to business, Krebs said he'd spent time during the thirty-five-day government shutdown pondering mission and priorities. (He also "thanked" Congress for the shutdown, always the canny team player, aware of the importance of messaging both for the DHS ranks and for the real boss at the White House.)

Krebs identified four priorities guiding his work: Chinese threats to the telecom supply chain, securing federal networks, securing industrial controls, and election security.

"My team has a clear understanding of what we need to be looking at over the next 18 months," Krebs said. He pointed to cross-cutting initiatives like the ICT supply-chain task force and development of criteria for a "qualified bidders list" to promote government contractors that met cybersecurity standards, a huge, tangible shift in the way the federal government did business that would, presumably, have a positive ripple effect across the entire economy.

Election security was the most high-profile issue for the new agency, with its efforts in the 2018 midterm and 2020 presidential elections under intense scrutiny from the public and Congress.

But rather than pulling CISA away from core critical infrastructure protection missions, Krebs said, the 2016 election hacks and disinformation campaigns created "a galvanizing moment" that redefined cybersecurity—and DHS's mission.

"People realized it's not about PII [personally identifiable information] or some movie North Korea doesn't like," Krebs said. "It was about our democracy. Election security is national security."

That, Krebs said, "was the 1957 *Sputnik* moment. . . . That showed me things were different."

Krebs said he was positioning CISA as "the nation's risk adviser . . . notice I didn't say risk manager." DHS was leading voluntary partnerships rather than demanding cybersecurity actions. Krebs loved one-two-three examples, so that voluntary approach translated into "Understand, Share, Act."

DHS was listening, he said, and learning that stakeholders in the cyber ecosystem were overwhelmed with information and needed context, which CISA would step in to provide by revamping its info-sharing efforts.

On risk, he noted that the agency was pulling back from the view of critical infrastructure as sixteen distinct sectors—like emergency services, health care, electricity, water, and telecom—a construct developed in the aftermath of 9/11 with an eye toward physical threats.

"You couldn't see the forest for the trees," he said. CISA was looking instead at the truly important functions within those industries and activities, the specific places adversaries would target. A long-awaited list of critical functions was in the works, he said, and the new approach also made clear that CISA needed "a better understanding of supply-chain issues."

Krebs said he could not "untangle" China from the telecom supply-chain issue, particularly regarding next-generation 5G networks. He said CISA and industry partners were "working on risk management for 5G" and trying to better "scope" the problem.

On securing the government's own computer networks, he noted that the agency's efforts included the emergency government-wide directive put out during the government shutdown, highlighting that CISA's work never ceased. Further, CISA's critical infrastructure efforts, he said, "are really focused on industrial control systems . . . an area where we had the least understanding." He mentioned a recently launched program to secure natural gas pipelines that included DHS "boots on the ground" along with electronic sensors and self-assessment tools for pipeline operators.

Finally, on election security, Krebs noted that 1,400 entities joined the new election information sharing and analysis center in its first nine months—"the most ever" for a new ISAC, he said—while cyber sensors were issued for 90 percent of election systems by election day 2018. Krebs said a landmark tabletop exercise with state and local officials would become a permanent annual event.

The cyber efforts around elections highlighted the "collective defense" model he was trying to promote, Krebs said. "Everyone has some piece of information about what's going on out there—we've got to bring it together. . . . If you have anything related to election security, get it to me and I'll get it to the people who can do something about it."

It was all can-do, galvanizing.

"A lot of people are focused on threat, I need to determine what it means—so what?" Krebs told the RSA audience.

DHS had its mission and concrete objectives. It had a cyber leader in Krebs who was building off the work of Spaulding, Reitinger, Bruce McConnell, and others. And as always it occupied a precarious position within the political ecosystem, where a presidential outburst, a shutdown, or the departure of key personnel could upend its work. It was a department that desperately needed dynamism and a cause, which both Krebs and Nielsen were providing. But it also desperately needed some long-term institutional stability that could only come with the blessing of the person in the Oval Office.

Another earthquake was always going to come. On April 7, 2019, Nielsen submitted her resignation under pressure from Trump, who wanted a tougher approach to the border situation with Mexico. She had just returned from London, after cutting short a multicountry European trip—with a heavy focus on cyber issues—that reportedly infuriated the president.

Trump named Customs and Border Protection Commissioner Kevin McAleenan as acting secretary of DHS. McAleenan had no background in cybersecurity. An acting secretary was also running the Pentagon. Said former White House official Hathaway, "Too many 'acting's' in government right now. Definitely will be impacts—paralyzed decision-making."

On Capitol Hill, Democrats reacted sharply to the forced departure, while reiterating their border-related criticisms of Nielsen.

"This could not come at a worse time for the day to day management of the Department of Homeland Security and the over 220,000 employees that need leadership in order to best help keep the country secure," said Homeland Security Chairman Thompson. "There is now currently no permanent Secretary nor Deputy Secretary at the Department. The Department will quickly need proven, Senate-confirmed leaders in place that can work with Congress in good faith to help keep the country safe and to fix the Trump-inflicted situation at the border."

There was the cyber agency, CISA, to provide continuity, industry sources said with some measure of gratitude. "The existence of CISA provides an anchor, including symbolically," one source said. "But Secretary Nielsen's departure adds uncertainty to cyber relationships between industry and government. Among other things, the next secretary needs to enable public-private interactions that put America's adversaries on their back feet."

The former DHS official Mike Echols noted, "The departure of the Secretary is no surprise, just maybe the timing. CISA was a great achievement, as cybersecurity is risk management. However, leaders seem to have forgotten that people are the greatest defense we have to minimize cyber vulnerabilities leading to cascading consequences. [There is] nothing occurring in government that is inspiring to those hardworking employees who are looking for leadership."

Another industry source who worked closely with the department said, "Secretary Nielsen provided strong leadership on cyber matters as head of arguably the most critical cyber agency within the federal government. Without a knowledgeable and proactive cyber cabinet official at DHS and the elimination of the cyber coordinator position at the White House, the policy vacuum becomes even more pronounced, leaving a level of uncertainty that the nation can ill afford at this point in time."

Former DHS official Paul Rosenzweig, a Republican, underscored the nature of the problem in an April 8 tweet: "Trump is destroying DHS because it won't break the law for him and it won't implement his absurd policies. That any Republican allows this to stand, much less any Republican who cares about national security, is a blot on their character that will never wash out."

At DHS, skilled and earnest professionals were trying to manage—and lead—cybersecurity in the midst of an absurdist playhouse.

Trump was asked by reporters on April 10 whether he might consider naming White House adviser Stephen Miller—a thirty-three-year-old conservative activist and political kneecapper, who long pushed for the hardest possible policy on the border—as the new DHS secretary, a move that might give even GOP senators pause. *Washington Post* reported that Miller had been racing around behind the scenes to undermine Nielsen and encourage Trump to get rid of her. The chances of him winning confirmation, if nominated, would range from slim to none, but Democratic senators would surely relish the chance to grill the Trump insider under oath on a range of topics that could make the White House squirm.

"Stephen is an excellent guy," Trump said. "He's a wonderful person. People don't know him. . . . He's been with me from the beginning. He's a brilliant man."

But that was really beside the point.

"And frankly there's only one person that's running it," Trump told the reporters. "You know who that is? It's me."

Truer words had never been spoken.

On May 17, the Daily Beast reported on a memo sent to CISA employees, seeking volunteers to go serve at the border.

"The Department of Homeland Security's cybersecurity agency—which also works to protect schools and places of worship—is urging staffers tasked with handling cyber threats to set their day jobs aside and go on mini-deployments to the U.S.-Mexico border after an earlier request from headquarters failed to recruit enough officials, according to an email obtained by The Daily Beast."

The news site reported, "The effort to send more employees to the border comes amid concerns that the agency's focus on the influx of migrants at the border is siphoning off DHS officials who should be handling other threats—especially to elections. DHS's other components, including its intelligence arm, have also been asked to send volunteers to the border. It is unclear if those components have found enough volunteers to satisfy headquarters."

The next week at a hearing on Capitol Hill, Representative Langevin cited "361 cyber vacancies" at CISA and asked Acting Secretary McAleenan whether it was "appropriate" to free up CISA staffers for border duty amid the personnel shortage at the agency.

CISA's leadership would make a "risk-based decision" on who to free up in asking for volunteers, "like in any other national disaster," McAleenan replied. He said he wouldn't support allowing "mission-critical" cyber employees to go to the border. But "if they have lawyers" just hanging around the CISA offices, maybe they could go to the border. "It will be up to their leadership," the acting secretary said.

The same day at another event, Krebs said two cybersecurity professionals from CISA had volunteered to assist at the border out of the twenty or so employees at the agency who responded to an administration-wide request for government volunteers.

"I think the whole issue has been overblown," Krebs said. "We will assure it doesn't have an operational impact" on CISA.

And yet it showed clearly where the priorities were, as communicated to CISA by DHS's top office and ultimately the White House. Meanwhile, McAleenan would resign as acting secretary in November 2019, meaning that the department would get its fifth leader in less than three years.

7

Watchdogs, Wireless, and Cyber

TELECOMMUNICATIONS WAS ONE of a handful of "lifeline" industries that included electricity and the financial system: sectors where a cyber disaster could have a catastrophic effect rippling across the economy and costing lives and fortune. They were all interrelated and interdependent, but electricity and finance were highly regulated and complied with extensive cybersecurity rules written by government agencies. Telecommunications, including wireless, satellite, and other services, was covered by both state and federal reliability standards, but nothing as specific on cyber as those other industries faced.

Telecom was testing the proposition—partially embraced under Obama and more so under Trump—that an industry-led approach to cybersecurity was not only equal but actually superior to a regulatory approach. The telecom industry's shining lights on cyber were thrilled to have the bandwidth to pursue cybersecurity strategies and efforts without an omnipresent government directing the process, but they also realized the tremendous stakes and risks of their position.

"If this doesn't work, we're screwed," an industry source said as the telecom sector prepared to take the lead, in tandem with the tech sector, on an initiative to combat botnets. Tech and telecom were increasingly intertwined in terms of the cyber threats they faced—and in their desire to avoid direct government control of the process.

Under President Obama, the Federal Communications Commission was a front-line agency in the nation's cybersecurity fight. Obama's FCC chairman Tom Wheeler wanted industry to lead on cybersecurity, but he also wanted the commission to have a hand in the process and ensure that efforts really were being undertaken—and really did work. That changed as soon as President Trump took office.

"I'll be on my knees praying for the next three years that a bombshell doesn't drop," Wheeler said after the first year of the Trump administration's work in the telecom space.

Trump's man at the FCC, new chairman Ajit Pai, immediately moved to revoke Wheeler's "net-neutrality" rules designed to ensure equal access to the internet that were accompanied by a sweeping cybersecurity program. Both went into the bureaucratic waste basket. Also gone: an ambitious Wheeler-directed plan to match cybersecurity elements with the rollout of 5G wireless networks.

Pai was a former corporate lawyer for the telecom sector, a staffer on Capitol Hill and at the FCC and Justice Department, and a graduate from Harvard and the University of Chicago School of Law. He was a champion of free-market economics and the power of the business community to innovate its way forward with new technologies that would deliver new goods and services as well as security and enhanced consumer privacy protection. Pai didn't believe the commission should be telling industry how to secure telecom systems or directly overseeing their actions.

The summer before he would become chairman, then-commissioner Pai suggested the FCC could have a "complementary role" alongside the Department of Homeland Security, but it should not be "in the driver's seat" on cyber policy. In a conversation with Inside Cybersecurity at an industry event, Pai said the commission should endorse "a level playing field" on privacy requirements and that then-chairman Wheeler's broadband privacy proposal "is the opposite" of that. He said Wheeler's proposal would lead to "highly prescriptive" security requirements on internet service providers.

As the new chairman in 2017, Pai made clear that he believed Wheeler had vastly exceeded his authority in the cybersecurity realm. Pai moved to pull the commission out of cyber policymaking, with one exception: Faced with troubling allegations about Chinese telecom firms, Pai initiated a targeted process to shore up part of the supply chain in the telecom sector. He was looking to set new security rules around a fund designed to extend advanced communications services to rural communities, with an eye toward blocking use of routers and other network products made by Huawei, for instance.

But this looked like a narrow initiative, at least initially, and overall the FCC was leaving cybersecurity to others, including DHS on network security and ensuring the system didn't go down in a cyberattack. DHS was not a regulatory agency; it would partner with the telecom industry to guard against broad cyber threats as opposed to setting expectations for the sector that could be enforced with regulatory penalties. Wheeler protested that his own approach was actually light-touch regulation, but he wanted ways of ensuring adequate and ongoing efforts against a threat that never slowed down or stopped evolving.

With the FCC standing down on cyber, more responsibility for security at the consumer level was in the hands of the Federal Trade Commission (FTC). The FTC eagerly assumed the role of "cyber cop" under the Obama administration as well as under the Trump-appointed commission leadership. But there could be a legal gap in the role the FTC was being handed, related to its ability to enforce reasonable standards on privacy and security at the telecom companies previously regulated by the FCC.

A Democratic member of the FTC, Terrell McSweeny, argued in 2017 that her commission simply wasn't legally empowered to regulate the cybersecurity and privacy practices of broadband service providers, which she said left consumers unprotected as the FCC's security rules were withdrawn. "The Federal Trade Commission does not have jurisdiction over the security and privacy practices of broadband, cable and wireless carriers," McSweeny wrote in an op-ed for *The Hill*.

At the Federal Communications Commission, Pai along with fellow Republican commissioner Michael O'Rielly had served as the opposition to Wheeler's aggressive agenda on broadband, related security issues, and next-generation services. Wheeler saw a critical government role in shaping the economic and security landscape around these new technologies and consumer services. Pai and O'Rielly proclaimed Wheeler's agenda a vast regulatory overreach and seemed little concerned with the security implications.

Industry groups offered strong support for Pai's selection following tense relations with Wheeler over the commission's authority to set cybersecurity requirements and the scope of such rules. Pai suggested a more modest FCC role in which the commission would largely defer to industry on cybersecurity.

Telecom industry leaders on cyber responded by asserting that there would be no security vacuum. They were deeply engaged in cyber initiatives already and would eagerly jump into more during the early part of the Trump administration. Leaders in telecom and other fields knew that the cyber threats were real, as were the regulatory threats if they didn't take steps on their own to improve security.

But communications was a "backbone" industry sector, and if the telecom system went down, the US economy went with it. That's why Wheeler had empowered his FCC security chief—retired rear admiral Simpson—to craft a security framework for the sector. One of Simpson's jobs in the navy had been to stand up the telecom system in Iraq during the US-led occupation, so he understood operating in hostile environments with real bullets flying around.

At the FCC, Simpson would pull a bemused smile amid the constant barrage of criticism from industry, an antagonism that the admiral always believed was misplaced and missed the essential points of his security concerns.

Simpson and Wheeler both were strong believers that the telecom system was a prime target in the ongoing, multifront war in cyberspace, its networks constantly eyed by nation-state adversaries, terrorists, activists, and run-of-the-mill cyber thieves.

The vulnerabilities to the telecom system weren't unknown in the Trump White House. Staff on the National Security Council produced a document, Axios reported in early 2018, suggesting the US government take over and lead a "moonshot" to stand up a next-generation wireless network within three years.

Axios said the document it obtained was "older" and subsequent versions might have deemphasized the nationalization idea. "We don't comment on documents allegedly leaked from the deliberative process," an NSC spokesman said at the time.

In any case, Pai sharply rejected the proposal to "nationalize" the development of 5G wireless networks as a way to win a technology and cybersecurity arms race with China.

But the NSC document came amid what critics called a cyber policy vacuum around 5G created by Pai's moves away from cybersecurity initiatives launched under the previous commission leadership.

"So, now the White House awakens to the consequences of their actions. That the next generation wireless network is vulnerable to cyber threats is a situation the Trump FCC has exacerbated," Wheeler said in a blog post on the Brookings Institution site. "That the Trump Administration national security staff is considering government ownership of the means of production and the essential network for the 21st century is mind-boggling. Apparently, just waking up to what they were told during the Transition, but was ignored by the Trump FCC, their response is to attack the competitive market and suggest government can do it better."

Pai reacted quickly when the news broke, saying in a statement that a government-led 5G effort would be "a costly and counterproductive distraction."

"I oppose any proposal for the federal government to build and operate a nationwide 5G network," Pai said. "The main lesson to draw from the wireless sector's development over the past three decades—including American leadership in 4G—is that the market, not government, is best positioned to drive innovation and investment."

Pai added, "What government can and should do is to push spectrum into the commercial marketplace and set rules that encourage the private sector to develop and deploy next-generation infrastructure. Any federal effort to construct a nationalized 5G network would be a costly and counterproductive distraction from the policies we need to help the United States win the 5G future."

Debate over cybersecurity aspects of 5G was first stoked early in Pai's term as chair, when he quickly rescinded a July 2016 order and rule that allocated spectrum for 5G wireless and fixed broadband networks, and had required licensees to submit statements of their network security plans. Pai also withdrew a "notice of inquiry" crafted by Simpson under Wheeler's leadership, a forward-looking, even visionary document on building in security as 5G was developed.

"For the first time, we had an opportunity to deal with security at the outset of a new generation of technology," Wheeler told Inside Cybersecurity. "The standards would've included cybersecurity. This is an abrogation of responsibility."

Wheeler, however, also firmly rejected the idea of nationalization as an answer to 5G challenges.

In April 2017, Pai issued a request for comment on streamlining rules related to 5G rollout, which did not address cybersecurity issues. The idea was to eliminate bureaucratic obstacles in order to get 5G into the field as quickly as possible—and before the Chinese could get there. The move was sharply criticized by Simpson.

"The failure to include cybersecurity as one of the inquiry's topics for 'barrier reduction' will defer an important dialog across the IoT [Internet of Things] ecosystem on cybersecurity risk," Simpson said. "The commission cites several public safety IoT applications of 5G and is apparently ready to let county and municipal governments figure out how to address cybersecurity risk after 5G arrives on the scene."

Following Pai's remarks on nationalization, Simpson said, "The FCC is squandering the opportunity for U.S. leadership in that space." He cited a "huge disconnect between [Pai's] FCC and the rest of the Executive Branch" on the urgency of cybersecurity challenges facing the telecom sector.

Initiatives on 5G security were under way through various venues, including at a working group under the FCC's Communications Security, Reliability and Interoperability Council, known as CSRIC (insiders pronounce it "sizrik"). Another was taking place at the Commerce Department's National Telecommunications and Information Administration. Amid the nationalization brouhaha, administrator David Redl said NTIA would work with government agency partners and industry to deploy 5G in a way that protected the national interest and ensured security. "Security in both the device and the network itself will be important," Redl said.

But Redl would suddenly resign without comment in the spring of 2019. Reports attributed his departure to policy disagreements with Pai and dissatisfaction with the administration's overall approach to 5G and other issues.

Coupled with the repeal of the FCC's net-neutrality rule and related security requirements, and the Trump administration's wild swings between laissez-faire and nationalization on 5G, critics found serious "backsliding" on cybersecurity under Pai's leadership.

Telecom industry representatives, however, said their cyber posture was solid and continued to improve thanks to the sector's embrace of the National Institute of Standards and Technology's framework of cybersecurity standards, related industry-led work conducted in 2014–2015 by CSRIC and other initiatives.

In pushing back on the leaked draft NSC memo, one industry source cited "intense collaboration" between industry and government on the security of 5G, but also on issues like combating botnets. "It's difficult to understand how nationalizing infrastructure would lead to significant improvements in cybersecurity," the source added.

A CSRIC working group was charged with preparing a strategy on 5G cybersecurity, due for delivery in 2019. But when it came in March of that year, it largely recommended further study along with efforts to ensure that industry "best practices" were widely shared.

It felt like a punt.

Wheeler and Simpson, in separate interviews with Inside Cybersecurity, argued that the FCC had intentionally downgraded its approach to cybersecurity, which by definition would have a negative impact on the sector's cyber efforts.

"It's the law of human nature—if you don't have to, you won't do it," Wheeler said.

"The theme of the Trump FCC has not been one of having a vision but one of undoing things—starting with saying 'we don't have jurisdiction over cybersecurity,'" Wheeler said. "We had a vision on cybersecurity, on privacy, net neutrality, [providing broadband service under the low-income] LifeLine [program]. They don't have a vision, it's been erasure on each one."

Wheeler pointed to Pai's moves to rescind the July 2016 order and rule requiring 5G spectrum licensees to submit statements of their network security plans, and withdrawal of a "notice of inquiry" on building in security as 5G was developed.

"For the first time, we had an opportunity to deal with security at the outset of a new generation of technology," Wheeler said. "The standards would've included cybersecurity. This is an abrogation of responsibility."

In an October 2, 2018, interview with Inside Cybersecurity, Wheeler complained, "They are overlooking the steps necessary to fulfill 5G's promise, including on cybersecurity, economic efficiency and expanding coverage" of next-generation service to communities throughout the country. "I thought our job was to protect American consumers," Wheeler said. But Pai "believes what's good for the companies is good for the consumers. That's a basic difference in the role of government, and it's very difficult to get to security through Pai's approach."

Well into 2019, the FCC consistently declined to respond to questions on 5G cybersecurity efforts in the aftermath of the NSC memo.

Simpson told Inside Cybersecurity that the FCC under Chairman Pai redefined the commission's cybersecurity responsibilities, which harmed efforts to ensure the cybersecurity of 5G, among other damaging side effects.

"It's clear that Pai doesn't believe cybersecurity fits within the FCC's national security and homeland security charter," Simpson said. "It's also clear that a huge gap remains between NSC concerns regarding loss of U.S. leadership in the development of secure 5G and solutions that leverage the power of the market. This FCC is not closing that gap."

The "good news," Simpson said, is companies "increasingly understand that cybersecurity is part of their risk environment and has to be included in their risk assessments. Boards are getting better." But he said "there are still a lot of companies in the telecom space that don't have the expertise to make assessments on their own. They think they'll weather the storm and then respond. At the FCC, we had the obligation to work with the sector to make them more cyber-ready."

That sense of cyber mission was gone under the current FCC leadership, he said.

Simpson pointed to the repeal of the net-neutrality order as a move with substantial cybersecurity implications, notably in the scrapping of related privacy and data-security rules. "The net-neutrality order provided the high-level framework that supported work on the privacy and security order," Simpson said. "That order said that the same privacy and security goals should exist in broadband that the FCC always looked out for with telephony services."

Simpson added, "Of course the technical details of the rules were different and the privacy and security order matched the reality of consumer internet experience today. It put consumers in the driver's seat for their 'web clicks' while giving ISPs great flexibility to allow consumers to 'opt out' of specific privacy protections. If the net-neutrality repeal stands, it would be that much harder to address shortfalls in privacy and security in the future."

The net-neutrality order under Wheeler placed internet service providers under Title II of the 1934 Communications Act, while repeal would move them back to Title I. The difference, for the layperson, was that Title II entities were subject to more direct regulation and reporting requirements, anathema to telecom companies. But Simpson strongly rejected industry arguments that the FCC was "going back to Ma Bell or the railroads" in the way it intended to exercise Title II regulatory authority. "That was just a smokescreen," he said.

Overall, Simpson said, "There is no affirmative mechanism for the FCC to assess cybersecurity risk in the telecom sector. Because there is no mechanism, the FCC has stepped away entirely from trying to help drive improvements in the sector."

Among industry leaders, the nationalization question was a diversion and, they said, unfairly minimized their own security work, which continued at full tilt both in collaboration with government and on their own.

Telecom sector sources believed the Trump administration was committed to collaboration—rather than government dictates—on cybersecurity, despite the leaked NSC memo. Industry sources called the nationalization idea "a lead balloon" and "unrealistic." One source said, "Anything that creates fear, uncertainty and doubt will dampen innovation and development of cybersecurity products." The source added, "I think the White House is looking for more engagement with the [telecom] sector," while citing "an ongoing dialogue with top officials at the White House and in the agencies. But there's no evidence that there's a desire to reverse the policies reflected in the 2017 executive order on cybersecurity that was based on the collaborative model."

In addition to Trump's May 2017 executive order, this industry source and others pointed to the January 5, 2018, report by the Commerce and Homeland Security departments on botnets—a top priority for the Trump White House—as further evidence of administration commitment to collaboration in contrast to the nationalization idea.

"The Jan. 5 report to the president set very specific expectations on government and industry to work together to resolve the most serious cyber threats," the source said. This work "is dependent on intense collaboration between industry and the U.S. government, across industries and in coordination between the U.S. government and like-minded foreign governments."

However, "a more prescriptive model, or more interventionist government activity wouldn't accomplish more than is envisioned in the Jan. 5 report through collaboration," the source said.

"The security of the sector was good to begin with and improves every day," a source close to the wireless industry told Inside Cybersecurity. The National Institute of Standards and Technology's voluntary framework of cybersecurity standards was "the cornerstone of our work [and] we're always adding new improvements that incorporate the lessons we're learning."

Meanwhile, two years after Pai began scaling back the FCC's cybersecurity role, stakeholders said the lines of responsibility between the FCC and Federal Trade Commission had yet to be fully defined. Still, the telecom sector stressed that cyber initiatives were proceeding and effective, including through security partnerships overseen by DHS.

"The FCC has morphed itself to be an expert adviser agency rather than a lead agency" on cybersecurity, said Gregory Guice of the law firm McGuire-Woods and a former FCC legislative director. "That's a big shift, to cede that territory. But Pai—and some lawmakers—said DHS was better suited to oversee network security."

Guice observed, "The parade of horribles hasn't happened. That doesn't mean it won't, but cybersecurity was not so affected, despite the intense hyperbole around repeal of net neutrality and other moves by Pai."

Two years into the Trump administration, "The FCC has become incredibly circumspect on cybersecurity," David Turetsky, Simpson's predecessor as FCC security chief, said in an interview. "I have a lot of respect for the FTC's role and expertise, but the FCC has withdrawn more than it should have."

DHS was getting the broad, secure-the-networks side of the equation, but it remained unclear exactly how the FTC would pick up the consumer security side and help ensure ordinary people were protected from hacks before they happened, rather than just penalize a company after cyber thieves had already run off with their Social Security and credit card numbers.

Guice said, "We haven't yet heard the FTC's voice in its role," suggesting that "in some ways, the commission was still awaiting legislation" that would clarify and expand its role, a wait that would last for years. "What do we want the FTC to be—that is still to be determined."

Republican chairman Joseph Simons as well as many congressional Republicans and Democrats supported spelling out more robust legal authorities for the FTC in areas like data security and online consumer protections.

"In my view, we need more authority," Simons said before a House Energy and Commerce subcommittee in July 2018. "I support data security legislation that would give us three things: one, the ability to seek civil penalties to effectively deter unlawful conduct; two, jurisdiction over non-profits and common carriers; and three, the authority to issue implementing rules under the Administrative Procedure Act, and we should consider additional privacy authority as well."

The FTC in 2018 and 2019 led a series of public workshops on data security, privacy, and related questions.

In early 2019, Abigail Slater, special assistant to the president for cyber policy at the National Economic Council, said there was "violent agreement" that the FTC's authority should grow and it should be allowed to issue fines when companies break privacy and data security promises for the first time.

But the Trump White House didn't seem ready to weigh in with proposed legislation to make it happen. And in the spring of 2019, Simons walked back some of his earlier statements and stressed that new authority for the FTC should be narrowly tailored.

"I have substantial concerns, and please do not do it," Simons told lawmakers, addressing the idea of giving the FTC rulemaking authority under the Administrative Procedure Act. "Do not give us broad rulemaking authority."

The FTC was comfortable as a cop, an enforcer, but it didn't really want to be a cybersecurity regulator. At least, it didn't want to be the body that defined digital security rights and responsibilities. Lawmakers should be doing that, FTC chairman Simons implied.

As roles were being sorted out, Guice asked, "Are consumers at greater risk due to the change in oversight? I don't think that's what's come about. Operators are still being very responsible—there are market factors and other things that encourage good behavior."

In the telecom sector, Guice said, "at its core, their networks are highly engineered to ensure the security of the service. They know the network has to be always on. FCC reliability rules still make sure it's an 'always on' service."

Noting a January 11, 2019, letter to Pai from new House Energy and Commerce chairman Frank Pallone (D-NJ) on protecting consumers' privacy, Guice said industry players "know they're under the microscope. That has a disciplinary effect."

Guice said, "A lot of effort at the carriers goes into ensuring traffic is clean and validated," adding that "the harm comes from outside their networks."

Turetsky observed the FCC "has been pretty reticent about asserting its jurisdiction on cybersecurity over the past two years, with one glaring exception," noting the proposed rulemaking on supply-chain issues intended to block rural communities from tapping the Universal Service Fund to pay for telecom equipment made by certain Chinese manufacturers.

"They put out a trial balloon—I assume the White House pushed this—but it seemed very out of whack with Pai's overall approach," Turetsky said.

But on the larger question, Turetsky said "one strength" of the FTC's historic approach to enforcement was that its "'unfair and deceptive practices' standard is flexible and can be applied in different ways." He noted the calls for rulemaking authority but asked, "How would rulemaking be more effective and flexible than what they have now? I don't think it's a no-brainer to give the FTC regulatory authority."

Turetsky clarified that "it's not a good idea to just take companies at their word." This showed up in the way Facebook handled consumers' data, he said. "That this could happen without action by a regulator or enforcer is very disappointing. We need a fundamental revamping of privacy policy."

On security, Turetsky said, "The FTC says it doesn't have the tools it needs, but you can argue that cybersecurity has improved more than privacy has over the past two years. There are more incentives toward cybersecurity than toward privacy," Turetsky explained. "Companies aren't oriented in their DNA against cybersecurity like some are against privacy," he asserted.

And still, he said, "the market doesn't incentivize security investments appropriately. Companies don't face all the costs of a breach. I'm a market guy and it's a rational thing: A company will rationally look at its vulnerabilities and costs, and if the cost of harm is smaller—because consumers bear the rest of the cost of a breach—they'll invest less in cybersecurity."

Government oversight—from somewhere—was intended to bridge that gap. "Companies need to behave reasonably," Turetsky said, and when they do, "they shouldn't get hammered when they're breached." Looking to the FTC, he said that commission "historically is about enforcement. Obviously . . . the telecom sector likes FTC enforcement over FCC enforcement, because the FTC enforces across sectors and has to allocate its resources more broadly. Having a dedicated cop isn't as desirable from the telecom's perspective, for their business interest," Turetsky said with a laugh. But finding the right balance between the two commissions has been an issue for about twenty-five years, he added.

Overall, Turetsky said, "It's arguable that there are benefits to greater attention to telecom's network security than we'd get from the FTC alone—telecoms are the super highways that connect consumers to perpetrators. The consequences of how we manage that are very important."

He said an expanded FCC role "could be important," adding that "how the networks are built and managed given their role in the cybersecurity ecosystem is very important."

Turetsky also said, "I think increased consequences for unfair or deceptive acts or practices pertaining to cybersecurity is both valuable and important. Companies decide how much to invest in cybersecurity and ensuring compliance with their promises. Companies may choose to invest too little if the consequences are not severe enough, especially given the chance they may not get caught at all, and even if they are caught, the cost of the resulting harm is borne partly by others in society and not them under our present system."

On the industry side, Robert Mayer of USTelecom said the FCC had been the proper venue several years earlier, when federal officials and industry were jointly crafting a cybersecurity strategy for the telecommunications sector.

But the threats and challenges evolved and the nature of the government-industry engagement needed to evolve as well.

"Regulation won't keep up with the attacks, it's a static process," Mayer said. "But there is an understandable interest by government that industry is pursuing reasonable activities."

He pointed to industry-government engagements on botnets, malware, internet routing, and other security issues. "We are actively engaged with DHS, the National Institute of Standards and Technology, the National Telecommunications and Information Administration and other agencies to understand what government is concerned about and what we should do to address those concerns."

These engagements were part of a "whole-of-government" approach to cybersecurity that went beyond what the FCC could accomplish, Mayer said.

And he said the FTC was an attractive venue due to its "broader purview grounded in reasonableness. They provide industry with insight on how they view 'reasonable,' and the beauty is that it evolves."

Mayer stressed that beyond the jurisdictional issues and roles for the two commissions, "It's more important to recognize that many agencies have interest and expertise on cybersecurity, rather than just focus on legal ambiguities."

Jurisdiction could be nothing more than turf and budget, as was often seen on Capitol Hill. It could also be the deciding factor between an effective government approach to a problem and useless paper shuffling. Would the shift of alphabet-soup regulators from the FCC to the FTC undermine or damage cybersecurity? That remained undetermined.

Former FTC commissioner McSweeny said in early 2019, "At the time [in 2017], I was very critical of Congress's moves and Chairman Pai's moves to weaken the FCC's authority and take the FCC off the playing field on security and privacy. The expert regulators, like the FCC on networks, are well positioned to handle network security and privacy as the cops on the beat."

McSweeny, now a partner at Covington & Burling, was appointed to the Federal Trade Commission by President Obama and served from 2014 to 2018. Previously she served at the Justice Department, as a White House adviser to Obama and Vice President Biden, and on Biden's Senate staff.

She said, "The FTC does a fantastic job on consumer data protection and privacy, but there are exemptions for common carriers. The current commissioners have called for removing those exemptions—I was very pleased to see that. It can be very difficult for the FTC to proceed on privacy and security because of the exemptions."

She highlighted a February 2018 ruling that went against the telecom industry in the US 9th Circuit Court of Appeals, which said certain "activities" of common carriers were not covered by those exemptions. The court, in reversing an earlier ruling, held that AT&T could not claim an exemption from FTC oversight for services unrelated to its "common carrier" status. Because AT&T—and every other common carrier—now offered a broad range of services well beyond phone service, the distinction was incredibly important. "That was good," McSweeny said of the ruling, "but it would also be good to eliminate the common carrier and nonprofit exemptions" in statute. There was broad, bipartisan support for Congress to pass a law codifying such a move, including from current chairman Simons, she said.

"The FTC's authority—assuming the common carrier exemption isn't a barrier—is a very broad authority to protect consumers. It has found weak security practices to be unfair practices," McSweeny said. "Inherently, enforcement that's ex post occurs after something has gone wrong."

McSweeny noted, "One of the challenging things in the telecom industry is cybersecurity best practices do evolve—it's a very dynamic space and there have been expressions from the telecom industry on evolving best practices that are very important. Best practices in the space are being updated."

She added, "You need to have steps in place to detect vulnerabilities, to receive reports and remediate. The FTC—and previously, the FCC—DHS, the Department of Transportation, others are emphasizing this. . . . [And] state attorneys general have their own authorities."

Further, she said, "Cybersecurity is well-understood in all industries as essential to brand reputation and trust, so we've seen a tremendous amount of progress on cybersecurity. No one on the government or industry side thinks there will be perfect security. One of the complaints about FTC authority is what does 'reasonable' mean? I understand that criticism, but in 2019, there is a good baseline understanding of what reasonable cybersecurity practices are."

Echoing many of McSweeny's points, Maureen Ohlhausen, a Republican commissioner who served on the FTC for over six years—including a long stint as acting chair before Simons was confirmed—argued that the commission aggressively enforced both security and privacy standards and continued to be a tough cop on the beat with the tools it had. She supported legislation giving the FTC explicit authority to enforce standards for telecom entities, as well as the power to assess civil penalties.

"The Federal Trade Commission Act only gave the FTC authority to get redress, so you have to find the causation," Ohlhausen said in a February 25, 2019, interview. "That's hard to do, that's why civil penalty authority is particularly important. Causation is hard to attribute."

So, rather than being forced to precisely calculate the consumer damage caused by a specific hack and the use of stolen data, civil penalty authority would allow the commission to set a reasonable penalty against the company for failing to protect that data.

When the settlement with Equifax was announced in July 2019, Chairman Simons noted, "I want to flag an important aspect of this settlement and a key message for Congress: The [Consumer Financial Protection Bureau] and the states were able to obtain civil penalties for this breach by a major financial institution. The FTC could not."

Simons said, "Fortunately, other agencies were able to fill in the gaps, this time, but that will not always be the case, which sends the wrong signal regarding deterrence. For this reason, I renew my call for Congress to enact federal data security legislation that gives the FTC authority to seek civil penalties for first-time violations."

But in general, the current FTC structure and authority in some ways were more beneficial to consumers than counting on sector-specific regulatory agencies like the FCC to write cyber rules, Ohlhausen argued.

"The FTC has been able to use its authority very well," Ohlhausen said. "There have been a lot of enforcement actions and that's under-appreciated."

That authority was flexible and capable of evolving along with technologies as well as with changing public preferences around privacy. "We have to be careful about being too prescriptive," she said. For example, iron-clad rules on how companies could collect and use location data from smartphones, for instance, could inhibit services that consumers want.

The FTC was also well situated to address the increasing "convergence" of services within industries such as telecom, which no longer followed the lines of the regulated industries of years past. "Thank God the FTC has this general authority," she said, or the government would have no way of enforcing consumer protections as industries evolved in unimagined ways. The commission needed some more statutory authority in areas like civil penalties and data security, sure, she said, but the FTC as constituted was still the best place for finding that balance between giving consumers control over their data and allowing innovation to flourish.

On regulatory authority and possible gaps, Ohlhausen said dropping the Title II classification of common carriers "put the FTC back on the beat," and its authority was further enhanced by the 9th Circuit ruling.

Regulatory questions aside, the case was not closed on telecom cybersecurity. In January 2019, the news service FierceTelecom reported, "In what should be a cautionary tale for enterprises, communications service providers were targeted by 65% of the distributed denial-of-service [DDoS] attacks in the third quarter of last year, according to a new report."

The news service said, "While it's not unexpected that DDoS attacks are taking aim at communications service providers (CSPs), it's how they are doing them that is of concern. According to Nexusguard's 'Q3 2018 Threat Report,' the new methods of attacks exploits [*sic*] the large attack surface of ASN-level (autonomous system number) CSPs by spreading tiny attack traffic across hundreds of IP addresses to avoid detection. Nexusguard said the continued discovery of new attack patterns should serve as a warning for enterprises to pick service providers with the best DDoS-proof systems."

The telecom sector's representatives said they were taking unprecedented steps to secure the networks. Pai's FCC was largely leaving the private sector to it, with some assurance that the security of the nation's critical communications backbone was being looked after through collaborations between industry and various agencies. And the industry was clearly investing the time of its top people as well as massive resources into security.

But unlike in other sectors on other issues, like environmental protection, for example, there wasn't a well-developed "watchdog" community of public interest groups that would keep track of telecom's cyber efforts—other than on consumer privacy—and keep an eye on the regulators, too. There were informal backstops, the testers and security pros who would call out industry for lax or flawed security procedures or general laziness on the issue.

And there were Wheeler and Admiral Simpson up on the bridge, repeatedly sounding a warning. Wheeler wrote in a January 21, 2019, op-ed for the *New York Times*:

> The Trump administration's so-called "race" with China to build new fifth-generation (5G) wireless networks is speeding toward a network vulnerable to Chinese (and other) cyberattacks. So far, the Trump administration has focused on blocking Chinese companies from being a part of the network, but these efforts are far from sufficient. We cannot allow the hype about 5G to overshadow the absolute necessity that it be secure.

The former chairman concluded the piece:

> The Trump administration has been told that cybersecurity is an "existential risk." The new Congress should use its oversight power to explore just why the administration has failed to protect against that risk, especially when it comes to the next generation of networks.

It may have been unclear through two years whether anyone in a position to do something about it was listening. Early in year three, the administration sent out a series of signals that it was in fact paying attention. The coherence and effectiveness of its responses, though, remained to be determined.

On April 12, 2019, Chairman Pai went to the White House to stand alongside Trump in announcing new steps designed to help the United States beat China and others in the race to deploy 5G. Pai told reporters on a conference call earlier that day that security was "a top priority" when it came to 5G. But that was only after he was prompted to address the issue by a reporter. It didn't sound like a top priority, or at least not on par with the priority of getting 5G up and running.

"So far, this Administration's interventions on 5G have done more harm than good," Democratic FCC commissioner Jessica Rosenworcel said on April 12. "From imposing tariffs on 5G equipment to alienating allies on 5G security to falling behind the rest of the world on critical mid-band spectrum, the White House has yet to offer a workable plan for US leadership. On top of that, allies of this Administration are muddling our efforts with persistent talk of a nationalized 5G network. I hope today's announcement offers better because our global leadership is at stake."

At the White House, it was actually Trump who gave a nod to the security side of the 5G equation. He stressed the deployment of "secure 5G networks" as he called the global competition on 5G "a race we must win." The next-generation networks "must be secure, they must be strong and they must be guarded against the enemy, and we do have enemies out there," Trump said.

Former FCC chairman Wheeler, asked that day for comment, said, "You know how I feel about the Trump FCC killing our 5G cyber efforts."

Pai struck again on security just a week later, announcing that he would move to block China Mobile from obtaining a license to provide services in the United States. Pai said in a blog post:

> After a lengthy review of the application and consultation with the U.S. intelligence community, in 2018, the Executive Branch agencies recommended that the FCC deny China Mobile USA's application due to substantial national security and law enforcement concerns that cannot be resolved through an agreement with the company (called "voluntary mitigation"). Notably, this is the first time the Executive Branch has ever recommended that the FCC deny an application due to national security concerns. Based on this recommendation and the full public record in this proceeding, I have determined that approving this application would not serve the public interest. At our May meeting, the Commission therefore will vote on an Order that would deny China Mobile USA's application.

The commission was actually asserting a cybersecurity role, on a case-by-case basis. That wasn't reassuring to the Democrats now in charge of the House.

House Energy and Commerce chairman Pallone, addressing the FCC commissioners directly at a hearing on May 15, 2019, said that body was failing to meet its mission on security.

Running through a litany of complaints, Pallone said, "Even more shockingly, when the Trump Administration took over, the new FCC deliberately walked back its role in cybersecurity, leaving Americans vulnerable. I'm hopeful things will change, but I fear even if they do, we're starting from behind, because of the decisions this Commission has already made."

While the FCC took action on China Mobile, its limited process on restricting companies that posed a national security risk from US 5G networks—aimed at funding for rural telecoms—was apparently on hold, pending the commission's receipt of a list from the Commerce Department of entities meeting the criteria. But there was more to come in this space from the Trump administration as 5G, security, and China suddenly moved into the spotlight in the spring of 2019.

Meanwhile, FTC chairman Simons in March 2019 stunned some in industry by voting with two Democratic commissioners—and against his two Republican colleagues—to advance a proposal requiring financial firms to implement cybersecurity controls including encryption and two-factor authentication.

The commission's existing approach "provides direction to financial institutions on how to protect data security—importantly, while not being overly prescriptive—in an area where standards continuously evolve," the two dissenting Republicans said. "The current proposal, however, trades flexibility for a more prescriptive approach, potentially handicapping smaller players or newer entrants."

But Simons went with the argument of the FTC's professional staff, which wrote, "While our original groundbreaking Safeguards Rule from 2003 has served consumers well, the proposed changes are informed by the FTC's almost 20 years of enforcement experience. It also shows that, where we have rulemaking authority, we will exercise it as necessary to keep up with marketplace trends and respond to technological developments."

It was a direct cybersecurity mandate on industry that was as specific as—or more specific than—rules issued by any sector-specific regulator. It suggested the FTC might reshuffle the cyber regulatory deck in unexpected ways, with implications for telecom and every other sector.

There was yet another wrinkle in the telecom realm. In new and different ways, the tech and communications industries and another security-minded arm of the government—the military—were looking at ways to work together. Outside the push and pull of regulation, the Pentagon was taking a fresh look at critical technologies under one initiative, while under another the leaders of the communications, electricity, and other sectors were discussing with the military ways to ensure the nation's vital systems were secured against hacks, electromagnetic pulses, or whatever new threat could be dreamed up in the digital age.

The administration and lawmakers alike saw roles for the Defense Department in helping to both secure technologies and defend the telecom and computer networks run by the private sector. As such, the Pentagon was also tasked with developing an unparalleled partnership with the private sector operators of critical infrastructure.

"DOD is working first with financial services, communications and electricity," said one industry source active in cyber intelligence and pointing to the quiet nature of the engagement. "I don't have much visibility in what they are doing," the source acknowledged. "On a more general level, Cyber Command is working hard to declassify and send indicators through DHS."

Suzanne Spaulding, formerly the top cyber official at DHS as well as a CIA veteran, noted that "DOD's focus has traditionally been on mission assurance. They will look at how their dependence upon critical infrastructure could impact their ability to carry out their mission, and find ways to mitigate that risk. This might mean becoming less dependent upon civilian infrastructure, for example by developing micro-grids for military bases. Where that isn't feasible, it may mean trying to find ways to help shore up the resilience of that infrastructure, very likely working with DHS and sector-specific agencies."

But, she added, "they have not traditionally focused on protection of critical infrastructure beyond that needed for DOD mission assurance. Can't say if that's changed in this administration."

It did seem to be changing, at least in increments and potentially with major implications.

For instance, the Defense Department let it be known in February 2019 that it was directly part of the effort to secure the new 5G wireless networks expected to speed development of the Internet of Things and other hallmarks of the twenty-first-century civilian economy.

"Secure and resilient 5G telecommunications is vital to the security and prosperity of the United States, and DOD is working closely with our industrial and research partners to develop comprehensive and innovative solutions for both the Department and commercial industries. The United States and our allies and partners must demand nothing less than robust, trusted, and secure next-generation communications systems," Acting Defense Secretary Patrick Shanahan said in a February 26, 2019, statement.

And starting in January 2019, the communications sector and the military's Northern Command launched a collaborative effort on cybersecurity and other challenges that telecom industry leaders characterized as "the first major engagement" between the industry and the armed services on confronting these issues at a strategic level.

Leaders of the Communications Sector Coordinating Council, the sector's Information Sharing and Analysis Center, and representatives from major wireless and wireline communications companies met in Colorado Springs with the senior leadership of Northern Command, the unified joint-services command specifically responsible for homeland defense and nonmilitary issues like disaster relief.

The telecom leaders proposed that the dialogue continue through the auspices of DHS's National Risk Management Center.

"This was a seminal event," said Robert Mayer of USTelecom, who also served as chairman of the Communications Sector Coordinating Council. "They brought the top brass and they were very impressed with our abilities and we were very impressed with their abilities. . . . The commitment to engage further has been confirmed by them and by us."

Kathryn Condello, vice chair of the coordinating council and senior director for national security at CenturyLink, noted that while the Federal Emergency Management Agency "organizes support in emergencies like hurricanes and wildfires," it was Northern Command that provided troops and services to the response.

"This is a longstanding role for the Department of Defense," she said. "The new wrinkle is they're now taking a deeper look at their role and needs. If there were an [electromagnetic pulse] or cyber incident, would they still be in position to help? They are taking a coordinated view of all critical infrastructure, including telecom, to secure their own mission."

The military and telecom sector were discussing "how to work together collaboratively and systemically, rather than contractually, to ensure they are in a position to help in an emergency," Condello explained.

"This is the beginning of a collective effort by telecom to share capabilities and engage at the right points with Northern Command," Mayer said. "We've invited them to engage in the collective efforts of the National Risk Management Center and they indicated there have been discussions about this between Northern Command and DHS leadership."

Mayer noted that DHS and DOD "have a shared objective: resilience." He called Northern Command "a major resource in 'consequence management.' Their motto is 'We have the watch,'" Mayer observed, saying, "This is a logical place for us to start the conversation."

This was a new, nonregulatory approach: a commitment between two massive entities—the military and the nation's privately run telecom system—to share what they knew and what they were doing. It was potentially a giant step in a new direction. This new relationship could provide an important bulwark in a cybersecurity crisis.

For the industry participants, it was a tangible demonstration of the sector taking responsibility for cybersecurity in an innovative way. The telecom sector was picking up the challenge created by Trump's FCC moving out of the cybersecurity business. As noted, the stakes were as high as they get and the results were TBD.

8

It's a Marvelous Night for a Moonshot

In places, the Trump administration was following the cybersecurity "building blocks" approach of the Obama years, with a little more public emphasis on technological solutions. Its decisions to launch a cyber "moonshot" to secure the internet within a decade and to take on "botnets"—robot armies of captured computers and personal consumer devices, turned against all kinds of targets—were supported across the cyber community as worthy, if generic, goals.

This "moonshot"—unrelated to that memo on 5G nationalization—might even capture the public's imagination and enlist support through an "only you can prevent cyberattacks" campaign.

Likewise, the administration was updating cyber tools like the "NIST framework" and implementing a law to upgrade government technology and safely shift programs to "the cloud."

The National Institute of Standards and Technology's "framework of cybersecurity standards" turned five in 2019 and was still the government's most popular cybersecurity offering, a relatively simple guide for companies and others to organize their thoughts and activities around cybersecurity. Insurance companies, government regulators, and corporate board directors all asked as a benchmark question, "Are you using the framework?"

These initiatives were where the resiliency of the nation's governing system, and the skill of cyber professionals, could be proven, even amid a chaotic political environment. It would also test the ability of consensus-based collaborations to survive in a toxic political atmosphere.

Cybersecurity experts often stressed that cyber wasn't primarily a technology problem—it was one of people, policies, and commitment. Sharply focused efforts to develop and deploy the latest technology get you part of the way. Such progress was easily undermined by vacillations in policy or hard-to-decipher pronouncements from up top. That was true in any company, and it was true in the government.

The cyber pros within and advising the Trump administration settled on legitimate priorities and by 2018 were deep into policy work that promised to yield significant security rewards. The administration's botnet report, released in May 2018, launched a new phase in government-industry collaboration on cybersecurity, framed by a landmark effort to define roles and responsibilities—and by enormous stakes.

The country's cybersecurity challenge was growing amid increasingly sophisticated botnet and distributed denial-of-service attacks, commented one industry veteran of government-stakeholder engagements, "and there's more pressure on federal agencies to make things happen." Massive DDoS attacks pushed government and private sector defenders to the limits of their abilities and showed that bad actors could actually win these pitched battles in cyberspace—and even win this war. With that in mind, the source said, "This is an important opportunity to show that industry can take the initiative, work with government and show results."

Government officials wanted the private sector to use its expertise and resources and play a leading role in combating botnets. Industry was generally happy to oblige, and its representatives stressed the potentially transformational nature of the collaborative process itself.

"There are things the U.S. government can do, but there are limitations," said Kent Landfield of the security firm McAfee. "They need to pull in the industry stakeholder community," he said, adding that the government side heard and responded to that message as it got rolling on the botnet strategy.

"A Report to the President on Enhancing the Resilience of the Internet and Communications Ecosystem against Botnets and Other Automated, Distributed Threats" was crafted by the departments of Commerce and Homeland Security and fulfilled a key requirement of Trump's May 11, 2017, executive order.

"DHS has developed ways to improve our protection of the federal networks, work more collaboratively with our private sector partners, and reduce the threat of automated cyber-attacks from botnets. The work undertaken reflects months of extensive research and collaboration with the private sector," then-secretary Nielsen said in a May 2018 statement.

"Automated, distributed threats are a systemic challenge that no one actor—government or commercial—can solve," said Redl, then of the Commerce Department and DHS's partner on botnets. "Over the past year, we heard from industry, government, academia and civil society on the importance of working together and developed a roadmap to protect the Internet from botnets. Now that we have itemized the challenges, we look forward to getting to work on concrete actions to accomplish these goals."

The report was expected three weeks earlier, on the anniversary of the executive order, but "it was worth waiting for," commented USTelecom's Mayer. "It took a little more time to get agreement between Commerce, DHS and the White House, but that's essential to a whole-of-government approach. This gives confidence to industry that [implementation] will be pursued in a uniform way without duplication."

Mayer said the requirement in the report for a status update to the president in 365 days showed "a serious effort to track progress." The report also signaled recognition that "regulation is too static," Mayer said, and suggested government could play a "facilitating" role in addressing international aspects of the botnet challenge.

Botnets were the issue at hand, but government and industry representatives alike were crafting a response plan that could define public-private roles and responsibilities on cyber for years to come.

John Miller, the Information Technology Industry Council's vice president of global policy and law, said, "Successfully combating botnets and bolstering cybersecurity across the global digital economy will only happen if industry and government work together. We look forward to rolling up our sleeves and working with government and ICT partners to implement the recommendations in the report."

USTelecom and ITI spearheaded a new joint venture—the Council to Secure the Digital Economy—that was "developing and promoting an international guide to anti-botnet baseline security practices for key segments within the ICT sector," according to ITI. This effort recognized the intersection between technology and communications, and the blurring of lines between what used to be entirely separate and distinct industries. Tech and telecom products and services were merging, and they increasingly represented a single, vast attack surface for hackers.

The collaboration and statements of support were important, and the report was a good first step, Admiral Simpson told Inside Cybersecurity. But the follow-on strategic approach to this growing threat to the internet still needed to include a central role for the Federal Communications Commission. If the new administration hadn't been so determined to reverse previous FCC work on cybersecurity, he said, some of the goals already could have been accomplished.

"The report is a good [start] and hopefully will be a 'call for action' for measures to address this significant and growing threat to public safety, homeland and national security," Simpson said in a detailed email response to Inside Cybersecurity.

"By and large this report does a good job of cataloging previously well-known best practices for botnet risk mitigation," Simpson said. However, "it 'kicks the can down the road' in many areas and falls well short of an implementation plan commensurate with the risk to critical infrastructure from botnets and other automated and distributed threats."

Simpson said, "We can hope that as the president receives the report, he'll direct his staff to raise the priority of cybersecurity risk reduction and put forward a more aggressive plan knowing that our nation-state adversaries are well aware this is a growing national security Achilles heel."

"Still," Simpson added, "this is an important step forward."

The report "clearly recognized that edge device security currently is an externality in the market, with insufficient incentives to close the gap," Simpson said. The admiral went on to say, "Yet it curiously avoids articulating a role for the agency [the FCC] best positioned to address many of the issues outlined in the report."

Further, "It does not effectively communicate the urgency of the issue with respect to critical infrastructure and is a weaker approach than advocated by the prior administration, shifting much of the burden" to the Pentagon and federal agencies, basically to use their purchasing power to compel suppliers to improve the security of their products.

Simpson wrote, "While referencing much of the cyber work done by the FCC, the report doesn't include the FCC in its prescription for future action and instead draws upon the very weak authorities of the FTC, with limited rule making, technical standards and enforcement potential. The Obama FCC concluded that a market-based approach would be a much less expensive (and more effective) way to address IoT and other edge device botnet security shortfalls than one in which DOD does the R&D and drives new solutions through procurement rules."

Simpson said, "Failure to use market-based incentives and penalties risks further erosion of U.S. leadership in the market as other governments define market parameters influencing global products"—including the European Union's General Data Protection Regulation and 5G initiatives, as well as China's cybersecurity laws—"and potentially places overseas and deployed U.S. personnel at risk where their communications ride over non-U.S. infrastructure. The Obama FCC made expectations clear for ISPs to lead risk reduction for botnets."

The report "urges voluntary adoption of best practices . . . yet providers and other ecosystem stakeholders have not widely adopted many of those for which this report recommends," Simpson wrote. "The report does not provide a compelling analysis to suggest that a continuation of this policy approach will now lead to different results."

It was a towering challenge, and it wasn't clear to Simpson that the expedition was properly equipped to make the climb.

In the fall of 2018, the federal government released a roadmap on how it would implement the recommendations in the botnet report. It detailed steps on security of the IoT and of the internet, new technology, public awareness, and other issues. The roadmap foresaw a major role for industry and would be followed by an update to the president a year later, keeping up the pressure for progress.

It was a crammed government document—dense but slightly more readable than most, perhaps. It was, in essence, a true government battle plan for organizing resources and confronting the scourge of botnets. It wasn't accompanied by a Churchillian call to action from the president. Obama might've been inclined to launch a new cyber initiative, figuratively, with a champagne bottle across the bow, but not Trump. The current president tweeted once about his 2017 cyber executive order and once about his decision to elevate the status of the military's Cyber Command, but he wasn't going to gush about a botnet campaign.

It was left to the pros to largely speak among themselves within the cybersecurity community that would do and closely follow the work. It was unfortunate this wouldn't get a wider audience, because it truly underscored important work that was taking place on cyber—which, alas, would come to a temporary halt just weeks later when the government shut down in the budget fight over Trump's border wall.

According to a blog post by Commerce's Diane Rinaldo and NIST's Kevin Stine, "The government and private sector spent a year developing the report in an open and transparent process. The report maps out an ecosystem-wide view of the botnet threat, and lays out actions that could dramatically reduce the threat of botnets and similar attacks."

This was how the government intended to fight DDoS attacks launched by botnets.

"This is just a starting point and the road map will evolve to address the rapid changes in digital technologies and the threat environment," they wrote. "The departments will track progress through regular stakeholder meetings as well as a workshop. In addition, the departments will provide a status update to the President that reviews progress, tracks the impact of the road map, reassesses the botnet threat, and sets further priorities."

Commerce's Evelyn Remaley explained, "We're really viewing [the roadmap] as a tool for the community to use to keep us all accountable to each other. This goes a long way toward the first line of effort in the roadmap," which was centered around developing a security baseline for the consumer Internet of Things, she noted.

Reviews of the DHS-Commerce "roadmap" by security pros were positive, if somewhat guarded.

"This policy formulation is in the same state as many other pieces of cybersecurity policies and proposals—it enumerates many good ideas but will not be effective without strong regulation with incentives. While awareness is important, regulation is necessary for success," said Andrew Howard, global chief technology officer of Kudelski Security.

An alliance of telecom and tech industry groups, in a move coordinated with the government, released its own report on how the private sector would organize to combat botnets. USTelecom's Mayer told Inside Cybersecurity, "With 20 billion connected devices expected by 2020, the risk of disruptive activity to our global digital ecosystem has never been greater. Any hope for changing this deteriorating trajectory rests with collective and coordinated actions across the information, communications and technology sectors."

He added, "This realization is the foundational underpinning that brought 14 global infrastructure providers together in the Council to Secure the Digital Economy, which just released the 2018 International Anti-Botnet Guide urging organizations around the world to adopt a set of baseline security practices."

Government and industry sources saw the two reports as complementary. Kudelski's Howard stressed that "cooperation between the government and the private sector is not only essential, it is required. There is no single stakeholder that can address this problem alone. This challenge, like many security challenges, requires broad commitment across the board to have any impact. If one part of the ecosystem, such as product manufacturing, does not improve, improvements by other parts of the ecosystem will be dampened."

"I appreciate the spirit of the roadmap," said Kurtis Minder of the cybersecurity reconnaissance firm GroupSense. "It is detailed in the objective and stakeholder organizations which would contribute. It is so preliminary/academic, though, I cannot comment on its effectiveness. Many of the objectives do not have defined timelines and while I'm sure each organization has assigned an owner to implement and collaborate, it isn't outlined here. Of most interest to me is the threat sharing components. Intelligence is a fundamental part of building a security program, happy to see this included in the roadmap."

He said, "My overall thoughts are that while this document primarily focuses on infrastructure and vulnerable IoT and networked systems, that some focus on the marketplace that drives the economy behind these [botnet] attacks would be fruitful. A 'follow the money' approach, if you will."

There was, however, an underlying problem: A year after the roadmap release, the government's botnet effort was proceeding so quietly as to be almost imperceptible. Stakeholders were engaged, for sure, though the same government and industry people were also engaged in multiple other initiatives on top of their regular day jobs. But there was little effort to connect the botnet initiative—identified by the Trump White House as perhaps cyber priority number one—to the public in any meaningful way. One might wonder whether the Trump White House, with no cyber coordinator, had lost interest.

The government promised at least one public workshop to gather input and gin up some attention (and many were hoping for more, spread around the country), but nearly a year into the effort, a government official would only comment that "it's in the early planning stages."

What should have been a central feature of the overall effort—engaging the public and using this as a cyber educational tool—was instead just one extra chore that officials might or might not get to as they raced to meet the deadline for delivering a report to a president who wouldn't read it.

With the botnet work silently unfolding, another cyber initiative was aiming even higher—metaphorically speaking.

Perhaps mindful of Trump's fondness for the grandiose, a body of presidential advisers, chartered by law with providing recommendations on securing communications systems, called for a dramatic initiative patterned after the effort to put an astronaut on the lunar surface before the end of the 1960s, a "moonshot" to secure the internet within ten years.

It set 2028 as the target for a secure web, though that date might have to float thanks to government shutdowns.

The President's National Security and Telecommunications Advisory Committee in November 2018 intoned:

> The United States is at an inflection point: simultaneously faced with a progressively worsening cybersecurity threat environment and an ever-increasing dependence on Internet technologies fundamental to public safety, economic prosperity, and overall way of life. Our national security is now inexorably linked to cybersecurity. Therefore, the Nation must build on past efforts and current strategies to seize the opportunity to strategically reorient from a largely reactive, incremental cybersecurity posture to a proactive approach that boldly assures digital trust, safety, and resilience for all Americans. Achieving this audacious outcome will require strong national leadership, political will, and a

> sustained whole-of-nation investment over an extended period. The U.S. Government can take immediate actions that lay the foundation for this long-term shared cybersecurity vision for the Nation, while simultaneously yielding near-term benefits that ensure continued technological global leadership.

The advisers, top executives from major companies in critical infrastructure sectors, called for a rare "aspirational statement of strategic intent" from the very top level of the US government, inspiring a "collective" national campaign on cybersecurity evocative of the 1960s effort to send astronauts to the moon.

They recommended creating a senior-level Cybersecurity Moonshot Council, chaired by the president or vice president, which would craft a "strategic framework" with six "pillars" as a starting point: on technology, human behavior, education, ecosystem, privacy, and policy. It was to be based on establishing a "whole of nation" approach to cybersecurity, with "whole of government" and "whole of industry and academia" components.

"Leadership must start with a bold aspirational statement of strategic intent, as the United States has done just a few times historically when facing existential challenges," according to the report. "The President's National Security Telecommunications Advisory Committee [NSTAC] believes cybersecurity represents one of the 21st Century's greatest challenges, and one the United States simply must enduringly address as a matter of national strategic imperative."

Therefore, "to communicate this, the Administration, at its most senior levels, must deliver a clear aspirational and inspirational vision as a catalyzing force for national activities. It must declare a national strategic intent to: Make the Internet safe and secure for the functioning of Government and critical services for the American people by 2028." The report noted, "The differences between the characteristics of President Kennedy's moonshot vision and those anticipated of a moonshot for cybersecurity, however, are numerous. Principally, the success criteria for a Cybersecurity Moonshot Initiative will be less precise and measurable because its achievement will be a societal transformation rather than a singular, visual triumph."

It was bold, and it did link to JFK, both of which could appeal to the current president. It was also complex and demanded a serious commitment of attention, which might not be so appealing to Trump. Perhaps that's why the advisers suggested that either the president or the vice president could chair the moonshot council. This might be more of a Mike Pence thing. In a discouraging sign, the report would sit on Trump's desk for months. (Whenever the report physically made its way into the Oval Office, it landed on the famous Resolute Desk, used by both Trump and JFK.)

On its merits at the start, Admiral Simpson called the moonshot initiative "a nice idea, not clear that it hasn't devolved into a few companies working on proprietary methods to obfuscate internet externals . . . not sure this scales to a free and open internet." Simpson said, "It will be interesting to see if NSTAC members commit to individual actions or just glittering generalities. The actual moonshot was a committed government program with healthy funding, clear milestones and a strong commitment to staying on track."

In comparison with that defining effort of the 1960s, Simpson noted the ponderous bureaucratic language and timelines around the proposed cyber moonshot. "After six months," he observed, "the NSTAC reported out that they will 'next discuss the subcommittee's planned next steps for the study, a preliminary step in a longer, iterative dialogue between the NSTAC and U.S. Government counterparts on the cybersecurity moonshot concept. Informed by this discussion, the subcommittee will continue developing a cybersecurity moonshot action plan, focusing on the following near-term areas: 1. Providing definitional clarity around the cybersecurity moonshot vision and high-level organizing principles; and 2. Developing a detailed strategic framework for launching a coordinated, whole-of-nation approach towards achieving that vision.'"

Taking a deep breath, Simpson said that language was "not quite the Agile Epoch, with scrums driving incremental, tangible results . . . but better than not having a goal."

Senior Trump officials were enthusiastic about the plan, but they also tried to inject some realism.

Inside Cybersecurity's Mariam Baksh quoted Grant Schneider, the federal chief information security officer and top cyber director on the National Security Council: "There is no planting the flag here, there isn't a pinnacle solution or something that we're going to be able to have pictures and posters and movies about saying 'this is the moment we were secure in cyberspace.' Unfortunately, it's not an end state, it's continuous."

Baksh reported that Jeanette Manfra, a top cyber official at DHS, "said there is a benefit to setting a timeline, but that the moonshot is more about making a call to action and expanding the sphere of people paying attention to cybersecurity." She quoted Manfra: "Although we do like the concept of 'let's set a timeline for ourselves' to achieve a series of things that will build a more secure infrastructure, sort of maybe the negative of calling it a moonshot is really you're talking about an entire ecosystem that we're trying to shift. I think it's important that it's a broader community that actually cares about this. It can't just be the security people who care about this. So that, to me, is getting a generation of children who actually understand what it means to be a responsible digital citizen."

Baksh noted that "Manfra also said, because people are naturally lazy, security should be opt-out, rather than opt-in."

Government itself wasn't necessarily lazy, but it usually moved at a glacial pace. The real moonshot initiative of the 1960s was attached to a political booster rocket and moved rapidly; the cyber moonshot was more typical. On March 11, 2019, Politico reported, "Planners hope this year to establish a series of 'grand challenges,' and next month have their second set of military academy meetings around the country to broaden input, Tom Patterson, vice president and chief trust officer of Unisys, told MC. The project still doesn't have a council to lead some of its tasks, however, something Patterson said was delayed by the government shutdown."

Maybe this would lead to securing the internet in a decade, and maybe, like Admiral Simpson said, it wasn't quite the Agile Epoch. Trump still hadn't signed off on the report six months after its submission, revealing a lack of Kennedy-esque urgency. Leaders from Unisys, Palo Alto Networks, and other firms were trying to press ahead, including with well-attended stakeholder events at the navy and air force academies. But a senior administration official would only say on May 22 that "the White House received the NSTAC 'moon shoot' report and is evaluating its recommendations as part of the Administration's National Cyber Strategy implementation efforts. We have no other comment."

As with the effort on botnets, the public engagement/educational aspects were being neglected. The advisers' call for "a clear aspirational and inspirational vision as a catalyzing force for national activities" was largely ignored. The 2028 target for securing the internet may have been too close for the president's comfort. If he served two terms, Trump would be only three years into retirement when the public began blaming him for failing to deliver on a promise to secure the internet.

Still, these were big initiatives, the botnets and moonshot efforts, with high stakes, important buy-in from the cyber community, and realistic plans of action. What about the voluntary, collaborative cyber North Star of the Obama years, the NIST framework of cybersecurity standards?

A three-day NIST "Cybersecurity Risk Management Conference" in Baltimore in the fall of 2018 included presentations and discussions on metrics, mandatory uses of voluntary tools like the framework of cybersecurity standards, and binding commitments on cyber in international trade agreements.

And—even with once-verboten words like *mandatory requirements* in the air—there were no reports of industry representatives' hair catching fire. With hundreds of industry types and security pros filling the conference rooms at an Inner Harbor hotel, the hard, in-the-weeds work of cybersecurity continued, almost blissfully oblivious to the Trump administration's daily dramas.

The discussions were about core issues, who would do what to secure digital life, and how responsibilities would be assigned and enforced. It was a relief, for many, from the politically charged and disorienting atmosphere an hour away in the capital.

"We are not calling for regulation—that's not in my charter," Matthew Barrett, then the NIST program manager for the cyber framework and master of ceremonies at the conference, stressed to Inside Cybersecurity.

In fact, discussions about the role of mandated cyber requirements and ways of measuring the effectiveness of business cyber activities marked a noteworthy evolution in the industry-government engagement that began with the launch of the cyber framework process in 2013. The framework was released in 2014 and became the focal point of government-industry discussions on cyber; earlier in 2018, NIST had produced an updated version with plenty of input from industry. It also committed to regular conferences to discuss the document and broader cyber issues with the cybersecurity community, an annual event that promised to be the premier venue for community interactions.

The Baltimore meeting was the first formal gathering since the framework update had been released.

Businesspeople at the Baltimore conference were not cheering for new cyber regulation—far from it—but there was less anxiety on the industry side that cyber policy would boil down to a binary choice between compulsory rules and flexible, industry-driven strategies.

A few months earlier, a former Pentagon official's call for mandatory use of the framework of cybersecurity standards by critical infrastructure operators caused a stir, running counter to how some security professionals saw the recently updated document and its role in securing the cyber ecosystem.

"The framework gets misused in a regulatory context, it can't be a check list," said Vikram Phatak of NSS Labs. "People keep looking for check lists and easy audit buttons," Phatak said in an interview with Inside Cybersecurity. "But when [a government] auditor comes back at you with a check list, that obliterates the intent" of the framework.

Former Defense Department official Eric Rosenbach, speaking before the Senate Homeland Security and Governmental Affairs Committee on April 24, 2018, said, "Congress can do more to incentivize the private sector to act. In particular, Congress should . . . mandate that critical infrastructure providers adopt the NIST Cybersecurity Framework."

Mandatory use of the 2014 framework wasn't a new concept, of course. Federal agencies were in the process of adopting the framework for their own systems under Trump's executive order. And the House Intelligence Committee in its Russia hacking report said certain federal funding for securing state election systems should be tied to adoption of NIST standards.

Military leaders throughout the Obama years made clear their uneasiness with a voluntary, business-led approach to cybersecurity for critical industries that provided essential services like electricity and communications to almost all of the armed services' bases across the United States.

On the flip side of this coin, the financial sector under the leadership of the Bank Policy Institute was trying to rationalize the panoply of rules it faced by customizing the NIST framework to its needs and streamlining regulations around the framework's structure.

That tracked with one of the core elements of Obama's 2013 Executive Order 13636, which mandated development of the framework while calling for regulatory streamlining. The latter point was often cited by business leaders as a piece of unfinished business from that executive order, which might come to pass under Trump.

NIST officials said framework version 1.1 brought them closer than ever to the long-held goal of positioning the framework as a flexible, adaptable tool suitable to any cybersecurity environment. The underlying voluntary nature of the framework was widely seen by business groups and security experts as essential to that proposition.

"We've never been closer to having a singular structure for alignment" of the tools and principles contained in the cyber framework with how organizations of various types were designing their cyber efforts, Barrett said in an interview in April 2018.

Barrett said NIST in version 1.1 sought to "affirm" the framework's value in "expressing compliance with one's own cybersecurity plans," but also to recognize industry concerns about language on compliance being used in a regulatory context. "We came back quickly [in the 1.1 document] and said it's about industry's internal use of the framework," Barrett said. "Of course, regulators are a part of our stakeholder group, but we acknowledge that 'compliance' is a confusing term."

It was unlikely at the time that the Republicans who controlled all the congressional committees would be interested in imposing a framework mandate on the private sector, although many Democrats (and even some GOP senators, such as Susan Collins of Maine) called for legislating specific cybersecurity requirements for critical infrastructure.

There was at least a chance that dynamic would change when Democrats took over the House in 2019. And even a Senate Republican-led committee in early 2019 issued a bipartisan report, based on the Equifax hack, suggesting that use of the NIST framework should, perhaps, be made mandatory for entities that held citizens' sensitive data. But conversations with private sector security experts and industry representatives suggested that mandating the use of the framework by private sector entities risked missing the point.

"Folks see the framework as very helpful," Phatak noted, "but it's not helpful when it gets misconstrued by the auditor types." Phatak said his own security firm "consciously aligns" with the functions in the framework, noting, "The NIST framework moves the discussion away from fear and uncertainty and doubt—which is what vendors try to sell sometimes—into science and objective reasoning."

He said, "The framework is a good touchstone for sophisticated companies and we've incorporated some of it into our day-to-day operations. Our clients are larger companies and they are very familiar with it."

For regulators, Phatak said, a better approach would be to "encourage companies to properly measure risk and respond—if you know the risks, you can mathematically determine the appropriate [security] investments."

John Holmes, general counsel at Forcepoint, said his firm also tailored the framework to its own internal security needs. "We're a cybersecurity company but we have to secure our network and it's very helpful," he said in an interview. "The threats are too pervasive—nobody feels 'too secure.'"

Added Forcepoint's Sean Berg, "NIST has this public-private partnership down—that's the right way to go." The framework was a valued tool, these security professionals said, and its use should be encouraged.

"It's been a great public-private partnership to point to when working with other agencies, and we think the revised framework is a great risk-based approach, and what industry would like to see," Pamela Walker, the senior vice president for the Public Sector at the Information Technology Industry Council, told Inside Cybersecurity. "The industry overall, our members have been supportive of the framework, it's a tool to be able to measure your cyber capabilities, your risks, it allows you as an organization to figure out where you need to move to improve your cyber posture," Walker said. "So it's been a great tool."

But these sources were eager to make the point that the public-private partnership component—as opposed to regulatory mandates—was the secret sauce that made it effective.

A few months later, much of the discussion in Baltimore on mandatory uses of the framework focused on government itself, as the Trump administration and countries ranging from Israel to Uruguay required its use throughout their executive branches.

Compared to earlier years, the US government's evolving embrace of "risk management"—propelled by Barrett and DHS's Krebs, Manfra, and Kolasky, who had served under Obama and been promoted in the Trump years—was making industry less nervous about the broader regulatory implications of requiring federal agencies to use the framework, and more comfortable in formally assuming responsibility for cybersecurity without fearing a regulatory bludgeoning. Risk management implied making choices, and the government was signaling a level of trust with its industry partners—to be on top of their own cyber posture and to choose to emphasize security where they were finding the most risk.

To be sure, the conference program in Baltimore was dominated by discussion of industry initiatives, security products and services that were popping up across industries and domains, and nonregulatory collaborations in places like the DHS's Information and Communications Technology Supply Chain Risk Management Task Force and DHS's new National Risk Management Center.

Supply-chain cybersecurity was "clearly a top-priority issue for industry and government, and [the task force is] a great opportunity for a broader set of stakeholders to drive proactive solutions," said ITI's John Miller. DHS's Kolasky said the risk management center he led was "bringing government and industry together to think strategically" about these issues.

In addition to those very nonregulatory topics of discussion, software industry representatives discussed their own emerging framework for secure software development, modeled on the NIST cyber framework.

NIST's Barrett noted that regulation "often happens when we have market failures, but there are great things happening in cyber where there aren't market failures." Against that backdrop, he said, "there is a change in tone around measurement and metrics."

"There is a market desire to demonstrate trustworthiness," Barrett said, adding that "we've been waiting for a sign that this is the right time" to engage on metrics. "We need to create a thriving process" on metrics, he said, and "this will be a focus in the coming months."

Measurement and metrics was one of the most contentious issues on the agenda during NIST cyber conferences in years past. And it still stoked anxiety among industry groups concerned about how government might use such information. But there was clearly a narrowing of the gulf of distrust on this issue, which—again—could be attributed to a government embrace of risk management, and which in turn changed the perception of what federal officials might do with these metrics.

Broaching the regulatory matter from another angle, the opening keynote at the conference was delivered by Leo Simonovich, the vice president and global head of industrial cyber and digital security at Siemens. He helped spearhead a voluntary "charter of trust" already adopted by a number of global manufacturing, tech, telecom, and other industry heavyweights. But he also called for binding commitments in trade agreements in order to fully implement international cyber standards and a "regulatory framework" around cybersecurity.

"Security has to be more than a seatbelt or airbag in the digital world," Simonovich said.

Barrett downplayed the idea that Simonovich's statement was a call to regulatory arms, but said, "The charter of trust is interesting—it's an agreement to behave a certain way. Those principles are the basis for dialogue. When Leo says 'standards,' he's talking about formal and informal agreements on how we operate."

And yet what the Siemens executive suggested amounted to binding requirements for industry enforced by governments.

The simple consideration of such standards constituted a change in attitude and perhaps an opening for dialogue less rooted in regulation versus nonregulation, and perhaps more about both security and cost effectiveness—and appropriate places to assign responsibility.

The Baltimore conference provided a venue for such dialogue across cybersecurity issues. That it didn't bog down or grow contentious suggested a new maturity level—generally the goal of cyber efforts—in the government-industry relationship around cyber policy. How did we get to this point?

February 12, 2019, was the five-year mark since the NIST framework of cybersecurity standards was unveiled at an Obama White House ceremony that featured senior government officials and representatives of major industry groups and companies, after a one-year collaborative process launched by Obama Executive Order 13636.

"It's difficult to think of any partnership initiative in the last five years that has had a more profound impact on our collective ability to manage cyber risk," said USTelecom's Mayer. "The CSF has become the cornerstone for communicating risk within organizations, across organizations, and with domestic and international civil, industry and government stakeholders. What is most indicative of its lasting impact," he said, "is that we are finding ways to apply the framework construct to an emerging array of threats from IoT to botnets to supply chain and more. It remains a model for stakeholder collaboration and a robust and accountable public-private partnership."

The framework was offered in 2014 as a way for entities to voluntarily organize their cybersecurity efforts. Its voluntary nature was stressed by NIST officials and their industry partners. The framework included no mandates or other inducements for companies to use it.

"I remember back on the day of the launch, several critics suggested that without specific high-cost incentives, like tax cuts, the framework would never be successful," said Ari Schwartz, now of the firm Venable but then a cybersecurity director on Obama's National Security Council. "While there have been some small incentives—insurance-oriented for example—I believe that those of us that felt that industry already had enough incentive to move to a more risk management-oriented process, if presented, have been proved correct," Schwartz observed.

Suzanne Spaulding, who led cyber efforts at the Department of Homeland Security during the Obama administration, noted that the framework "was initially conceived as a way to pull together best practices from the private sector and make them generally available, but that turned out to be the least important part of the framework." Spaulding said, "Having best practices in one place helps but they were already out there. What has been most valuable is actually the structure and lexicon for companies and governments to use in thinking about and planning for cyber risk management."

She added, "I would say the biggest problem is the failure of the government to uniformly apply the framework as various departments and agencies, particularly regulatory agencies, issue guidance to the private sector."

Benign neglect from the White House allowed the framework to continue to evolve organically, but it also deprived the process of the kind of energy that propelled its uses and value initially.

But as Scott Aaronson, the Edison Electric Institute's vice president for security and preparedness, put it, "Protecting our nation's interests in cyberspace requires government and industry working closely together. The development of the NIST cybersecurity framework five years ago represented a proof-of-concept for how public-private partnerships can effectively address cyber threats and vulnerabilities. Five years later, the shared perspective on cybersecurity, the common language developed through the process, and the ongoing collaboration fostered by the framework continue to make industry and our nation more secure."

Josh Magri, the Bank Policy Institute's senior vice president, said, "The creation of the NIST cybersecurity framework could yield as many benefits for the country as the development of the National Highway System." Magri went on to say, "With respect to shared risks, the framework evidences the power and applicability a multi-stakeholder, public-private partnership can have versus a more typical top-down regulatory approach. For the financial services industry, the NIST cybersecurity framework formed the foundation of our sector's cybersecurity profile, an assessment synthesizing various supervisory expectations and ordering them so as to reduce the 'Tower of Babel' that was developing around cyber risk management."

Even the Pentagon was using the framework to organize its approach to cybersecurity for its own internal systems. It helped power a cost-effective approach to cyber risk management at the Defense Department that aligned in many ways with how the framework was employed by the private sector, according to senior National Security Agency official Pat Arvidson.

"How excited we are about the cybersecurity framework and what DOD has been able to do with the program," Arvidson said, offering a defense/national security take that complemented and mirrored the observations of many industry stakeholders on the fifth anniversary of the landmark NIST document. "We used data from our networks combined with the NIST framework to make informed decisions on buying down risk," Arvidson said of a 2015–2016 process undertaken at the Pentagon.

Arvidson explained the Pentagon in 2015 wanted to examine the effectiveness of its spending on cybersecurity "and realized we didn't understand the threat correctly," a position probably familiar to many corporate executives. He used an analogy of Godzilla standing outside a building, with engineers on the first floor seeing the threat one way and executives upstairs seeing it differently. "Everyone looks at the threat through an independent lens and no one looks holistically, so we waste a tremendous amount of money," he said, speaking broadly of a problem that affected all types of enterprises.

Arvidson said DOD was able to "figure out what the adversary was trying to do" on the department's networks and where it was attacking; it was also able to develop "a good profile of the attacker. . . . Then we used the NIST framework to match how well each of our capabilities matched to each aspect of the threat," Arvidson said. "Now we had a coverage map of how we're being attacked and our capabilities, and that determined how much we were over-spending," he explained. "The point is," Arvidson said, "to be able to look out of any window and see all of Godzilla."

The framework speaks to boardroom executives as well as security officers, he said, calling it the "Rosetta Stone of cybersecurity."

NIST director Walter Copan offered a soup-to-nuts review of his agency's sprawling cyber portfolio during the 2019 RSA Security Conference in a speech that showed how much was in the works down at the boiler-room level of government's interaction with industry, businesses, and the world.

"Collaboration is NIST's wheelhouse," Copan said before an audience of industry representatives and cyber professionals. "It's wonderful to be part of a nonregulatory agency." Copan cited a significant change over the past few years, with business leaders taking a much more proactive role on addressing cyber risks. "It's no longer an information technology issue, it's being engaged at the C-suite level," he said.

Spurred by that broad development and the specific requirements of Trump's cyber executive order, Copan said NIST was "enhancing" a separate risk management framework and working to explain how that tool could be used in tandem with the landmark framework of cybersecurity standards. "NIST is committed to ensuring even more organizations know about the cybersecurity framework" and how to use it to allocate resources, he said.

"NIST sees the risk management framework and the cybersecurity framework as complementary," Copan said, "but we understand how this can be confusing. . . . Over the next year, you will hear more from us on how the two can work together."

Also in support of the Trump executive order, NIST and industry were working on a "practice guide" for securing Internet of Things devices from distributed denial-of-service attacks, Copan said. "These kind of partnerships can yield immediate value. . . . It's about understanding the environment in which IoT devices are connected."

Could NIST and other agencies, plus their private sector partners, pull all of this off? Could they use the policy orders crafted in Trump's White House as both the fuel and framing documents for major government-industry endeavors, while steering clear of—or, more accurately, completely ignoring—the political firestorms the president was eagerly fanning?

Maybe, thanks to the professionals involved.

As NIST's Jon Boyens put it during the late 2018 Baltimore conference, "Trust is incredibly important."

9

We'll Always Not Have Paris

One high-profile cyber development at the end of 2018, year two in the age of Trump, was very much in line with the president's worldview: shunning an opportunity to collaborate with allies by rejecting a landmark "Paris call" on cybersecurity for the world community.

Sixty-six states signed the "Paris Call for Trust and Security in Cyberspace," and 347 private sector entities signed the related "Cybersecurity Tech Accord" and "Charter of Trust" that Siemens's Leo Simonovich had promoted at the NIST Baltimore conference. US allies such as the United Kingdom, Germany, and Japan signed the Paris call. The United States, Australia, and Israel were among the countries that declined to sign, along with China, Russia, and Iran.

The US government didn't formally spell out its reasons for declining to endorse the global declaration crafted by French president Emmanuel Macron on common cybersecurity principles, despite support from major players in US industry. It was a bit hard to imagine Trump's predecessor ignoring a global agreement embraced by US businesses and allies alike, but this was a disruptor presidency, and getting in a dig at a dashing—some would say self-righteous—French president played well with Trump's political base, and even with a few savvy members of the cyber community.

Supporters of the Paris call committed to working together "to increase prevention against and resilience to malicious online activity; protect the accessibility and integrity of the Internet; cooperate in order to prevent interference in electoral processes; work together to combat intellectual property violations via the Internet; prevent the proliferation of malicious online programmes and techniques; improve the security of digital products and services as well as everybody's 'cyber hygiene'; clamp down on online mercenary activities and offensive action by non-state actors; [and] work together to strengthen the relevant international standards."

It all sounded good and perhaps could lead to structures and engagements to actually get that kind of cyber work done. But a number of cybersecurity strategic thinkers downplayed the significance of the Paris call, regardless of business community backing.

James Lewis of the Center for Strategic and International Studies dismissed the whole Paris exercise.

"The Paris thing was a lot of hot air, so not signing it was a nice gesture," said Lewis. "My first question is why didn't they hold it at Versailles?"

Others had practical concerns about the call but wondered why it provoked such disdain from the US side.

"No idea what the reasoning here is, but the U.S. has been avoiding multilateral solutions in the past two years," commented Toomas Hendrik Ilves, the former president of Estonia currently at Stanford and a leader in efforts to rally democratic nations behind a common cyber strategy.

He said the Paris declaration moved somewhat in this direction, but he cautioned, "I fear there is too great a chasm between authoritarian and liberal democratic countries even on what should be under discussion for something like this to work. I would go for just liberal democracies that respect freedom of speech."

Along with the UK and Japan, for instance, the list of signatories included a variety of nondemocratic governments.

However, Ilves didn't discount the idea that the United States could eventually find a way to sign. "I am sure that with major U.S. companies already on board, there is always a way to join," he commented.

The US business community weighed in with support for the Paris call as a long list of tech companies, including Dell, Microsoft, Cisco, and Facebook, signed the "Cybersecurity Tech Accord." Manufacturers from various industries signed the "Charter of Trust."

US Chamber of Commerce executive vice president Neil Bradley said in a statement, "The Paris Call makes the compelling argument for global dialogue to enhance the trust, security, and stability of cyberspace. The Chamber supports the important goals of the campaign and is committed to working with all signatory governments and other stakeholders to combat malicious cyber activity that harms individuals, targets critical infrastructure, undermines democracy, and threatens peace among nations."

Bradley added, "The Chamber also prioritizes enhanced enforcement, effective deterrence policies, and increased cyber defenses through industry-led standards, best practices, and risk-based frameworks. Preserving an open, innovative, and secure online environment that fosters commerce can only be achieved through enhanced international cooperation between states, civil society, and the private sector."

The World Economic Forum issued a statement from Troels Oerting, head of the Centre for Cybersecurity: "We're facing a new wave of globalization that is driven by technological advances of unprecedented scale and speed. While we welcome the opportunities arising from this transformation, cyber criminals welcome them, too. I'm convinced that organizations that hope to fend off these new threats on their own will pay a high price. Only through global cooperation can we hope to win the day. That's why the Forum has chosen to support the Paris Call."

After a few days of silence on the matter—a haughty silence, perhaps, that the French could appreciate—a State Department spokesperson said the United States was supportive of the cybersecurity goals outlined in the Paris call, but it had problems with specific elements of the document and would continue to push ahead on international cyber norms of behavior through multiple avenues.

"Although the United States supports the objectives of the Paris call, we had reservations with certain elements of the text itself," the spokesperson told Inside Cybersecurity. "We understand that a number of governments and other stakeholders have endorsed the document. We welcome their engagement in the discussions on these issues at the Internet Governance Forum and in various other fora going forward."

One private sector source who was not impressed by the Paris call suggested the Trump team "didn't see a point in signing on to something that largely aggregated other things and seemed to be the product of Microsoft and the French without a lot of transparency in its drafting or ultimate purpose."

The handful of democratic governments that declined the invitation to sign, the source said, "did not want to see yet another 'process' and despite assurances it would not launch one, Macron . . . suggested a lot of future 'process,' [while also] hitting French favs like regulation, taxation and control. The statement itself is mostly milquetoast and I doubt it will have lasting effect."

The State Department spokesperson noted, "The United States strongly supports efforts to promote greater stability in cyberspace. Our recently released National Cyber Strategy affirms that the United States promotes 'a framework of responsible state behavior' built on international law and adherence to voluntary non-binding norms of state behavior that apply during peacetime, which is consistent with the Paris Call."

The spokesperson added, "We have also introduced a resolution at the United Nations General Assembly aimed at further advancing international dialogue among States on these critical international security issues in cyberspace."

This was a rare example of the United States, under Trump, taking a hard line but also taking care to wrap it in diplomatic niceties. The president and his team largely resisted any gratuitous shots at the French president over the cyber initiative. However, there was little progress in the ensuing months, prompting Microsoft CEO Brad Smith to issue a renewed call for commitment to the "Paris call" during the annual World Economic Forum in Davos, Switzerland.

But Trump and his economic team skipped Davos amid the government shutdown of that winter and likely were little impressed by Smith's desire to bring everyone together. The administration was looking to take a hard line with the less subtle fist of the military, as with the strike on the Russian Internet Research Agency.

Despite the Trump administration's official disdain for the Paris call, the Department of Homeland Security was finding the industry-led "charter of trust" to be helpful. DHS, in partnership with a "relatively small set of vendors," was setting up events organized around the "charter of trust" as part the campaign to secure industrial control systems. These were the systems that kept large industrial processes running, so it was a clear sign that the cyber pros on the ground were finding value in something that might be shunned at the political level.

It demonstrated once again that an engaged cybersecurity team could find practical value in all kinds of places while keeping its head down amid the political firefights.

10

Frenemies in Beijing

THE CONFLICT WITH THE RUSSIANS—as with the Soviets decades earlier—was portrayed as a zero-sum clash between two nation-states; one's success was perceived as a mortal threat to the other. For Americans, in *Star Trek* terms, it was always the Klingons versus the Federation, with the Russians as an embattled, aggressive, perennial foe to the US-led "Federation" of liberal democracies. In some ways, that might be a comforting political allusion.

A Trekkie might see a different rival in China: the Borg, an antagonist that would absorb and take over those liberal democracies' very own structures. If that was the political allusion of choice for the competitor or adversary in Beijing, it was not comforting.

From Wikipedia: "The Borg co-opt the technology and knowledge of other alien species to the Collective through the process of 'assimilation': forcibly transforming individual beings into 'drones' by injecting nanoprobes into their bodies and surgically augmenting them with cybernetic components. The Borg's ultimate goal is 'achieving perfection.'"

The bit about forcibly transforming people and injecting nanoprobes was a stretch, but the goal of a new perfection, defined in Beijing rather than Washington, wasn't so far off. And the entire US political establishment was intent on chasing this dragon. It extended to concerns—some might say paranoia—about Chinese-made subway cars for the DC Metro as US senators fretted about espionage systems rolling around under the city, embedded in the trains.

It wasn't quite "nanoprobes," but it showed a sensitivity to China's ambitions and capacities that was becoming acute, if not distorted by fear.

In the real world, the Chinese government's goal, which seemed to have plenty of popular support at home, was political and economic superiority within a new global order, with explicit target dates: 2025 for major advances in technology and other emerging fields under a "made in China" program; and 2049 for a vast realignment of the global ordering, coinciding with the one hundredth anniversary of the communist victory.

It was audacious and unsettling for the nation that currently occupied the number one spot in the global order. But it was also worth remembering, as the United States debated or managed to actually craft cybersecurity strategies toward Beijing, that China was far from the political-socioeconomic monolith often projected onto the screen for American policy debates. The Chinese government's hand reached deeply into the private sector, with a guiding national industrial policy that aided technology and other industries, and a military-intelligence complex that likely could, ahem, *encourage* collaboration with authorities in sensitive cyber areas.

But China also had 120 companies on *Fortune*'s 2018 "Global 500"—126 US companies were on the list, still number one—and these firms all had managers, shareholders, and boards of directors who were mostly interested in profit, just like their American counterparts.

And they, too, had hackers to contend with. Remember that tour through the "dark web of Asia"? Those hackers taking payment in Chinese currency reflected the crackdown on bitcoin in China, and also the fact that plenty of bad actors were operating within the country and targeting its growing wealth. Grady Summers of FireEye wrote in *Security Week*, "Chinese organizations have a huge target on their backs. As compared with the West, life in China is more dependent on online and mobile services, which increases the motivation of threat actors."

The ubiquity of these cyber problems might make cooperation between the United States and China a little more conceivable to audiences in both countries. Plus, President Trump and Chinese president Xi Jinping formed something of a mutual admiration club early in Trump's term, though CSIS's James Lewis commented the Chinese leadership in those first days was frequently "baffled" by the new president.

But within a year, the souring of the US relationship with China was front-page news. Repeatedly, the Trump administration and China clashed over trade issues, with US cyber complaints thrown into the mix. Trump signaled that tough US actions targeting specific Chinese companies and whole industries might go away if Beijing just agreed to lower barriers to US products and buy more American stuff.

There was no underlying principle to the approach; it was strictly transactional. And it made it very difficult to try to bring China into a process of global norms around cybersecurity.

Cheap Chinese steel exports, barriers to US farm products and manufactured goods, and opening up the Chinese tech sector were among the issues Trump White House and trade officials wanted to get at, the ones candidate Trump railed about during the 2016 campaign. At the same time, lawmakers with security beats in Congress were all over Chinese telecom products in particular and the cyber vulnerabilities they might carry. By early 2018, cyber concerns about China were increasingly zeroing in on consumer devices manufactured in that country—by companies from all over the world, including the United States—and then, more darkly, on the role of Chinese firms in building 5G networks in the United States and elsewhere.

Here was a cyber-related matter where Congress was going to move ahead on a bipartisan basis, and relatively quickly by congressional standards. The idea that China posed an existential threat to the United States in the 5G race swiftly became an article of faith, and a source of near-panic, in Congress. That was fine with the Trump team, as the security issues matched up neatly with the administration's trade negotiating objectives. Trump's negotiators could use lawmakers' concerns as a hammer in the trade bargaining with China, or disregard them, as the moment demanded.

But the policy lens narrowed rapidly on Capitol Hill—first to prohibiting the US government from purchasing any personal devices or telecom equipment from companies like Huawei, and then to keeping those companies out of the supply chain for the equipment needed in the 5G buildout.

Some observers were warning from the start that the approach was too narrow, too company focused, when this was really a battle over investment, innovation, and for hearts and minds internationally. The United States could keep cheap Chinese phones and routers out of its markets, but the mammoth Chinese companies were constructing the telecom infrastructure all over the globe. For one thing, the Chinese government was offering sweetheart deals throughout the developing world for countries to use Huawei products in their telecom systems. For another, US allies didn't immediately share the same deep security concerns. And—a big supply-chain problem—only a few non-Chinese firms were actually making the products needed to build 5G networks.

But there was a significant, legitimate concern shared across the political spectrum and policy community in the United States: If China built much of the world's next-generation information and communications technology structure, what was the likelihood that privacy and digital rights would become global norms?

At the Senate Intelligence Committee's 2018 annual hearing on global threats, Chinese-based telecom and IT companies were a frequent topic—quite a bit more so than during the previous year's threats hearing—and legislation was promptly introduced in 2018 that would ban two of those firms, Huawei and ZTE, from US government contracts.

The leaders of US intelligence agencies like the CIA and NSA, under questioning from Senator Tom Cotton (R-AR), agreed with the concerns about security risks associated with the products and said they would not recommend using them.

Across the Capitol, House Intelligence ranking member Adam Schiff said, "The equipment they produce is very much a risk to U.S. agencies. We can't rely on their integrity. Something like this bill ought to move."

The legislation targeting Huawei and ZTE attracted cosponsors throughout the year as lawmakers jumped on the campaign to highlight cyber dangers from China. Schiff was a cosponsor of the House bill while Cotton and Senator Marco Rubio (R-FL) offered the Senate version.

The Chinese companies strongly rejected the accusations against them. A US-based spokesman for Huawei said, "Privacy and security are critically important to all of us these days and we must all be cautious to protect our personal and family and professional data from compromise. In a world in which every information technology solution is the product of global supply chains, authorities should also be cautious not to brand one or another supplier as 'more vulnerable' than others—this is misleading at best, dangerous at worst."

ZTE also issued a statement: "ZTE is proud of the innovation and security of our products in the U.S. market. As a publicly traded company, we are committed to adhering to all applicable laws and regulations of the United States, work with carriers to pass strict testing protocols, and adhere to the highest business standards."

For context, it wasn't just Chinese companies being singled out: products from Russia-based Kaspersky Lab were banned under a Department of Homeland Security binding operational directive, a surprising and novel move by DHS at the time.

Some cybersecurity leaders questioned the efficacy of going after individual companies in this way.

"My view, then and now, is it doesn't make sense to make procurement decisions based on the headquarters location of the company whose name is on the box," said Bruce McConnell, formerly the top cyber official at the Department of Homeland Security and now global vice president at the East-West Institute. "All of these products are from the global supply chain—all come from the same place as Huawei."

But the winds on Capitol Hill were already blowing in a certain direction, and in January 2018 a powerful House Republican promised a new push to prohibit federal purchases of telecom products from Huawei and ZTE, while those firms—and some observers—questioned whether the legislative effort was based on competitive economic worries as much as cybersecurity concerns.

Representative Mike Conaway (R-TX) put his weight behind a bill banning the products, saying it was cybersecurity. Huawei said it was all economic politics. And some unaffiliated cybersecurity professionals said it was a combination of economic protectionism and legitimate cyber issues.

The Chinese companies did not have contracts with the federal government, but such a legal ban would deliver a reputational blow as they sought to broaden their reach into the US market. Industry sources said inexpensive phones and routers from Huawei and ZTE were increasingly popular with smaller US companies and individual consumers. More important for some American firms, if they decided to do business with the Chinese companies, their own US government contracts would be at risk.

Conaway and twelve cosponsors on January 9, 2018, introduced the bill targeting government purchases of Huawei and ZTE products. Conaway was a senior member of the Intelligence Committee and took over the panel's high-profile Russia investigation in the spring of 2017, after Chairman Devin Nunes stepped aside from the probe amid criticism of his tight ties with the Trump White House. Conaway also served on the Armed Services Committee's investigations panel and chaired the influential House Agriculture Committee.

"Chinese commercial technology is a vehicle for the Chinese government to spy on United States federal agencies, posing a severe national security threat," the Texan said in a statement. "Allowing Huawei, ZTE, and other related entities access to U.S. government communications would be inviting Chinese surveillance into all aspects of our lives. This legislation falls directly in line with President Trump's policy of putting American national security interests first, a policy I'm proud to support."

Retired representative Frank Wolf (R-VA), who for many years led efforts as a House Appropriations subcommittee chairman to scrutinize the cybersecurity of Chinese tech products, praised the legislation and called Conaway a "well-respected member of the Intelligence Committee."

"I think it's a good idea," Wolf told Inside Cybersecurity. "This is a big problem—the Chinese are spying on us and the technology can be embedded in their products."

It was widely reported in January 2018 that an unnamed group of lawmakers pressured AT&T not to partner with Huawei on its new Mate 10 Pro smartphone, citing cybersecurity issues. Conaway was not part of that group, according to his office.

The AT&T arrangement was set to mark "the first time that a major U.S. carrier will sell a Huawei phone for its main service," the *Silicon Valley Business Journal* reported in December. But AT&T in January dropped out of that partnership.

The Huawei phone "is still coming to the U.S., through open channels like Amazon, Microsoft Store, Best Buy, [and] Newegg," a company official based in the United States said, hopefully, before the full force of US hostility hit the fan later in the year.

The sudden, intense congressional interest in Huawei and ZTE raised the question: Was there new information in early 2018 on cybersecurity issues related to the products? No new information was offered publicly, and the legislation itself referred to a February 2015 FBI "intelligence note" as the most recent documentation of a potential security issue involving Huawei, along with a 2012 House Intelligence Committee report.

On ZTE, the legislation highlighted a 2017 guilty plea by the company "to conspiring to violate the International Emergency Economic Powers Act by illegally shipping U.S.-origin items to Iran."

Huawei dismissed the allegations cited in the legislation. The company official called the FBI intelligence note "a cartoonish rehash of the unsubstantiated 'vegetarian'" 2012 House Intelligence panel report. Representative Dutch Ruppersberger of Maryland, the one original Democratic cosponsor of Conaway's bill, was a ranking member of the Intelligence Committee in 2012.

Many cybersecurity practitioners on the industry side contacted by Inside Cybersecurity suggested there were no new security alarms related to the companies. The Department of Homeland Security did not respond to requests for comment, but it also hadn't made any moves like it did in 2017 with the binding operational directive to get Kaspersky products off federal systems.

"There have been no new 'red flags' [on Huawei and ZTE] but the assessment [of a potential risk] hasn't changed," one private sector cybersecurity source said, referring to concerns raised in 2011 and 2012 government reports suggesting links between the companies and the Chinese government.

"What has changed," the industry source said of Huawei and ZTE, "is now they are beginning to eat market share and getting a better reputation, and that makes it enticing to go after them."

The source said there "are legitimate concerns" about security, but also noted that other governments, including the United Kingdom, had come to "trust" the Huawei products.

In the United Kingdom, the security of Huawei products was assessed under a special arrangement between the British government and the company.

The Huawei Cyber Security Evaluation Centre certified the security of the products for British government use. The body "opened in November 2010 under a set of arrangements between Huawei and [the British government] to mitigate any perceived risks arising from the involvement of Huawei in parts of the UK's critical national infrastructure," according to its oversight board, which was chaired by the chief executive officer of the UK's National Cyber Security Centre.

Amid the gathering fury in Congress, the July 2018 report from the oversight board concluded that "in the year 2016–17, HCSEC fulfilled its obligations in respect of the provision of assurance that any risks to UK national security from Huawei's involvement in the UK's critical networks have been sufficiently mitigated. We are content to advise the National Security Adviser on this basis."

In 2019, China and the European Union's regulators came to an understanding on how the cybersecurity of 5G products would be assessed. Mobile phones were one thing, but equipment for next-generation 5G networks raised fundamental national security issues. "Huawei welcomes the objective and proportionate approach of the European Commission's recommendation on 5G security. Huawei understands the cybersecurity concerns that European regulators have. Based on mutual understanding, Huawei looks forward to contributing to the European framework on cybersecurity," the Chinese company said in a statement.

And in the summer of 2019—in the midst of the US international push to blacklist the Chinese products—the head of data security for the German government would part ways with his US counterparts by saying, "I think the risk is manageable."

The Huawei official based in the United States argued that the products were widely trusted across the globe.

"Indeed, the facts are that Huawei is trusted by governments and commercial carriers and consumers across over 170 markets, connecting over one-third of the world's population with network solutions, and over 150 million global consumers with consumer solutions, the latter last year alone," the official told Inside Cybersecurity in 2018.

"There is no there there," the official said, noting that many brands of smartphones were made in China. "Everyone's building in China. This is a political game, nothing more." The source emphasized that "Huawei is not owned, directed or subsidized" by the Chinese government.

But a spokeswoman for Conaway explained that the lawmaker "at the start of every year reviews national security threats" and was offering his bill as a "tangible solution" to an ongoing problem.

The industry security source quoted above said the government could have legitimate concerns about the company, but also noted the wide-ranging ramifications of publicly banning a company's products.

"It may be inappropriate to tell a private company that they can't use a cheaper alternative," the source said; a government ban could have such an effect on the private market.

However, in the end, a ban on government purchases of Huawei and ZTE products was the simplest, most visible step lawmakers could take to show they were fighting Chinese efforts to infiltrate the US telecom supply chain, and not incidentally, to knock off a key competitor to US companies. The effectiveness of the policy was TBD.

How would Congress actually do this? The vehicle would be the annual policy bill for the Defense Department crafted by the House and Senate Armed Services committees. The fiscal year 2019 National Defense Authorization Act banned federal procurement officers from purchasing telecommunications equipment made by Huawei and ZTE, and video surveillance and telecommunications equipment produced by Hytera Communications, Hangzhou Hikvision Digital Technology, and Dahua Technology. The procurement ban took effect in August 2019, while government contractors would be banned from using such products themselves effective in 2020. The Chinese companies filed legal challenges to the ban.

But the question was never fully answered: What kind of threat, if any, did Huawei and ZTE actually pose?

As the digital news service TechCrunch put it in January 2019:

> But there's a problem. Years of congressional hearings and "inconclusive" hardware inspections have presented a mixed picture on the threat that Huawei may, or may not pose. Despite the fact that the company's founder and president is a former officer in China's People's Liberation Army and the company remains heavily funded by the Chinese government, there's also no public, direct evidence that Huawei is using its equipment to spy on network traffic inside the U.S. or any other country. In any case, Huawei can't prove a negative, so all it can do is allow governments to assess its devices—which has so far found some issues but nothing conclusive to tie it to Chinese espionage actors. That's the crux of the argument: nobody thinks Huawei is spying now. To get caught would be too dangerous. But nobody knows that it won't spy in the future.

Beyond the Huawei saga, technology was a key part of the US-China trade war that erupted in 2018, and the administration's decision to link cybersecurity and trade objectives was a profound one. In the Huawei case, the confluence of security and global tech industry competition, once grasped by lawmakers, spurred quick action to enact bans and root Huawei and other equipment out of government systems and American supply chains. That was a policy approach initiated in Congress, not the Trump administration, but the White House happily went along because it served a purpose in the trade war realm.

However, it soon appeared that the administration—Borg style, perhaps—would subsume the security side of the China issue in its trade agenda. Next to immigration and building a wall, the trade fight with China was perhaps President Trump's top policy priority. But there were deep splits within both parties in Congress, and within the larger cyber policy community, on whether cybersecurity could be effectively addressed in trade negotiations.

Among Senate Democrats, Intelligence ranking member Warner didn't believe a trade deal could accomplish much of anything on these cybersecurity issues. "Don't confuse trade with security policy," he warned in a June 2019 speech at the Council on Foreign Relations. Using Huawei's access to US markets and the buildout of fifth-generation wireless networks "as a trade chip would be a disaster," Warner said.

Years of classified intelligence briefings had darkened his view of China's motivations and likely actions, he said, gradually shifting him into the China-hawk camp. Beijing wasn't moving fitfully but steadily into the global economic and political order; it was determined to steal from, undermine, and ultimately replace the existing US-led international structure.

Many security hands agreed: China wouldn't give up its well-oiled hacking machine no matter what was written into a trade deal; it needed to be confronted consistently and forcefully across cyberspace, much as the United States had pushed back against Soviet ambitions in the earlier Cold War.

Senate Democratic leader Schumer, however, firmly believed that the trade talks gave the United States its greatest point of leverage with Beijing to wring out concessions in the cyber realm. It wasn't ideal, but it was the best available option. That position was backed, to a degree, by policy experts ranging from cyber diplomat Chris Painter to China hawk James Lewis.

Painter believed China could be moved to change its behavior when it was shown to be in China's interest and the United States applied the appropriate pressure. The 2015 Obama-Xi antihacking agreement was an example. Lewis's view was more pessimistic: that China had set a course ultimately leading to confrontation with the United States, but that it could be budged in different directions along the way through punishment and rewards.

At the White House, National Security Adviser Bolton called punitive tariffs on Chinese products "a little shock therapy" that could alter China's behavior in cyberspace and elsewhere. Specific cybersecurity initiatives aimed primarily at China were beginning to unfold at DHS and other agencies. But as lawmakers and security officials hunkered down to address Chinese threats to the US supply chain for telecom products—the most serious threat vector in the US-China cyber contest—it became clear that the Trump White House viewed those efforts as little more than a bargaining chip in trade negotiations.

The White House zigged: While battling with China in a tit-for-tat exchange of tariffs on semiconductors and soybeans, the president in June 2018 shockingly decided to overturn legally imposed US sanctions on Chinese telecom ZTE. Trump believed this gesture earned him a chip in the game with China's Xi Jinping, costing him nothing.

And it zagged: In December 2018, the Trump administration took it up a notch and linked China to specific hacking activity aimed at US intellectual property. The Justice Department announced new indictments while the departments of Homeland Security and Energy sent out related warnings and details about ongoing "malicious" cyber activity emanating from China. The White House was expressing a new urgency about the Chinese cyber threat at the same time it was squeezing for a deal in the trade talks.

The Justice Department always argued that indictments were motivated by specific crimes, with absolutely no link to the trade game going on in a separate government domain. And DOJ always had plenty of technical evidence to back its legal actions against Chinese entities.

Deputy Attorney General Rosenstein said in December 2018, "Today, the Department of Justice is announcing a criminal indictment of two computer hackers associated with the Chinese government. The charges include conspiracy to commit computer intrusions against dozens of companies in the United States and around the world. As with all American criminal charges, individual defendants are presumed innocent unless proven guilty in a court of law."

Rosenstein said, "This case is significant because the defendants are accused of targeting and compromising Managed Service Providers, or MSPs. MSPs are firms that other companies trust to store, process, and protect commercial data, including intellectual property and other confidential business information. When hackers gain access to MSPs, they can steal sensitive business information that gives competitors an unfair advantage."

He added, "The indictment alleges that defendants worked for a group known to cyber security experts as APT-10. These groups are designated as APTs, or Advanced Persistent Threats, because they use malware to gain access to computer networks and exfiltrate data over an extended period of time."

Secretaries Nielsen and Pompeo put out a joint statement, saying, "The United States is concerned that this activity violates the 2015 U.S.-China cyber commitments made by President Xi Jinping to refrain from conducting or knowingly supporting 'cyber-enabled theft of intellectual property, including trade secrets or other confidential business information, with the intent of providing competitive advantages to companies or commercial sectors.' China has also made this commitment with G20 and APEC members as well as in other bilateral statements."

Here was a Trump administration action that drew bipartisan support in Congress, along with skepticism about the president's commitment.

Senator Warner weighed in: "The Department of Justice, and in particular Deputy Attorney General Rod Rosenstein, should be congratulated for their work on this announcement. DOJ's recent moves to hold China accountable are important in exposing some of the threats posed by China as it attempts to pursue economic and technological dominance over the United States."

Warner also offered a broader policy view, saying, "While legal action is important, a truly effective response will require a coordinated approach with our allies and a comprehensive strategy to protect our national security and enhance U.S. competitiveness and resiliency. We have to punch back against China's malign activities—but we also have to do more than play defense if we're going to truly check China's bad behavior."

In the very first days of the 116th Congress in January 2019, Warner and Senator Rubio introduced a bill that would establish an office within the White House itself to combat intellectual property theft by China and to secure the supply chain for critical technologies. House members introduced their version a couple of weeks later. The lawmakers were underlining their perception of the threat with a thick marker and trying to put responsibility for acting right in the heart of the White House. Such an office could provide much-needed coordination on China policy and—unspoken by the lawmakers—serve as a counterweight to any presidential impulses to abandon cyber concerns in the quest for a trade deal.

Lawmakers were hungry for action on China and wanted more.

Representative Langevin said, "Stealing commercial secrets to prop up companies is not the behavior of responsible states, and the United States and her allies must stand up to this reckless behavior. I commend the Deputy Attorney General for leading a whole-of-government response to Chinese cyber-enabled economic espionage. We are joined by our international partners, many of which have also been victimized by China's campaign of relentless state-sponsored theft. Collective international action, rather than going it alone, is the best way to make it clear to China that their actions are unacceptable."

Langevin said that Trump "should immediately take steps to sanction not just the parties directly involved in breaking into these managed service providers but the Chinese companies that benefited from this illicitly acquired intellectual property. Chinese business leaders need to understand that if they make a Faustian pact with their government, they will not be welcome in the international community."

Indictments could be seen as a solid policy move, nuanced and hitting on important cybersecurity considerations. But would the policy angles be pursued, or would the president undermine his national security team?

"We're doing very well with China," Trump told reporters on January 14, 2019. "They're having a hard time with their economy because of the tariffs. We're doing very well with our economy. We're at records, our unemployment numbers just hit a record, another record. We're doing extremely well with the country. We're doing better than any country right now anywhere in the world. China wants to negotiate."

It was about relationships, he said, not policy. "I have a great relationship with President Xi because it's good to have relationships with Russia, and China, and Japan, and India. And I have relationships with almost everybody and that's a good thing, not a bad thing. I think that we are going to be able to do a deal with China. . . . I can tell you, we are getting things that, before I became president, you would have had no chance at getting. They would have laughed at your president's face."

China, meanwhile, was all about policy—one aimed at eventually dominating the global digital economy.

"Cyber policy is tied up with trade policy and it's hard to see where one starts and the other ends," said retired admiral Simpson. "Cyber actions taken to impose costs for prior years' intellectual property theft seem to blow hot or cold depending on how the trade negotiations are doing. Efforts to address supply-chain weakness appear to focus on a few Chinese service providers without effectively addressing highly interdependent manufacturing and assembly concerns for Western companies."

Simpson said, "Instead of blunt force tools aimed at a few companies, it would be more effective over the long term to communicate national goals to restore domestic alternatives in the supply chain and set expectations for an informed supply-chain risk management program in our markets. The [National Cybersecurity Strategy] may be headed in that direction, but it's not clear at this point and they have been reluctant to engage regulators in this area to incent meaningful change."

At the same time, "Congress, similarly has been bore-sighted on two Chinese companies instead of pushing for greater attention in our domestic markets towards good overall supply chain risk choices."

And, he said, "China has become a more and more attractive commercial alternative in many overseas markets. Whether we like it or not, China is a commercial force to be reckoned with around the world, and our actions seem to myopically focus on the domestic market without due attention being paid to our continuing loss of global ICT market share."

Simpson said, "At the highest levels, President Trump's negotiation style has served to normalize national leaders that were formally pariahs among rest-of-world governments. This appears to have benefited China's expansion of broadband market share around the world, where the Belt-and-Road initiative includes expansion of broadband capabilities that are hard for developing countries to turn down."

And, he said, "The Trump administration does not seem to have a counter to China's growing international ICT strength, taking a market-based approach domestically that does not appear to be closing our own nation's digital divide at a satisfying rate and does not have affirmative policies oriented towards expanding U.S. telco presence in foreign markets as a national goal."

Simpson noted former Google CEO Eric Schmidt's observations "that in the next decade the world will very likely see two separate internets: China-centered and U.S.-centered. If we don't make security a priority in the commercial internet, we may wake up one day to an internet based in a capitalist China—albeit with all the social/human rights concerns—that has better, more predictable security. Will retail and banking gravitate to a more secure home? Can't imagine that today . . . but could we lose our dominant e-economy position in the future?"

Admiral Simpson agreed with an important point in the Trump 2018 National Cybersecurity Strategy, saying, "U.S. dominance is not guaranteed. I don't see how the NCS sufficiently moves the needle for a U.S.-centric, open internet with predictably secure user experiences while the Chinese continue to make steady advances in e-economy, innovation, security laws and rules supporting an aggressive international ICT leadership agenda."

To be sure, the Trump administration wasn't shy about calling out Chinese activities in cyberspace. Officials—and the president—believed it helped in the trade fight, as Simpson noted, and the Chinese provided the US side with plenty of fodder for complaints. And not incidentally, it moved the narrative away from Russian influence campaigns and hacking.

Just after the Department of Justice announced the hacking-related indictment against Russian military officers in the fall of 2018, Vice President Pence in a speech claimed an even graver challenge from China across a range of military, trade, and human rights issues—backed by that country's aggression in cyberspace.

The claim wasn't off base, but this line of debate was being offered by White House officials and GOP allies on Capitol Hill as if it were an either/or proposition. In fact, the Chinese could be aggressively using cyber tools to steal US intellectual property and taking steps to match or surpass America as a cyber military power, while the Russians waged a sophisticated campaign that supported many of Trump's domestic political goals, stoked divisions within the United States, and damaged this country's standing internationally. The two propositions weren't mutually exclusive in any way.

Cybersecurity was not the prime focus of Pence's speech at the Hudson Institute—itself a target of Chinese hacking, the vice president noted—but he accurately identified cyberspace as one of the key domains in an intensifying struggle between the United States and China.

And he specifically called on Google to end development of the "Dragonfly" app—an unconfirmed project to create a search engine for Chinese users—which he said China would use to strengthen censorship and surveillance, and for those in media and academia to stand up to China in various ways.

Pence, in theatrically mournful tones, said that despite Trump's best efforts to develop "a strong personal relationship" with Chinese president Xi, "the American people deserve to know" that China "is using a whole-of-government approach to advance its interest in the United States," including interference in US elections and "wholesale theft of U.S. technology."

Instead of cooperation, Pence said, "China has chosen economic aggression, which has emboldened its military." The United States under Trump, Pence said, was countering this and other global challenges through a major military build-up that included growing capabilities in the cyber realm designed to enhance deterrence.

Pence's speech came weeks after Trump signed an executive order on election security that the White House described as addressing foreign interference operations beyond Russia, to include China, North Korea, and Iran. Trump at the United Nations in June 2018 argued that Chinese interference in the US midterm elections was in response to his stance on trade, while the White House's cybersecurity strategy linked global economic competitiveness with defending against cyberattacks, an assertion linked to China, not Russia.

Pence asserted that Chinese influence and other campaigns significantly outstripped Russian operations that included cyber components, which he said were all designed to "undermine support for President Trump."

He pointed to newspaper ads and attempts to "leverage relationships" with the US business community in opposition to Trump-imposed tariffs on China, saying Beijing was "using wedge issues like trade to cause divisions."

While Pence charged an unprecedented campaign of "interfering in the domestic policy and politics of the United States," the actions he cited appeared to be markedly different from the issues cited in the indictments aimed at Russia. DOJ linked Russian conspirators directly to the Putin government and charged them with using distributed denial-of-service attacks, spearphishing, malware, and spoof domains, among other clear indicators of cyberattacks.

Ads in Iowa newspapers promoting the benefits of trade with China were certainly strategically placed. But they were also clearly public advocacy as opposed to hacking Democratic National Committee emails or Facebook traffic generated by dummy entities and spreading slanderous disinformation about a Democratic presidential candidate. The ads were about a specific trade policy, not about trying to sow political chaos. There was simply nothing comparable between the two cases, despite what Trump's team and allies were saying.

It was all part of preparing the ground for what Trump envisioned as a climactic confrontation with China over trade. His administration would put bright lights around anything that bolstered the case that China was a chronic abuser of the global free-trade system and was stealing America's technological know-how in order to best the United States in world markets with high-quality but cheaper goods, as well as gain military and cybersecurity advantages.

With the avid support of his trade representative, Robert Lighthizer, Trump was determined to stare China down on global trade, even to the extent of allowing some of his key constituents, like the farmers of Iowa and other states, to suffer short-term pain from losing access to Chinese markets as the trade war raged. Trump assured these rural voters, who had propelled him toward the Republican nomination in 2016, that the pain was temporary and would yield tremendous benefits in the not-so-distant future.

The Office of the United States Trade Representative (USTR) used China's cyber activities as a bazooka in the trade war.

Since 2015, an agreement between then-president Obama and Xi had set the terms of the two countries' cybersecurity engagement: traditional espionage would be countered and combated, but it was an expected activity by intelligence agencies and tolerated in a sense, while there would be no cyber snooping by the Chinese government, or related entities, to steal US trade secrets for the benefit of Chinese companies.

The 2015 agreement for several years largely worked as intended to reduce China's state-sponsored cyber espionage for commercial gain, according to a leading expert on cyber and foreign policy in July 2018, who warned the deal could crumble under the weight of the escalating trade war between the two countries.

"Most people think it's holding," James Lewis of the Center for Strategic and International Studies (CSIS) told Inside Cybersecurity. "You'll know the agreement is broken when the PLA [People's Liberation Army] goes back to stealing commercial information."

US trade officials that spring charged China with violating the agreement in a report that laid the foundation for some of the tariffs Trump was imposing on that country's products. But US industry leaders were much less willing to say the agreement had been a failure, although they also cited ongoing issues with China's behavior in cyberspace.

"There is a working consensus in U.S. circles that China's observable theft of American firms' IP by cyber means has decreased but not gone away," said an industry source who closely followed cyber and China-related issues. "Chinese leaders are certainly not conscious-stricken about past—and likely ongoing—misdeeds. [But] if there is a connection between the misappropriation of trade secrets and the imposition of trade tariffs, it's implicit, not explicit."

Lewis, at the time recently returned from Beijing, said Chinese officials told him that senior US officials had expressed an interest in resuming a bilateral dialogue on cybersecurity issues in the fall of 2018. He characterized this as an effort to improve cybersecurity ties between the two nations outside of the strained trade relationship. Lewis was a former Foreign Service officer and a key architect of highly regarded recommendations crafted for the past two US presidents.

Those talks wouldn't end up coming off.

Cybersecurity and probably every other policy area were affected by the wide-ranging tariffs being imposed on Chinese products by the Trump administration, and China's retaliation on US products, which triggered a global crisis over trade policy.

US trade officials, as part of their case against China in advance of imposing tariffs, explicitly pointed to violations of the 2015 agreement but publicly offered only one specific example, and that involved a Chinese technology company, Boyusec, which "cybersecurity firms have linked to the Chinese government."

"I'd point to the DOJ's indictment . . . of Boyusec as an example of continuing intrusions for the theft of IP that is connected to China," a senior administration official said, while declining to comment on whether the 2015 agreement was holding.

The Office of the US Trade Representative in a so-called Section 301 report in the spring of 2018 detailed a wide-ranging case against China on its technology policies, including twenty-five pages devoted to "Unauthorized Intrusions into U.S. Commercial Computer Networks and Cyber-Enabled Theft of Intellectual Property and Sensitive Commercial Information."

"For over a decade, the Chinese government has conducted and supported cyber intrusions into U.S. commercial networks targeting confidential business information held by U.S. firms," the USTR report stated. "Through these cyber intrusions, China's government has gained unauthorized access to a wide range of commercially-valuable business information, including trade secrets, technical data, negotiating positions, and sensitive and proprietary internal communications. These acts, policies, or practices by the Chinese government are unreasonable or discriminatory and burden or restrict U.S. commerce."

However, the Boyusec indictment was the only specific case since 2015 that involved the type of commercial spying that Obama and Xi had agreed was out of bounds.

Still, the report stated,

> Notwithstanding an apparent decline in the observed number of cyber incidents, the continued use of cyber intrusions by the Chinese government targeting U.S. companies remains a serious problem. State-sponsored cyber intrusions originating from China into U.S. commercial networks occur alongside China's institutional framework for promoting its industrial and technological development through a state-led model in which state-owned enterprises and national champions are the recipients of extensive state support. In sum, the evidence indicates that China continues its policy and practice, spanning more than a decade, of conducting and supporting cyber-enabled theft and intrusions into the commercial networks of U.S. companies.

The report did offer numerous examples of cyber-snooping observed by US private sector cybersecurity firms, but many of these cases may have fallen "in bounds" under the Obama-Xi agreement, observers said.

"It's really confusing but the consensus view is that the agreement doesn't ban espionage, it bans espionage for commercial purposes," CSIS's Lewis said. "It doesn't mean the Chinese stopped spying, but it does mean they put more resources toward traditional espionage."

Lewis said the 2015 agreement helped Xi's internal efforts to professionalize the Chinese military. "Xi wanted the PLA to be a real professional military, and it isn't," Lewis said. "He said, 'do your day job, don't do corruption on the side.' . . . This agreement helped."

But, he noted, "they can move resources from military to commercial targets" if they decide to abandon the deal.

The USTR report said, "The United States has been closely monitoring China's cyber activities [since 2015] and the evidence indicates that China continues its policy and practice, spanning more than a decade, of using cyber intrusions to target U.S. firms to access their sensitive commercial information and trade secrets."

It stated, "[T]his report has drawn upon information in the public domain from both private parties and U.S. law enforcement. However, publicly available information necessarily represents only a fraction of all relevant activity."

The State Department in the summer of 2018 was "monitoring" China's commitment to a 2015 agreement that it wouldn't use cyber espionage for the commercial gain of its domestic industries, and might "pursue opportunities for continued dialogue" on the matter, according to a statement provided to Inside Cybersecurity by a department official.

The United States—publicly, at least—had not used any tools related to the 2015 agreement itself to signal that it believed China had violated the accord.

"It's fair to say that [the agreement] had an effect on their behavior," said Christopher Painter in an interview about the 301 report and the State Department's comments. "It created a measurable expectation of behavior" that China subsequently accepted in agreements with the G-20 and other countries, including Japan and Australia, Painter pointed out.

"If the Chinese government is sponsoring [prohibited] activities, the U.S. has tools, including formally notifying them of violations and using sanctions," Painter said. "China committed to no espionage to benefit the commercial sector and that created accountability—and the U.S. didn't give up anything to get that, our options are still on the table."

Painter added, "The State Department is saying, 'we're looking closely, we have all these tools.' . . . If they violated the agreement, I support taking action. But it's not clear [from the 301 report] that they have violated the agreement."

The State Department, in its statement to Inside Cybersecurity, did not cite any specific violations of the 2015 agreement but said, "For the past several years, we have consistently raised our concerns to China regarding cyber-enabled intellectual property theft. Our persistent engagement led to an unprecedented set of cyber commitments announced during President Xi Jinping's September 2015 state visit. Those commitments included an agreement that neither country's government would conduct or knowingly support cyber-enabled theft of intellectual property for commercial advantage. . . . The United States is closely monitoring China's adherence to these commitments."

State noted the USTR report, saying, "The Section 301 investigation concluded that China conducts and supports unauthorized intrusions into, and theft from, the computer networks of U.S. companies to access their sensitive commercial information and trade secrets."

The State Department did not comment on the specific allegations but said, "We consistently and candidly raise our concerns regarding cybersecurity with the Chinese at every level. We remain committed to holding China accountable through a variety of mechanisms, and will pursue opportunities for continued dialogue when appropriate."

An industry source added, "There is a working consensus in U.S. circles that China's *observable* theft of American firms' IP by cyber means has decreased but not gone away."

Painter suggested China would not resume state-sponsored cyber espionage for commercial gain even if the current conflict with the U.S. over trade issues intensifies. "If relations with the United States become so bad, China has a number of options. But the agreement [still] makes sense for them for a number of reasons, including that similar language was agreed to with other countries as well."

Painter said real progress had been made, both for the United States and for its allies, adding, "It took two years of pressure to bring them to the table in 2015."

Noting language in the 301 report citing the 2017 indictment of Boyusec, Painter said, "If [the Trump administration] can conclude that it was state action, not players 'associated' with the government, that's a real concern."

By the fall of 2018, State, USTR, and other arms of the federal government managed to get on the same page as far as China using cyber as a tool to advance its commercial goals. A USTR update on its section 301 case argued forcefully that China's illicit cyber activities were accelerating, in violation of the 2015 agreement and international law.

> China shows no sign of ceasing its policy and practice of conducting and supporting cyberenabled theft and intrusions into the commercial networks of U.S. companies. This illicit conduct provides the Chinese government with unauthorized access to intellectual property, trade secrets, confidential business information, technical data, negotiating positions, and sensitive and proprietary internal business communications.
>
> The White House National Cyber Strategy, published in September 2018, concluded that "China engaged in cyber-enabled economic espionage and trillions of dollars of intellectual property theft." The White House Office of Trade and Manufacturing Policy also noted China's prevalent use of cyber-enabled theft (as well as physical theft) in acquiring technologies and intellectual property in strategic sectors. As the next section demonstrates, China's cyberenabled theft against the United States has increased in frequency and sophistication since the March 2018 issuance of USTR's findings.

There was plenty of smoke around Chinese activities in cyberspace and even its explicit policies. There was bipartisan support in Congress for pushing back, hard. Even the tech sector, anxious about the punishments it might receive through its operations in China, was on board for a tougher stance.

But as with so much during the Trump age, industry sources and policymakers worried that the president's negotiating style could be completely misunderstood by the Chinese, with unknown results. One Chinese company might be banned, another could be blessed. Or, perhaps worse, Trump could drop cybersecurity complaints against China and abandon deterrence and other cyber policies toward the country in exchange for a deal, on paper, that met his campaign promises on issues like steel imports.

The Trump administration, at first, blatantly neglected security in the race to get 5G telecom networks up and running before foreign competitors such as China and South Korea could seize the competitive heights. Then, as the China trade talks hit a critical phase in the spring of 2019, 5G security suddenly became a top priority for the administration. The president himself suggested that his top priority could change, given the state of the trade talks.

The libertarian CATO Institute, which championed the Trump administration's economic policies in some areas, basically called out the China policy as trade protectionism cloaked in cybersecurity. The United States in the past had argued that Beijing used cybersecurity as a smokescreen for everything from political censorship to trade restrictions. Now, it seemed, Trump was leading the United States down a similar path in which cybersecurity was a new excuse for trade barriers.

CATO author Daniel Ikenson said the US security concerns around Chinese tech products were based more on "innuendo" than fact and suggested, "No other government is as affronted by China's push to achieve technological preeminence as is the U.S. government because the U.S. economy is the incumbent in that space."

"Meanwhile," Ikenson wrote, "following a decade of evolving indigenous innovation policies intended to catapult China into a position of global technological preeminence, the Chinese government has begun implementing a set of new laws that effectively require imported ICT products and components to be secure and controllable. U.S. companies are interpreting that to mean that there will be delays and other uncertainties that adversely affect their supply chains and that they will be forced to provide Chinese authorities with proprietary information about their products, which could compromise their intellectual property and deter trade, investment, and the scope for collaboration in these industries."

He wrote, "All countries have legitimate concerns over privacy and national security, but China is the principal country addressing these concerns by requiring foreign companies to transfer their technology and to surrender their brand and operating control in order to do business."

Ikenson said actions taken by both sides in the name of cybersecurity were "among the most serious sources of trade policy tension" between the two countries. "But those measures also have the effect of impeding foreign trade and investment to the point that economic protectionism—and not cybersecurity—seems to be the primary objectives of both governments," he wrote.

Despite denials, the timing of the administration's "hardline" actions on China had unmistakable similarities. As the two countries prepared for an important new round of bargaining on trade at the beginning of 2019,

Justice Department officials—with DHS Secretary Nielsen standing beside them before the TV cameras—announced still more indictments, this time charging Huawei officials with theft of US intellectual property, among other crimes. The trade war was being fought in the criminal courts as well as the traditional trade venues.

"Today we are announcing that we are bringing criminal charges against telecommunications giant Huawei and its associates for nearly two dozen alleged crimes," acting attorney general Matthew Whitaker said on January 28, 2019. "As I told Chinese officials in August, China must hold its citizens and Chinese companies accountable for complying with the law."

The top Democrat in the Senate, Charles Schumer of New York, followed up the next day by raising the same nagging concern: This kind of enforcement action had strong bipartisan support on Capitol Hill, he said, but would the president give it up in his quest to sign a historic trade deal? Schumer said, "I give the administration credit for having this suit go forward, but my message to President Trump now—don't back down."

He said the Trump team actually "has shown signs of being tougher on China" than the Obama administration ever was, but that Trump let ZTE "off the hook" in hopes of reaching a trade deal with President Xi. "Do not make the same mistake you made with ZTE by interfering with the Justice Department's prosecution of Huawei," Schumer warned. "The United States should not make any concessions unless and until China makes enforceable commitments to end all forms of theft and extortion of American intellectual property, which is exactly what Huawei is accused of."

A week later, just before Trump arrived on Capitol Hill to deliver his 2019 State of the Union address, Schumer took to the Senate floor to again note the China contradictions:

> In the last State of the Union, the president said, quote, "We will protect American workers and American intellectual property through strong enforcement of our trade rules." That's something I strongly agree with. But six months after the president said that, he decided to let a Chinese telecom giant, ZTE, a company that violated multiple trade sanctions and put our nation's security at risk off the hook and begin operating in the U.S. Now while some in the administration are pushing him to be tough on China, there are some who just want to sell out for a decrease in the trade deficit. That will not do the job.

Cybersecurity professionals would say the United States should never make any concessions, period, when it comes to cyber-enabled thievery—that cyber norms of behavior were not transactional but needed to be constant. In the age of Trump, it was now clear on Capitol Hill and throughout the policy establishment that cyber was a chip on the table in a different game, this one about global trade balances and, more important, the balance sheet for President Trump's political account.

That same week in January 2019, DNI Coats delivered his annual worldwide threat assessment to the Senate Intelligence Committee—drawing Trump's ire for seeming to offer information on Iran and North Korea that ran counter to the president's own assessments. The discordant notes would put Coats's job in jeopardy with a peeved president, according to news accounts at the time. But on China, Coats was in tune with Trump's hard line of that moment.

> China presents a persistent cyber espionage threat and a growing attack threat to our core military and critical infrastructure systems. China remains the most active strategic competitor responsible for cyber espionage against the US Government, corporations, and allies. It is improving its cyber attack capabilities and altering information online, shaping Chinese views and potentially the views of US citizens.
>
> [W]hile we were sleeping in the last decade and a half, China had a remarkable rise in capabilities that are stunning. A lot of that was achieved, a significant amount of that was achieved, by stealing information from our companies by inserting Chinese into certain labs or bringing back stolen technological properties.
>
> [W]e are concerned about the potential for Chinese intelligence and security services to use Chinese information technology firms as routine and systemic espionage platforms against the United States and its allies. [China] has the ability to launch cyber attacks that cause localized, temporary disruptive effects on critical infrastructure—such as disruption of a natural gas pipeline for days to weeks—in the United States.

A few weeks later, on February 19, 2019, Chinese trade officials were in Washington for pivotal talks in the negotiations over trade. If these officials picked up the *New York Times*, they saw this headline: "Chinese and Iranian Hackers Renew Their Attacks on U.S. Companies."

"The Iranian attacks coincide with a renewed Chinese offensive geared toward stealing trade and military secrets from American military contractors and technology companies, according to nine intelligence officials, private security researchers and lawyers familiar with the attacks who discussed them on the condition of anonymity because of confidentiality agreements," the *Times* reported.

The article went on to say, "Chinese cyberespionage cooled four years ago after President Barack Obama and President Xi Jinping of China reached a landmark deal to stop hacks meant to steal trade secrets."

The *Times* noted, "But the 2015 agreement appears to have been unofficially canceled amid the continuing trade tension between the United States and China, the intelligence officials and private security researchers said.

Chinese hacks have returned to earlier levels, although they are now stealthier and more sophisticated."

US officials and well-informed insiders repeatedly told Inside Cybersecurity that it wasn't canceled, per se, but noted that China's motivation for playing within US-set cyber rules of engagement was greatly diminished by the tariffs Trump was imposing as part of his trade fight with Beijing. Even if cybersecurity didn't top the agenda for the February talks, the state of play in cyberspace would be enormously affected by the outcome of the talks.

"Federal agencies and private companies are back to where they were five years ago: battling increasingly sophisticated, government-affiliated hackers from China and Iran—in addition to fighting constant efforts out of Russia—who hope to steal trade and military secrets and sow mayhem," the *Times* concluded. "And it appears the hackers substantially improved their skills during the lull."

Tom Corcoran, a former senior congressional intelligence staffer, said at an event in March 2019 that China "was running wild" prior to the 2015 agreement, essentially "smashing and grabbing" when it came to stealing US intellectual property. It wasn't entirely clear what brought China to the table in 2015, he said, but agreeing to clamp down on the hacking also fit in with Xi's anticorruption efforts aimed at the Peoples Liberation Army.

"It's picked up again, though not at the same smash-and-grab level," Corcoran said. "What's changed?"

Cue the Trump tariffs.

As a round of talks began on February 21, 2019, the cybersecurity policy community was looking for signs of a deal that covered intellectual property theft and reined in cyber-enabled economic espionage.

US Trade Representative Lighthizer led the US delegation in the face-to-face talks at the Old Executive Office Building next to the White House. The Chinese delegation was led by Vice Premier Liu He, who also held the title of special envoy of President Xi, which "implies that he may have stronger bargaining power," according to a pool report.

Trump set a March 1 deadline for talks with China to produce adequate trade concessions, or else he would begin imposing a second round of tariffs on $200 billion worth of that country's products. The United States imposed tariffs on $250 billion worth of Chinese goods in 2018.

But Trump told reporters on February 20 that March 1 was "not a magical date," suggesting some flexibility in the negotiating process.

On February 22, flanked by his trade team in the Oval Office and with China's Liu seated across from him, Trump announced that two days of talks in Washington were being extended through the weekend, telling reporters that a deal was now more likely than not.

"Ultimately, I think the biggest decisions and some even smaller decisions will be made by President Xi and myself," Trump said, according to a pool report. "And we expect to have a meeting some point in the not too distant future and I can only say talks are going along well, but we're going to have to see what happens. I think there'll be some points that this group won't agree on because maybe they're not supposed to agree on or allowed to agree on. And I think President Xi and I will work out the final points. Perhaps and perhaps not."

It was looking like a March confab at the Trump property at Mar-a-Lago.

In the meantime, negotiators were working on six "memorandum of understanding" (MOU) drafts, including one specifically on cybersecurity.

Senior US Chamber of Commerce official Myron Brilliant said progress was being made in the talks but that "gaps remain" on issues including cybersecurity.

"The MOUs being discussed make sense to us," Brilliant told reporters prior to Trump's Oval Office appearance, noting that negotiators "are getting closer to putting text down," but "I'm not sure the MOUs cover all that we're concerned about" or how they would be enforced.

Brilliant said that, on his recent visit to Beijing, Chinese officials suggested some of these issues could be resolved through "more dialogue," but he said, "We're not looking for it to be done through more dialogue. . . . We want it to be concrete in the text of the agreement."

Brilliant said, "One of the reasons we're more cautiously optimistic is the talks have gotten more in the weeds—the fact that they're putting things in MOUs is positive. . . . But there are gaps," he said, stressing that the agreement must be comprehensive and sustainable; "it can't be a short-term fix."

Chinese officials began with "a very narrow view" of the negotiations and seemed to believe they could "avoid" issues, including cybersecurity, subsidies, and industrial policy, "that greatly impede the ability of our companies to compete in areas protected by the Chinese government," Brilliant said.

He suggested an evolution in thinking on the Chinese side—as well as an ongoing debate within the Chinese government on whether to address these issues in the context of this negotiation.

US business officials recently had talks with "officials very close" to Xi, Brilliant said, and "there are still gaps in their understanding of how important it is to address those issues" and "how in the absence of structural reform, we won't have a comprehensive deal."

Brilliant said a comprehensive agreement must be sustainable, as well as enforceable, and have support from the business community, Congress, and the public—markers that could apply to cyber aspects including forced technology transfers and data theft.

On February 22, that Friday of positive notes about China, the Agriculture secretary, Sonny Purdue, put out a tweet: "In Oval Office meeting today, the Chinese committed to buy an additional 10 million metric tons of U.S. soybeans. Hats off to @POTUS for bringing China to the table. Strategy is working. Show of good faith by the Chinese. Also indications of more good news to come."

That was certainly a good sign for farmers. But the question hovered in the air: Would Trump give up cybersecurity demands—essential concessions from China, the cyber community believed—in exchange for a better soybean market in China?

Representative Bill Pascrell (D-NJ), a member of the Ways and Means Committee that oversees trade policy, quickly zeroed in on this issue. "I am encouraged by signs of progress, but remain concerned that the President will accept a quick offer of procurement of U.S. goods rather than fundamental reforms to China's systemic problems," Pascrell said in a February 22 statement. "USTR was right to investigate forced technology transfer and intellectual property theft in its Section 301 investigation. . . . We cannot accept meager offers of cheap transactions over long-lasting and needed reforms."

Trump and his top trade official claimed progress on those cyber-related technology issues as the talks extended over the weekend.

"The answer's yes, it's one of the structural issues. It has to be done properly and we've made a lot of progress in it, so whoever told you we weren't just didn't know what they were talking about," Lighthizer told reporters in the Oval Office.

According to the February 22 White House pool report, Trump also commented on whether a trade deal would address issues related to Chinese telecoms Huawei and ZTE. Products from those firms were being removed from US government systems, and the United States in January had filed those criminal charges against Huawei.

"Well, ZTE paid a big fine of $1.2 billion, which nobody's ever even heard of before. And we want everybody to compete and I guess it will be somewhat of a subject that we're talking about here. We'll be talking about it. We may or may not include that in this deal, Huawei and ZTE," Trump said.

On whether recent criminal charges against Huawei might be dropped, Trump said, "We're going to be discussing all of that during the course of the next couple of weeks and we'll be talking to the U.S. attorneys. We'll be talking to the attorney general, but we'll be making that decision. Right now, it's not something that we're discussing."

Overall, Trump told reporters, "I would say it's more likely that a deal will happen. . . . The fact that they're willing to stay for a quite a bit longer period, doubling up the time, that means something."

Chinese vice premier Liu He through a translator said, "From China, we believe that it is very likely that it will happen and we hope that . . . we'll have a deal. . . . The Chinese side is ready to make our ultimate effort," the translator concluded.

"We're going to have a signing ceremony," Trump said at a breakfast the next morning with the nation's governors. He was visibly thrilled with the weekend's work and seemed ready to sign. But what that deal would be wasn't clear quite yet.

Trump left the National Governors Association meeting to fly off for Hanoi, Vietnam, where he would hold his second meeting with North Korea's Kim Jong-un. That summit didn't produce the hoped-for breakthrough on shutting down the North Korean nuclear arms program—snagging over the issue of lifting US sanctions—but at his February 28 press conference in Hanoi, Trump offered high praise for Chinese president Xi's assistance with North Korea.

"I think China has been a big help," Trump told reporters at the JW Marriott hotel in Hanoi. "Bigger than most people know. On the border, as you know, 93 percent of the goods coming into North Korea come through China. So there's a great power there. At the same time, I believe—I happen to believe that North Korea is calling its own shots. They're not taking orders from anybody. He's a very strong guy. And they're able to do things that are pretty amazing. But 93 percent still come in from China. China has an influence, and China has been a big help." Trump added unbidden, "And Russia has been a big help too. As you know, there's a pretty small part of the border, but nevertheless significant—about 28 miles. And things can happen there too. And they've been a help."

What would come next in either the China trade or North Korean negotiations was still an open question at the end of February 2019, but security firm McAfee added an interesting angle with the release of a new report showing North Korea's ongoing aggressions in cyberspace.

McAfee on March 3, 2019, released "evidence tying the North Korean nation-state actor, the Lazarus Group, to the cyber espionage campaign discovered targeting defense, government, energy and critical infrastructure organizations across the world in December 2018—and still ongoing."

According to the security firm, "McAfee's Advanced Threat Research team has rare access to a command-and-control server used to execute 'Operation Sharpshooter' after being seized following the campaign's discovery. On top of identifying the infamous group as the threat actor behind the sophisticated and highly targeted campaign, the researchers used this unique cyber investigation access to unlock deeper insights into the group's tactics, techniques and procedures than ever before."

McAfee found "a new and much longer campaign timeline than originally thought—from a few months to year-long; Interesting shifts in industry and geo-targeting during the campaign's lifecycle—the suspected nation-state campaign pivoted to new targets recently, focusing on finance, government, and critical infrastructure industries globally, largely in Germany, Turkey, UK and US; [and] Evidence also points to the actor testing malware implants in a small and unsuspecting region of Africa prior to broader global attacks, leveraging infrastructure based in Namibia."

It wasn't the activity of a government seeking to find its place in the community of nations or to follow global norms of cyber behavior. North Korea was still a renegade in the cyber sphere, regardless of Trump's relationships with Xi and Kim.

In March 2019, the US-China trade talks were in overtime, with additional tariffs on hold as negotiators tried to finalize a comprehensive deal. Senior Trump administration cyber officials like DHS's Krebs and FBI director Christopher Wray were in San Francisco for the RSA conference, the largest annual cybersecurity confab in the world.

Wray told the audience that the cyber threat from China was broad, deep, and not getting enough attention, while stressing that growing US efforts to counter it had nothing to do with the ongoing trade dispute. Wray cited an "uptick" in hacking from China and said "the depth, breadth and scale of the Chinese espionage operation shocked me when I came back into government" in 2017.

Asked whether the US government's cyber policy toward China was linked to Trump's trade battle with Beijing, Wray said, "Not at all. This is not about trade, diplomacy or politics. It's about rule of law. We will follow the facts and I don't care what any foreign government says about it."

Wray said the indictments against Chinese government-linked hackers were only "one factor in a multi-dimensional effort," but he noted that hackers "prize anonymity," and calling them out reduced their ability to function. "And," Wray said, "it's a myth that they'll never see the inside of a U.S. courtroom." Hackers do travel, he said, and when they venture outside their safe havens, "we'll pick them up."

Wray said there was no individual or entity the FBI was "afraid to go after if they break the rule of law."

Wray's China comments tracked with remarks made at RSA by DHS's Krebs, who said China was at the heart of a major cyber threat to 5G wireless networks. On a panel alongside NSA cyber adviser Joyce, the former White House cyber coordinator, Krebs said China had "given us their playbook" with the "Made in China 2025" strategy. Telecom was central to China's economic ambitions, making it critical that the United States build out a secure

5G system, Joyce said. He noted that 5G would bring about economic change on a vast scale, comparing it to the introduction of smartphones and the developments that followed.

"It's really hard to lock down something of that size and magnitude," Joyce said. "That depends on trust." Krebs said ongoing DHS–Commerce Department–led initiatives brought the right members of the ecosystem to the table for these supply-chain efforts. "We're getting the people we need into the discussions," Krebs told Inside Cybersecurity.

Joyce, in comparing the China threat with the one posed by Russia, said Beijing was carefully pursuing a long-term strategy. "Russia is a hurricane, China is climate change."

Joyce said, "China is projecting its power to build itself up. We are figuring out ways to alter that dynamic."

Amid all of this, there was actually an operational level of cybersecurity between the United States and China that had been functioning throughout the ups and downs of the relationship since 2015.

Jeanette Manfra, now assistant director for cyber at the Cybersecurity and Infrastructure Security Agency, commented at RSA that "technical" info-sharing and conversations continued with Chinese counterparts, despite the tensions over trade—and Chinese hacking—that had ratcheted up over the previous two years.

Manfra said there were "shared interests" with China in cyberspace and pointed to efforts to build "back channels" as part of the 2015 Obama-Xi cyber agreement. The idea was to have "baseline relationships" and share information, she said, "and that still continues."

"We have a channel for technical exchanges" with Chinese cyber officials, she told Inside Cybersecurity.

As those bilateral trade negotiations appeared headed toward a denouement of some kind in March 2019, business groups, lawmakers, and various interests were taking last shots at influencing the conclusion.

The US Chamber of Commerce flagged a report showing that the so-called Section 301 tariffs, which Trump was brandishing as a weapon against intellectual property theft and other cyber-related Chinese policies, were having a heavily negative impact on the US tech and telecom sectors. "The report further finds that Section 301 tariffs, should they remain in place, would reduce U.S. GDP by up to $1 trillion within 10 years," according to the Chamber.

On Capitol Hill, Senator James Risch (R-ID), the new chairman of the Foreign Relations Committee, held a hearing on a "new approach for an era of U.S.-China competition."

A *Wall Street Journal* story on Chinese hacks aimed at the US Navy and a story about Huawei devices hooked up near US missile silos by rural telecom companies were submitted for the record.

Risch himself said, "The best example of this type of behavior comes from my home state of Idaho. Micron Technology, one of the largest producers of semiconductors in the world has had their intellectual property stolen by a Chinese company, patented in China, and then used to sue Micron in Chinese Courts directed by the Chinese Government. To its credit, the Trump administration imposed sanctions for this action, and brought criminal charges against those responsible."

"We need to be less diplomatic . . . China is attacking" in cyberspace, warned Senator Ed Markey (D-MA). Risch stood on the right side of the ideological pendulum in the Senate, and Markey was about at the same point on the left side. The China threat was forging bipartisanship, at least superficially.

James Talent, a former Republican senator from Missouri and now on the US-China Economic and Security Review Commission, observed that this was a historic point of inflection that would shape the future in much the same way that US and allied actions from 1945 to 1955 had shaped the Cold War with the Soviet Union for another thirty-five years. Congress and administrations of both parties "built the bipartisan foundations" for an ultimately successful decades-long struggle, he said.

"There are reasons the Chinese Communist Party is doing what it's doing," Talent said, and China wouldn't change unless given a "compelling reason" to do so. He said the Obama administration's military and diplomatic "pivot to Asia" was "all about China" and that the Trump administration and Congress were appropriately following a similar path. In fact, it was Obama and his pivot that "signaled the era of wishful thinking was over," said the former Republican senator.

But Talent warned that threats were imminent. He said the Chinese threat to the US supply chain for IT and communications "is going to get worse as 5G is rolled out," and he warned that "China is in major competition to control 5G. If they do that, we're not going to be able to trust anything."

He said China is "operationally aware of the capabilities of our systems . . . because they've reconnoitered it."

Whether this problem could be tackled in the trade talks was at least a trillion-dollar question.

Trump's former economic adviser Gary Cohn, who left the administration in disagreement with its tariff policy—and following the president's equivocal comments on a pro-Nazi rally that turned deadly in Charlottesville, Virginia—turned up in a March 13 radio interview with a scathing critique of the China negotiations. He suggested the White House was in "chaos" and that it was so "desperate" for a high-profile agreement that it would sell out to China on issues like intellectual property theft. A few lines on paper would dispense with the hacking issue, he suggested.

The former Republican White House aide's words weren't too far apart from Senate Minority Leader Schumer's warning in a floor speech the same week to stay tough in the negotiations.

"Do not get played," Schumer said March 11. "If you don't achieve what you set out to achieve—namely the permanent reform of China's most abusive trade practices—then walk away."

On March 14, Schumer took the floor again to say, "If President Trump caves to China for the sake of soybean purchases, he'd be trading America's future literally for a hill of beans."

People believing their own eyes and ears was a running problem during the Trump presidential term—he couldn't really mean that, could he?—and as the China talks seemed ready to wind down, the likely outcome was becoming more and more clear, for those who cared to acknowledge it: the president wanted to announce a historic deal, and little details like cybersecurity were likely to fall to the side.

Meanwhile, the talks seemed close, but the White House let it be known that they wouldn't wrap up in March, signaling that an April Mar-a-Lago signing summit might be more realistic.

The Chinese National People's Congress on March 15 took a step that seemed to meet one key US demand, prohibiting so-called forced technology transfers in which tech companies operating in China had to share with the government confidential details of their products. The Chinese government said it was about security, but there was no doubt the policy was really about extracting trade secrets from US and other tech manufacturers and passing them to Chinese companies. Outlawing such actions was a big step—symbolically, at least—by the Chinese government.

Back in Washington, as many were celebrating St. Patrick's Day on Sunday, March 17, the National Security Council's media affairs staffer sent a note to reporters saying there would be a rare tele-briefing Monday morning on 5G security issues. The session wasn't expected to "make news," the staffer said, but "we have received lots of questions on 5G security in recent weeks."

The 5G issue was tightly linked with the trade talks that were increasingly in the news.

Separately, DHS Secretary Nielsen was over at George Washington University that Monday morning giving a speech on the "state of the homeland." She, too, took a shot at 5G challenges, describing the threat from China as "cannibalistic," with China "using companies as a forward-deployed force to actually eat away at our security from the inside, from the supply chain."

"Because we do have a weak link in cyber, what we hope to do is identify these vulnerabilities, take them out whenever we can within DHS authority, and ensure that the average person or the average American really understands what they're up against, which is a nation state," Nielsen said.

Two "senior administration officials" were on the phone call with reporters on March 18, and they stressed that the overall approach to 5G security was "country and company agnostic."

Officials must be "mindful of past behavior," they cautioned, and whether companies and countries have a track record of following through on security promises or have histories of "bad behavior."

The United States was engaged in extensive discussions with allies on this point, the official said. Asked about the British government's evaluation center for the security of products made by Chinese telecom Huawei, the official said discussions continued with the United Kingdom.

The UK center certified the security of Huawei products, but the US official said its work "is purely technical," while the Trump administration had a "broader mandate" to develop a "level of trust" and security across the 5G ecosystem.

"The U.S. is going to ensure our networks are secure and reliable," a second administration official said, adding that "many of our allies" were engaged in similar processes. The official said, "We're trying to make sure we have good policy in place" that would allow the nation to build out 5G "in a holistic way."

The briefing was arranged for no particular reason, according to the White House, except for a lot of recent media interest in 5G. It seemed clear that the administration's approach to 5G security was about to come into the spotlight, thanks to the trade talks, and security officials wanted to be as proactive as their trade office counterparts in framing both expectations and outcomes.

At around the same time, the *Times of London* would later report, US intelligence officials, in talks with close allies, were making "the most serious claim" so far linking Huawei to Chinese intelligence arms.

"A Chinese telecoms giant that wants to supply vital technology for Britain's new 5G mobile network has received funding from branches of Beijing's state security apparatus, the CIA has told spy chiefs," according to the *Times of London.*

"American intelligence shown to Britain says that Huawei has taken money from the People's Liberation Army, China's National Security Commission and a third branch of the Chinese state intelligence network, according to a UK source," the London paper reported on April 22. "The US shared the claims with Britain and its other partners in the Five Eyes intelligence alliance—Australia, New Zealand and Canada—earlier this year, with the UK entering the final stages of a wider review into its next generation mobile network rollout."

On March 19, DHS's Krebs said China's threat to the security of 5G was "at the very top of that list" of his cybersecurity concerns, Inside Cybersecurity's Maggie Miller reported.

On March 26, Acting Defense Secretary Patrick Shanahan said China was stealing US technology at a "staggering" rate and raised concerns about possible Chinese dominance of 5G. "The rate at which China is systematically stealing U.S. and allied technology for its own military gain is staggering," Shanahan testified before the House Armed Services Committee. "Reversing this dangerous trend—one which could impact our troops on the battlefield—means acknowledging reality: Every Chinese company is at risk of being either a witting or unwitting accomplice in China's state-sponsored theft of other nations' military and civilian technology."

In April, the administration would ban China Mobile from providing telecom services in the United States. There was no specific smoking gun related to the firm; FCC Chairman Pai said the potential cyber risk was just too great.

Across the administration, top officials were drawing red circles around Chinese threats in cyberspace while the endgame seemed to be at hand in the trade talks. The White House announced Trade Representative Lighthizer and Treasury Secretary Mnuchin were heading to Beijing the week of March 25 to meet with Chinese vice premier Liu He, who would come to Washington the following week. How the words and actions of security officials squared with developments at the trade negotiating table was unclear.

As the trade officials parlayed in Beijing, the board set up to advise the British government on the cyber integrity of Huawei products identified significant concerns with vulnerabilities in the firm's software development process in its latest report released March 28, 2019.

"Overall, the Oversight Board can only provide limited assurance that all risks to UK national security from Huawei's involvement in the UK's critical networks can be sufficiently mitigated long-term," according to the report by the Huawei Cyber Security Evaluation Oversight Board to the UK's National Security Adviser.

Ellen Nakashima wrote in the *Washington Post*, "Most ominously, the spy agency, which oversees a center that vets Huawei hardware and software for bugs and security vulnerabilities, said it can provide 'only limited assurance' that the long-term national security risks can be managed in the Huawei equipment deployed in Britain, and that 'it will be difficult' to manage the risk of future products until the current defects are fixed."

The day after that story appeared, Huawei reported a 25 percent increase in its earnings in 2018, one sign that global consumers, at least, were more impressed by the company's low-cost offerings than they were by US and UK security concerns.

"Yet there are signs that US efforts to stop other nations from using Huawei equipment in their telecommunications networks may be having an effect. The company said sales of telecom equipment to carriers fell 1.3% in 2018," CNN reported. "At a press conference . . . rotating chairman Guo Ping said the decline was mainly due to investment cycles in the global telecom industry."

On April 4, Trump met again with Vice Premier Liu in the Oval Office and told reporters, "We've had tremendous discussions. We're getting very close to making a deal. That doesn't mean a deal is made, because it's not, but we're certainly getting a lot closer. And I would think with, oh, within the next four weeks or maybe less, maybe more—whatever it takes—something very monumental could be announced."

According to Trump, "we are rounding the turn." And on the other side of the turn, he said, was a deal that would get at hacking as well as soybeans.

"But it's a massive deal. It could be one of the—I guess it is, if you think about it, the biggest deal ever made. There can't be a deal like this—no matter where you look, there can't be a deal like this. This is—this is the granddaddy of them all. And we'll see if it happens. It's got a very, very good chance of happening. I think that it will be great for both countries."

Talks continued on intellectual property protections and theft, he said, adding, "whether it's our farmers or our technology people, all of them will be really happy. And I think China is going to be very happy, too."

"We have made great progress," Vice Premier Liu said. "I do think that because we got direct guidance by two great Presidents—President Xi and President Trump."

Trump added the next day, "The China meeting was a big success. I think we're going to have a . . . Look, we have a very good relationship. We're going to say . . . I don't want to predict the deal or not a deal, but we're very well along. We really negotiated probably the two hardest points very successfully for our country. And China understands. You know China has taken advantage of our country for 30 years. And we can't do that anymore, not with me."

He was tossing in the perfunctory cautionary notes, but Trump was also setting very high expectations for a major agreement in the coming weeks.

The skepticism was deep, especially among those in the business community who most wanted to see something done to alter China's cyber policies. Ann Beauchesne of Ridge Global expressed little confidence that a deal would curb Chinese theft of intellectual property or sway its behavior in cyberspace—despite the Trump administration's public declarations that these issues were high on the agenda in the negotiations.

China "will keep doing what they're doing and get better at hiding it," she said. "Actions speak louder than words and they continue to steal IP and other things, and this won't stop it."

The two countries were now eyeing a May conclusion to the negotiations between the deputies, with Trump and Xi wrapping it all up at a June summit. They were thinking the White House might be the proper stage.

If the Rose Garden were to be the backdrop for a signing ceremony with Trump and Xi, that suggested an agreement of historical scale addressing deep issues between the countries, including intellectual property and behavior in cyberspace.

On May 1, the *Financial Times* reported a story that should have been a bombshell but instead landed like a feather: The Trump administration was dropping its demands on intellectual property theft in the trade talks.

The administration, according to the *Financial Times*, was "likely to accept a watered-down commitment from Beijing as an alternative." The paper quoted a source who had been "briefed on the negotiations" as saying, "A lot of issues are being jettisoned from the negotiations because President Trump wants a deal."

If it were a trial balloon, former State Department cyber coordinator Painter told Inside Cybersecurity, it would be an "unfortunate one" and a poor negotiating tactic.

"It's an interesting turn because the only way to solve this IP problem is through a larger agreement," Painter said. "Maybe there's a phased approach here and the trade deal would be part of a longer process, but to take it off the table, you lose leverage. And it means you haven't addressed one of the larger things you set out to accomplish."

Painter said there could be thinking that the trade agreement—and lifting of some or all related tariffs on Chinese products—would moderate China's behavior in cyberspace, but he added, "I fear that the president feels he has to make a deal and this is all optics."

Painter said, "If you're not addressing the huge long-term issues like this—which go to the heart of our economic future—why do this deal?"

The former State Department cyber leader noted that China always denied the allegations that it hacked for commercial gain, but that consistent pressure brought the Chinese to the negotiating table in 2015 and led to an agreement between Xi and President Obama that such activities were out of bounds.

"The Chinese came to the table because Obama consistently made it a high-level issue," Painter said. "If you signal this isn't a core issue, the Chinese will keep doing it."

The next day, the Chamber's Brilliant expressed resignation over the Trump administration dropping demands on Chinese state-sponsored intellectual property theft from the trade talks, with US officials signaling they considered such hacking as a separate "national security issue."

Hacking of commercial IP for the benefit of Chinese companies "is a very important issue to be addressed in the U.S.-China relationship," Brilliant said May 2 on a conference call with reporters. "But it's also an issue that touches on national security and it may have to be addressed separately."

"I'm not saying that's a good thing but we're being pragmatic," said Jeremie Waterman, president of the Chamber's China Center. "It's not a surprise that they are stepping back in the context of these negotiations."

"We're certainly in the endgame," Brilliant commented. He said, "94.5 percent of the deal is done, but the last piece is still complicated."

He noted that, even with a deal, this "won't be the end of all negotiations with China."

The US Chamber officials also said the issue of potentially banning Chinese telecoms Huawei, ZTE, and others from the buildout of 5G wireless networks was now separate from the ongoing negotiations.

Painter told Inside Cybersecurity on May 1 that 5G "continues to be a big issue, but it's probably on a separate track" from the trade talks. "If they sweep in Huawei and ZTE into the trade deal and don't address IP theft, it's even worse," Painter said.

He added, "If you're using Huawei and ZTE as a bargaining chip, you're basically saying there's no way to mitigate that threat to the system. That's a poor message to the Chinese and to our allies."

Painter called it "telling" that Trump "hasn't signed the E.O. [on banning Huawei from US networks] that's been sitting on his desk for months. Is this a security risk you can mitigate or not?" he asked. "The experts say 5G makes it much harder if not impossible to mitigate."

With IP theft apparently off the table in the negotiations, Painter said, "the question is what does this deal become? They open markets to certain goods and we drop the tariffs? If so, it's going to be very difficult to make progress in other areas" like cyber-enabled IP theft.

James Lewis of CSIS observed, "It's interesting to me that the Chinese don't want to talk government-to-government about cybersecurity (sure, there are lots of Tracks, but those are largely for show because they are not connected to policymaking). So the real issue is how do we bring them to the table. The trade talks could have been leveraged, but the Chinese are really good at dodging serious discussion and I don't think that has changed."

"It is practical to focus on facilitating trade," one industry source commented. "But the U.S. is seemingly losing its leverage to address IP theft—the top cyber irritant between China and the U.S. 'If not now, when?' one could reasonably ask."

But maybe it was all moot anyway.

Trump on May 5 took to Twitter to say he would impose 25 percent tariffs on $325 billion worth of Chinese goods that had not yet been subject to US tariffs and would raise 10 percent tariffs on $200 billion worth of goods to 25 percent within a week, *Inside U.S. Trade* reported.

"The Trade Deal with China continues, but too slowly, as they attempt to renegotiate. No!" Trump tweeted.

In Beijing on May 7, a Foreign Ministry spokesperson was asked about the cyber relationship between the nations and the status of the 2015 agreement.

"How the US views this agreement, you should ask the US," the spokesperson said. "As for China's position, I have already said that we are willing to work together with the US and other relevant parties to jointly address cybersecurity challenges and jointly safeguard cyberspace security through dialogue and cooperation."

A reporter also asked about a new *New York Times* report that China had stolen and was using National Security Agency "cyberattack tools."

"I haven't seen the report you said," the spokesperson said. "Regarding the issue of cyberattacks, there are various voices from time to time, but the relevant parties have never produced tangible evidence when making accusations."

The spokesperson said, "Cybersecurity is a global challenge that requires the cooperation of the international community. China and the United States have a good foundation for cooperation in the field of cybersecurity. We hope that the US can continue to cooperate with China in this field. It is not constructive to always blame and give others a 'deduction of hats' without evidence."

The talks did continue in Washington, with Vice Premier Liu back in the Oval Office on May 9. But the tariffs came down on Chinese products, as promised, on May 10. And as was becoming a habit, the United States announced a new indictment aimed at Chinese hacking, just as the talks were getting started.

The US government on May 9 charged one named Chinese national and a hacking group with criminal counts related to the cyber intrusion at health insurer Anthem, and emphasized in a release the company's quick action to notify authorities of the incident and subsequent collaboration with the government.

The four-count indictment said the hackers illegally gained access to and installed malware on the networks of Anthem and three other companies. Further, "on multiple occasions in January 2015, the defendants accessed the computer network of Anthem, accessed Anthem's enterprise data warehouse, and transferred encrypted archive files containing PII from Anthem's enterprise data warehouse from the United States to China."

"The allegations in the indictment unsealed today outline the activities of a brazen China-based computer hacking group that committed one of the worst data breaches in history," Assistant Attorney General Benczkowski said in a statement. "These defendants allegedly attacked U.S. businesses operating in four distinct industry sectors, and violated the privacy of over 78 million people by stealing their PII. The Department of Justice and our law enforcement partners are committed to protecting PII, and will aggressively prosecute perpetrators of hacking schemes like this, wherever they occur."

After the latest tariffs, the trade talks froze before revving right up again with hints of a massive deal just inches away. It would go on this way through 2019.

But on the cyber front, there was never much reason to expect this to play out differently from the 2015 agreement. If there was a deal, it might lessen pressure on China—politically, legally, and perhaps militarily—from the United States for the foreseeable future, just as the Obama-Xi agreement had done. China was willing to sign a deal, and just like the British Crown and Sir Francis Drake, President Xi would have deniability if and when the Chinese used cyber tools to steal what they needed to steal to rapidly push their economy forward. Was there ever a chance that a Trump-driven trade agreement would end what an internal navy document, obtained by the *Wall Street Journal* and published in March 2019, called a "cyber siege" of the most sensitive navy systems by Chinese hackers? Probably not—no more than the Obama-Xi deal ended such hacking.

Senate Homeland Security chairman Ron Johnson sought to temper expectations well before the negotiations concluded, saying that regardless of the publicly expressed hopes, the trade agreement probably wouldn't be the mechanism for curbing Chinese cyber-enabled theft.

"I differentiate the things that can be enforced through law versus outright cyber theft and espionage," he said. "I'm not expecting their theft to be part of the trade deal. We have to address that through law enforcement and public exposure."

Asked whether the current efforts to indict and publicly shame Chinese elements were sufficient, Johnson paused and considered. "I always want it to be more, and to be more effective. But it's not easy to do."

The bottom line: The Trump administration wasn't changing the arc of history with its approach to China; at best, it was gaining yet another pause. Of course, that might've been the only feasible goal, but it wasn't what Trump had promised.

Using the trade talks as the venue for achieving cybersecurity goals was a gamble, and by the summer of 2019, it clearly hadn't paid off. The threat from China would have to be addressed through supply-chain, global engagement, and other processes that were, in fact, under way. But cybersecurity policymakers would still have to hold their breath that these efforts weren't eventually undermined at the trade table.

Increasingly, next-generation 5G was the issue most concerning policymakers, as Krebs had noted at RSA.

Krebs was seeing three specific threats from the Chinese products: vulnerabilities "on the box," meaning security flaws in the software design; software updates performed remotely from China that could be subject to government interference; and the "management of shipments," meaning the possibility of actual physical tampering with the products during shipping from China.

All of that was coming to a head on 5G.

On Capitol Hill on May 14, 2019, Judiciary Chairman Lindsey Graham (R-SC) and ranking member Dianne Feinstein acknowledged a lack of familiarity with 5G issues along with an acute concern about China's ability to infiltrate the telecom system.

Feinstein had been briefed, though, and she noted China's $400 billion investment in 5G and that it had installed ten times as many 5G stations across China than the United States had installed at home. If China helped build 5G in the United States, she said, it would gain an unacceptable espionage edge and the ability to extract data of all kinds from US networks.

"Should we move ahead with 5G?" Feinstein asked, a question that stunned telecom executives. "I begin to question the whole 5G thing because of the risk."

Graham asked, "How could anyone follow a risk-based strategy and buy from China? There is no way in hell that China can meet the [security] criteria because of the way they govern."

Krebs and State's Rob Strayer told senators that there were US-based suppliers for switching and routing equipment, but not for "Radio Access Network" equipment, three critical elements in the 5G buildout.

Krebs explained, "The concern regarding the growing presence of Chinese telecom equipment is particularly acute in the Radio Access Network portion of the network where there are a limited number of RAN equipment suppliers. There are four main purveyors of 5G RAN technology globally, none of which are considered United States–based, and the largest of which is Chinese-based. If Chinese manufacturers, who receive significant state support, continue to gain market share, there will be growing concern about the long-term viability of the existing supply chain for 5G and successor technologies."

James Lewis of CSIS testified at the same Senate hearing that China was aggressively trying to tip the scales in international standards-setting bodies in order to ensure its companies' products passed muster, while also noting the hesitancy of US allies to ban Huawei and others from their networks.

Lewis questioned the much-touted British government program for assessing the integrity of Huawei products and said, "A complete ban is the only way to eliminate this risk, but a ban appears so far to be politically unacceptable for the UK. The recent UK announcement that it would allow Huawei to supply the 'edge' but not the 'core' of 5G networks is an effort to mitigate the risk of using Huawei without imposing a complete ban."

Lewis said, "One explanation for the recent UK announcement that it would allow Huawei into its 5G infrastructure, under certain limitations, is that senior levels of the British government, alarmed by the possibility of major economic damage from Brexit, hoped to allay this risk by pursuing both expanded trade with China and a free trade agreement with the U.S." It wasn't just US policymakers who allowed economic issues to "trump" cybersecurity.

But Krebs assured the lawmakers that under the current US strategy, "by 2025 the United States will have the broadest adoption in the world" of 5G, though he acknowledged that Huawei "comes in cheaper" than rival companies with 5G products and that it would be important to ensure small and mid-sized US telecoms had adequate support to make their 5G purchases from other providers.

Internationally, Krebs said it was simply "not the reality" that entities in other countries would refrain from buying inexpensive Chinese telecom products.

Strayer pointed to a global campaign to persuade allies to follow the US lead on 5G and Chinese companies.

"As countries around the world upgrade their communications systems to 5G technology, we are urging them to adopt a risk-based security framework," Strayer said. "To this end, the Department is executing a global campaign on 5G security that includes strategic bilateral and multilateral engagements to convince our allies and partners of the seriousness of the need to adequately secure these networks."

Strayer added, "An important element of this risk-based security approach is a careful evaluation of hardware and software equipment vendors and the supply chain. The evaluation criteria should include the extent to which vendors are subject to control by a foreign government with no meaningful checks and balances on its power to compel cooperation of these vendors with its intelligence and security agencies."

Strayer said, "Two weeks ago, the Czech Republic hosted more than 140 representatives of 32 countries from around the world, as well as the European Union and NATO, to build consensus on a common approach to 5G security. This effort produced the Prague Proposals—a set of recommendations on how to build secure and resilient 5G networks based on free and fair competition, transparency, and the rule of law. Moving forward, the Prague Proposals will help guide our engagements with our partners and allies to build secure 5G networks."

He concluded, "We will continue our bilateral and multilateral engagements to ensure that telecommunications, the Internet, and all the critical services that 5G will enable are secure and reliable."

As noted, though, allies such as Germany had an entirely different view on how to approach China and the 5G challenge. There were processes under way, as mentioned, but much had been gambled on the trade talks.

And yet Krebs and Strayer also knew what was coming.

Late in the afternoon of May 15, the White House issued President Trump's executive order on supply-chain security, which in reality was all about Chinese companies and, most important, securing 5G—or at least that was the frame.

The order directed the Commerce Department to write rules prohibiting US companies and consumers from purchasing or importing information and communications technology and services "designed, developed, manufactured, or supplied, by persons owned by, controlled by, or subject to the jurisdiction or direction of a foreign adversary" that posed an "undue risk" to economic and national security.

Commerce, in the first tangible step, added Huawei to what was known as the "Entity List," explaining, "The sale or transfer of American technology to a company or person on the Entity List requires a license issued by BIS, and a license may be denied if the sale or transfer would harm U.S. national security or foreign policy interests."

"This is one of the promises that [Trump] made during the campaign and he has most certainly kept it today," a "senior administration official" said on a press call. "What the E.O. addresses is the fact that our information and communications infrastructure is literally foundational to the American way of life and that our prosperity and our security depend on how we balance economic benefit with security risks."

The official said, "Today, the President determined that the unrestricted acquisition or use in the United States of information and communications technology or services that are subject to the jurisdiction or direction of foreign adversaries augments the ability of those foreign adversaries to create and exploit vulnerabilities in information and communications technology or services, and that that can have potentially catastrophic effects and thereby constitutes an unusual and extraordinary risk to our national security, foreign policy, and economy."

The upshot: "The President is incredibly committed to preventing our adversaries from turning our own information and communications infrastructure into a liability as opposed to an asset," the official said.

Republican senator Ben Sasse said in a statement, "Let's cut to the chase: China's main export is espionage, and the distinction between the Chinese Communist Party and Chinese 'private-sector' businesses like Huawei is imaginary. The Trump Administration is right to recognize this reality and issue this order. Huawei's supply chain depends on contracts with American companies and the Commerce Department ought to take a careful look at how we can effectively disrupt our adversary."

Senate Intelligence ranking member Warner said of the executive order, "This is a needed step, and reflects the reality that Huawei and ZTE represent a threat to the security of U.S. and allied communications networks. Under current Chinese security laws, these and other companies based in China are required to provide assistance to the Chinese state. This executive order places a great deal of authority in the Department of Commerce, which must ensure that it is implemented in a fair and responsible fashion as to not harm or stifle legitimate business activities."

But Warner cautioned, "It should also be noted that we have yet to see a compelling strategy from this Administration on 5G, including how the Administration intends to work cooperatively with our allies and like-minded nations to ensure that international standards set for 5G reflect Western values and standards for security and privacy. Nor do we have a stated plan for replacing this equipment from existing commercial networks—a potentially multi-billion dollar effort that, if done ineptly, could have a major impact on broadband access in rural areas. A coherent coordinated and global approach is critically needed as nations and telecom providers move to implement 5G."

Industry leaders on May 15 offered public statements of support, recognizing the national security stakes involved but also hinting at their anxiety over the economic implications and logistical realities.

By contrast, a former US security official was sharply critical, saying, "It's a short-sighted blunt instrument that will come back to bite U.S. companies in global markets without creating any meaningful increase in our cybersecurity. Networks and supply chains will remain global and full of vulnerabilities, notwithstanding a feel-good ban on a few companies' products."

Another source said of initial expressions of support for the executive order from major business groups, "That would be *U.S.* industry groups, I expect. Why wouldn't they support it, it limits competition! How about the ones with significant markets in China?"

The technology industry—which epitomized the globalization under way in the digital economy—carefully raised its concerns with the executive order but pointedly didn't offer cheers.

According to the Information Technology Industry Council, "The Executive Order as written is extremely broad and would sweep all ICT equipment and services into its scope, and as such we are still analyzing the potential unintended impacts of the order on the tech industry, consumers, and innovation. We urge the administration, including the Department of Commerce, to run an open and transparent process and to work with industry as it moves forward with implementing this Executive Order to ensure that it furthers the important national security imperatives underlying the action while minimizing potential unintended impacts."

"I don't think it's surprising that national security concerns about Huawei equipment have brought us to this point," said David Turetsky, the former security chief at the FCC. "I think it's a little bit unfortunate that it happens in the midst of trade war because the national security issues have transcended any trade war solutions."

Turetsky explained, "The national security issues around incorporating Huawei equipment into U.S. 5G and other networks are real and should not be considered just another trade issue that can be resolved as part of whatever agreement between the U.S. and China ends the trade war. The trade war and the national security threats shouldn't be conflated and confused."

Chinese Foreign Ministry spokesman Lu Hao said shortly after the order was released, "No one will regard it as a constructive and friendly gesture."

Lu said, "China resolutely opposes any country's unilateral sanctions against Chinese entities under its own domestic laws. It also opposes the generalization of the concept of national security and the abuse of export control measures. We urge the U.S. to stop wrong practices and create conditions for normal business and cooperation between the two countries to avoid further impact on Sino-US economic and trade relations. China will take necessary measures to resolutely safeguard the legitimate rights and interests of Chinese enterprises."

It was all boiling down to one conclusion: The trade talks had reached the critical moment, and the Chinese hesitated. Or, say the Chinese, the United States hesitated. In any case, the Trump team had prepared the ground by first indicting another batch of Chinese nationals on hacking charges and then by implementing a next round of tariffs, even with China's top negotiator in Washington. When the talks clearly stalled, the administration fired a symbolic nuke, banning Chinese telecom products from the United States. The action was aimed mainly at Huawei—and it was figuratively the equivalent of a nuclear strike because that telecom was the symbol and pride of China's technological ascent.

The Chinese leadership had been puzzled by Trump early in his presidency. Two and a half years in, they were obviously completely flummoxed by his negotiating style. But there was little sign that cybersecurity was getting better as a result.

There were puzzled looks on the home front too.

"I'm concerned that the Trump action comes out of weakness and does not address the underlying strategic problem of declining U.S. technology leadership in global markets," observed retired admiral Simpson. "It does very little to address our actual risk exposure for U.S. companies and government personnel with roles in the larger international economy, and may do harm in the long run."

It was all clear as mud. Policies were flying about, but underlying strategic principles were absent.

Meeting with reporters in the Oval Office on May 23, 2019, Trump said, "But Huawei is something that's very dangerous. You look at what they've done from a security standpoint, from a military standpoint. It's very dangerous. So it's possible that Huawei even would be included in some kind of a trade deal. If we made a deal, I could imagine Huawei being possibly included in some form of or some part of a trade deal."

But how would such a thing look, he was asked.

"It would look very good for us."

But how would it work?

"Oh, it's too early to say. But, I mean, we're just very concerned about Huawei, from a security standpoint right now."

Cyber was just a card in a long game on trade. There had been no collaboration with industry in preparation for the executive order, and it had never been framed for public discussion. Work on actually implementing the order inched ahead within the federal bureaucracy, as if officials were unconvinced it would actually be implemented at all. The work was complicated and maybe it just took time, and, in any case, conscientious security-minded officials weren't deliberately slow-walking the effort.

But the real action was happening in the stop-and-go trade negotiations. The US officials hammering out the cybersecurity policy on China were well aware that the trade talks could easily upend their work. And in Beijing, why should Chinese officials believe the United States was committed to putting in place a durable cybersecurity policy? They could read and interpret Trump's comments too.

Because beneath the security trappings, it was about pressuring China at the trade negotiating table, not about striving to create a sustainable global structure for cybersecurity.

In October 2019, the FCC announced the rules to ban rural telecoms from using federal funds to buy Huawei and ZTE equipment. But the broader ICT supply-chain rule continued to meander through the bureaucratic process, undermining the sense of emergency that accompanied the May 15 executive order.

"It's difficult to imagine a more poorly executed process," one industry source said. "The lack of transparency and engagement with stakeholders is stunning."

Meanwhile at Huawei, a putative target of the executive order, chairman Liang Hua, announced a 23 percent increase in global sales for the first half of 2019, right in the middle of US efforts to persuade the world to drop the Chinese telecom. "American pressure 'has galvanized our people and reinvigorated the company,' Liang said," according to the Associated Press on July 30, 2019.

Something wasn't working in the Trump-mandated approach being pursued by US diplomats and trade and security officials.

11

The Investigation and Cyber

WELL, THIS DIDN'T LAST:

In the late winter of 2017, a little over a month into the Trump administration, an agreement between the Republican and Democratic House Intelligence Committee leaders appeared to put the panel on solid bipartisan footing for probing Russian hacking and other activities aimed at the 2016 election. The committee—and its Senate counterpart—played an essential role on cybersecurity policy and was often a bipartisan enclave amid the political stresses in Congress. This would be particularly important in the Russia controversy—if they could pull it off.

With the March 1, 2017, announcement by Intelligence Chairman Nunes and ranking member Schiff of a six-page "scoping document" for the probe, both the House and the Senate Intelligence panels now had bipartisan investigations under way.

The document was classified, but the panel said in a release that it would examine: What Russian cyber activity and other active measures were directed against the United States and its allies? Did the Russian active measures include links between Russia and individuals associated with political campaigns or any other US persons? What was the US government's response to these Russian active measures, and what do we need to do to protect ourselves and our allies in the future? What possible leaks of classified information took place related to the Intelligence Community Assessment of these matters?

Democrats, and even some Republicans, were already calling for a more comprehensive, higher-level investigation, particularly into alleged contacts between Trump's advisers and Russian operatives.

Senate Democratic leader Schumer on March 2 kicked off the demands for heads to roll, calling for the resignation of Attorney General Jeff Sessions—following reports of a Sessions meeting with the Russian ambassador in September 2016—and for the appointment of an independent prosecutor to investigate Russian interference in the elections. House Homeland Security ranking member Thompson called for Sessions to resign and for the creation of an independent commission modeled after the 9/11 Commission.

For his part, Sessions during his January 2017 confirmation hearing pledged to take a tougher stance toward foreign cyber aggressors.

Amid this intensifying political struggle, there were the makings of a serious bipartisan examination at the House Intelligence Committee, addressing the overarching issues as well as each party's prime interests in the affair. There was encouraging history at this committee: Schiff and Nunes, who took their positions atop the panel at the beginning of 2015, quickly forged a partnership that helped lead to passage of cybersecurity information-sharing legislation late that year.

Nunes was seen as a security hawk while Schiff was known as a strong advocate for privacy and civil liberties protections—he had voted against an earlier version of the cyber bill that eventually became the Cybersecurity Act of 2015. Their ability to work out compromise privacy language helped lead to a final breakthrough on legislation long sought by cyber policymakers.

The Nunes-Schiff March 2017 agreement seemed to resolve, at least temporarily, how the committee would approach the investigation. But the two lawmakers were still firmly planted on different sides of the partisan uproar over potential connections between the Trump campaign and Russia and the impact of hacking on the elections.

Nunes in a statement broadened the context of the agreement to emphasize this wasn't a Trump investigation. "The Intelligence Committee has been investigating Russia for years and warning about the Putin regime's hostile international actions, its aggression in cyber space, and its influential international propaganda campaigns," Nunes said, spinning the Trump election as a chapter in a long-running story. Congressional Republicans quickly rallied around this narrative and would cite it repeatedly: The Russians have always tried to disrupt our elections and divide our nation. The 2016 Russian operation was nothing new and had nothing to do with Trump specifically.

"The committee is determined to continue and expand its inquiries into these areas, including Russian activities related to the 2016 U.S. elections. On a bipartisan basis, we will fully investigate all the evidence we collect and follow that evidence wherever it leads," Nunes said.

Schiff, in his statement, inserted what Democrats saw as the real issue: the specter of collusion between a presidential campaign and a foreign power engaged in a cyberattack on America. "The House Intelligence Committee must conduct a bipartisan investigation into Russia's interference in our election," Schiff said. "We must follow the facts wherever they may lead, leaving no stone unturned, and that must also include both the Russian hacking and dumping of documents as well as any potential collusion between Russia and U.S. citizens. This investigation is a national security necessity and anything less than a full accounting of all the facts will be insufficient to protect the country and meet the expectations of the American people."

The two had different objectives, but it was a start. Even a small step was welcome, because it would be next to impossible to get going on any cyber policy work until the Russia/election controversy had been wrestled into some kind of contained space. The Russia affair was subsuming cyber policy discussions, much like the Snowden affair had intruded on any discussion of cybersecurity from 2013 to 2015. Edward Snowden's explosive 2013 leaks detailing US digital surveillance created an atmosphere of intense distrust around any government cybersecurity activities and repeatedly derailed attempts to pass cyber legislation in those years, even on topics that had little to do with the type of widespread electronic snooping that Snowden had disclosed.

It took years to get cybersecurity, as a policy matter, back on firm nonpartisan ground. But cyber as a preeminent national security issue, pursued in a thoughtful, nonpartisan way, was again at risk by early 2017, overshadowed by Trump and Russia.

That point was underscored a few weeks later, when House Homeland Security chairman McCaul scheduled a hearing to help get the cybersecurity policy ball rolling. A couple of reporters showed up, but dozens—including most of those on the congressional cyber beat—trooped into a Capitol Visitor Center hallway for what was billed as an impromptu briefing by Nunes on the Russia investigation.

Standing by a staircase and looking harried, Nunes said he was just back from the White House, where the subject had been government surveillance of Trump officials. Schiff didn't know about it and Nunes's own staff only had a faint idea of what was going on, but nonetheless Nunes arranged an impromptu press briefing in a hallway, in the name of transparency, he said.

Nunes said he'd seen "raw" intelligence suggesting "incidental collection" of information by US government surveillance units during the November 2016 to January 2017 presidential transition, on the "president-elect and his team." What he'd seen had "nothing to do with Russia," Nunes said, but it did show that Trump and associates were being "monitored."

The Huffington Post reported:

> Nunes caused a stir when, with no prior notice to his fellow committee members, he announced that he'd received information showing that Trump transition officials had been caught inadvertently in surveillance operations targeting

> suspected foreign spies, and that their names appeared in internal intelligence reports. No one seemed to know where Nunes had gotten this information, and the congressman, who went to the White House to brief the president on his findings, would only say that he had an anonymous source. He has refused to name his source even to Rep. Adam Schiff (D-Calif.), the ranking Democrat on the intelligence committee.

With that, the bipartisan scaffolding was knocked out from under the House Intelligence Committee's work on Russian election interference, right at the start. The scene was surrealistic, with Nunes not quite saying what he was trying to say, or why he was saying it.

The Huffington Post explained:

> Over the weekend, it was reported that Nunes ditched his own staff the night before making his announcement. On Monday, the news broke that he had gone to the White House grounds to use a Sensitive Compartmented Information Facility—basically, a room or area that meets certain rigorous security standards—to get the information that formed the basis of his accusations.
>
> This raised the distinct possibility that the White House itself had been the source of the information, and that it had given that information to Nunes so he could provide Trump with some cover for his baseless accusation that former President Barack Obama had wiretapped Trump Tower. (The FBI and Nunes himself have said there is no evidence to support Trump's claims.)
>
> The White House and Nunes both deny that there was any collusion, and the White House has argued that it is possible Nunes came to the grounds without anyone from the administration knowing about it.

"I don't know that members of Congress need to be cleared," Huffington Post quoted White House press secretary Sean Spicer as saying.

To that, Huffington Post wrote,

> But it's basically impossible to believe that someone from the White House did not at least know that Nunes was coming to use the SCIF to access the information that would form the basis of his now-controversial press conference.
>
> The timing of last week's events offered the first indication of possible coordination between Nunes and the Trump administration. Earlier this month, Trump told Fox News that evidence to back up his wiretapping claims would soon emerge.

Nunes was suggesting, without coming out and making the accusation, that the US government had been spying on candidate Trump. Reporters asked the questions in a variety of ways, but Nunes kept repeating that he just couldn't say any more—not right now.

It had the look and smell of a PR ploy designed to discredit from the start any accusations of improper connections between the Trump campaign and

Russians. The real issue, according to this line, was improper (if not criminal) surveillance by *the US government* of a presidential candidate. Whatever Russia had done was a sideshow and, as Nunes said in his earlier statement about the investigation, well, the Russians always did this kind of thing.

At the House Homeland Security Committee on March 22, Democrats pressed their case for an "independent, 9/11-style commission" to investigate the Russian campaign aimed at the US elections. But reflecting the panel's pragmatic bent, the session mostly focused on nuts-and-bolts policy questions, like the need for a better-defined deterrence policy, which McCaul and his panel of expert witnesses all agreed upon.

What happened between the Trump campaign and Russian operatives was a matter screaming for investigation, but the Russia affair raised more nuanced policy issues as well. These required cool examination if the United States was to have any hope of crafting an effective response, and McCaul's committee was one place where that might still happen on a bipartisan basis.

"Cyber was just the tool" in Russia's efforts aimed at the US elections, former White House cyber coordinator Daniel told Inside Cybersecurity at the Homeland Security hearing. "This was really about the 'influence operations' that Russia has always been adept at, going back to the czars. Cyber was just the vehicle, and focusing too much on the vehicle is not helpful."

But, he added, "We need to improve our sophistication in terms of thinking about the things you can do in cyberspace. It's not just about destruction. Cyberspace doesn't adapt to the rules of the physical world. For example, what does sovereignty mean in cyberspace?"

Former Department of Homeland Security cyber chief Bruce McConnell said the very "definition of cyber is expanding."

Cyber now involved information warfare and manipulation, beyond the historic view of cyberwar as attacks aimed at stealing from or destroying computer networks, McConnell told Inside Cybersecurity.

"This presents new policy problems—it's not just protecting networks, it's content," McConnell observed. "And what is the government role in protecting content?"

Overwhelmed by the politics of the Russia affair, Congress wouldn't get very far on these deeper cyber questions. For one thing, bipartisanship collapsed swiftly and completely at the House Intelligence Committee, sharply limiting its ability to offer advice at the strategic level. The atmosphere was less toxic at the House Homeland Security Committee, but that panel was also unable to launch and sustain a strategic discussion on cyber amid the Trump-Russia narrative.

One year after Nunes's hallway presser, House Intelligence Committee Republicans made their bid to dispense with the Russia affair, releasing a report and cyber policy recommendations in April 2018. "Congress should encourage the adoption of [NIST] cyber security standards, such as those adopted by the Elections Assistance Commission, by providing federal resources to state and local governments to facilitate such adoption," their report stated rather blandly.

In one case, the GOP committee report said, "The FBI cannot, and should not, force a victim of a malicious cyber event to take specific remedial measures. However, the FBI should update its internal processes to make it clear that if a victim is neither willing nor able to take remedial measures in the event of a significant national security cyber event, FBI leadership should contact the victim and engage at the leadership level."

That was aimed at the accusation that Democratic Party organs failed to act on FBI warnings about Russian hacking, and that the FBI's follow-up was inadequate. In another case, the GOP report said, "The Committee therefore recommends that notifications associated with state-sponsored cyberattacks should be conducted as soon as possible, and at the highest levels of the victim organization. If intelligence sources and methods are threatened by dissemination of information, the IC should work with the Department of Homeland Security to provide specific recommendations on what actions can be taken by system owners to defend their networks from the state-actor."

It called for linking federal election-assistance funding to the states to meeting security requirements. The report said DHS "should provide certain designated state and local officials appropriate security clearances to enable those officials to respond to election-related threats."

Overall, Inside Cybersecurity's Rick Weber reported, "The report finds no collusion by the Trump campaign and Russia, but faults both campaigns for bad judgment in the handling and response to widespread reports of hacking including into the email system of the Clinton campaign."

Many of the cyber recommendations were solid, if unspectacular. However, it was a one-party report, shunned by Schiff, the committee's top Democrat who would become its chairman after the November elections. The major takeaway was the damage done to the collaborative spirit at one of the most bipartisan committees, historically, in Congress.

Nunes filed a $250 million defamation lawsuit against Twitter early the next year that would come to dominate the headlines about an influential lawmaker with a key post on cybersecurity. In addition to the social media company, the suit targeted a Twitter user going by the handle "Devin Nunes' Cow." Whatever the legal merits of the case, that could be considered a tactical mistake, as @DevinCow quickly gained hundreds of thousands of followers, and media coverage of the congressman couldn't resist taking jabs.

"And yet, Devin, you can't bear being made fun of by a fictional cow. On Twitter," a *Los Angeles Times* columnist wrote.

Filing suit against critics seemed right out of the Trump playbook, and the mockery directed at Nunes was a bit Trump-esque as well. Although by the standards of Donald Trump—whose repertoire included ridiculing physical handicaps and personal tragedies—the ribbing of Nunes was all in good fun.

All in all, it was quite the change in perspective for Nunes.

Cows notwithstanding, the Senate Intelligence Committee by 2018 was contributing its own preliminary and third-party research reports on the 2016 elections, these on a bipartisan basis.

The Senate committee in its July 3, 2018, preliminary report strongly backed the validity of the intelligence community's conclusions that Russia sought to undermine Hillary Clinton and help elect Trump, two points that would seem obvious but at the time were strenuously rejected by Trump and his allies.

The next report from the Senate Intelligence Committee went into detail on how Russia was using social media against the United States.

"Increasingly, we've seen how social media platforms intended to foster open dialogues can be used by hostile foreign actors seeking to manipulate and subvert public opinion," Intelligence Chairman Richard Burr (R-NC) said in a statement. "This newly released data demonstrates how aggressively Russia sought to divide Americans by race, religion and ideology, and how the IRA [Internet Research Agency] actively worked to erode trust in our democratic institutions. Most troublingly, it shows that these activities have not stopped. As we work to address these threats, these reports are proof positive that one of the most important things we can do is increase information sharing between the social media companies who can identify disinformation campaigns and the third-party experts who can analyze them."

Lessons from the 2016 election were slowly coming into focus, within Congress and across government.

"I don't think we missed it," Rob Joyce would say in 2019 of the Russian campaign of 2016. "We have looked at influence campaigns before in cyberspace. It's what we do about it that's the challenge."

Joyce explained that there were efforts to respond in real time during that campaign, "but . . . trying to shape a reaction within a space—free speech—that's a hard place for America to go."

That caution was coming from a renowned NSA cyber warrior. It tracked with Bruce McConnell's assessment of two years earlier and made clear there were no simple answers here. An adversary had discovered a digital seam in the democratic space and exploited it to the hilt. It was the Russians this time, but it could be almost any foe in cyberspace.

Upending the US electoral system wasn't Russia's only objective, of course. The Russians were also flexing cyber muscles in their own neighborhood, offering a taste of what they could do if left unchecked.

Reuters reported in early 2019, "Hackers likely controlled by Russia are stepping up efforts to disrupt Ukraine's presidential election in March with cyber attacks on electoral servers and personal computers of election staff, the head of Ukraine's cyber police said."

And amid all this, what was coming in the US presidential election year of 2020?

Well, weaponizing social media was a revolutionary cyberattack method, *in 2016*.

Two security pros explained to a packed hall at the 2019 RSA conference in San Francisco that cyber aggressors, presumably Russian, would use a wider array of tools for "a massive campaign" aimed at destabilizing democracy in the United States.

"It's no longer social-centric," said James Foster, CEO of cyber firm ZeroFOX. "It's omni-channel for a massive campaign going forward," involving social platforms, email, websites, and the dark web.

This wasn't just an election problem; it was a cause for concern throughout the cybersecurity community. Tools developed and sharpened in these geopolitical battle spaces usually bled into other areas for financial gain or other purposes.

Meanwhile, official Washington in March 2019 was bracing for two momentous policy developments: resolution of the China negotiations, which might set the course for US-China cyber relations for a decade or more, and the Mueller Report, which might set the course for Trump's administration—and his life—for the next two years or more.

Asked by White House reporters on March 13 about the status of the Mueller Report, Trump said he had no idea on timing, but "I can only tell you one thing. . . . No collusion."

The pool reporter, David Jackson of *USA Today*, wrote that Trump "went on [a] long riff about the 'hoax' investigation, and how Democrats are blaming Russia for their defeat in 2016."

"You don't call Russia when you go to Florida," Trump said instructively.

The following day, the House voted 420–0 in favor of a resolution calling for the Mueller Report to be publicly released in its entirety. As with the end game in the China negotiations, lines were being drawn by players on all sides that would have dramatic effects later. "A bastardized version of that report will not fly," Schiff, now Intelligence chairman, said on the House floor.

The same day, the Republican-controlled Senate voted 59–41 to reject Trump's declaration of an emergency at the US-Mexico border. It wasn't enough to overcome the presidential veto issued on March 15—Trump's first in two-plus years—but it was a remarkable statement from Capitol Hill on independence.

A week later, the capital was buzzing with reports that Mueller would send his findings to Attorney General Barr at any moment.

On Friday morning, March 22, as he boarded Marine One on his way to a weekend at Mar-a-Lago, Trump told reporters, "I have no idea about the Mueller Report," when asked about timing.

But he did have an idea about where it should go.

"This is a continuation of the same witch hunt," Trump said. "They ought to go to work . . . get a lot of things done instead of wasting everybody's time."

At 5 p.m. that day, Barr acknowledged receipt of the Mueller Report at the Justice Department, and the frenzy was on. On Sunday, March 24, Barr sent lawmakers a four-pager with the topline of no collusion—though Barr said "it also does not exonerate him" on obstruction of justice allegations. The president and his allies claimed vindication and immediately swung to the offensive. Democrats demanded the report itself and vowed this was not over.

At Palm Beach International Airport on Sunday afternoon, Trump made a short statement:

> So, after a long look, after a long investigation, after so many people have been so badly hurt, after not looking at the other side where a lot of bad things happened, a lot of horrible things happened, a lot of very bad things happened for our country—it was just announced there was no collusion with Russia. The most ridiculous thing I've ever heard.
>
> There was no collusion with Russia. There was no obstruction, and—none whatsoever. And it was a complete and total exoneration. It's a shame that our country had to go through this. To be honest, it's a shame that your President has had to go through this for—before I even got elected, it began. And it began illegally. And hopefully, somebody is going to look at the other side. This was an illegal takedown that failed. And hopefully, somebody is going to be looking at the other side.
>
> So it's complete exoneration. No collusion. No obstruction.

The Russian government and politicians, media and analysts in that country also claimed complete vindication.

But Susan Glasser, writing in the *New Yorker*, noted:

> The fact that Mueller explicitly refused to exonerate Trump of obstructing the investigation suggests that there is much more for Congress and the public to learn.
>
> Yet that information, even if it is damning, will not change the single, seemingly straightforward fact of Mueller's core finding: no conspiracy with Russia. Trump cheered the Russian hacking of his Democratic opponent; he seemed to

publicly beg Putin to carry it out. But, according to Barr's summary of Mueller, he did not make it happen. "Can you obstruct a witch hunt?" Rich Lowry, the editor of the conservative *National Review*, asked Sunday night. The answer may still be yes, but there is no one who believes that, without an underlying high crime and misdemeanor, Congress would take the unprecedented step of removing a President from office.

The worry now is that the country is too fragmented ever to agree on a single narrative anyway. Trump has spent the better part of two years trashing Mueller, in a bid to destroy the credibility of whatever conclusions he produces; Democrats built Mueller up. Both sides now crave a definitive resolution that will never be achieved. This episode of the Trump Show seems doomed to end in a much-argued-about cliffhanger.

One lesson of the Trump era, whenever it is finally over, will be that absolutely nothing is absolutely clear anymore. The end of the Mueller investigation should have been unambiguously good news for the President and the country. That it was instead confusing, partisan, uncertain, and guaranteed to be fought over for months and years to come is hardly surprising. It is our new normal.

What, after all this, were the actual cyber lessons from Russia's innovative uses of technology, social media, and cyberspace as new cold war–like terrain? What were the lessons in the responses from technology companies, critical infrastructure, the Trump and Clinton campaigns?

These questions were lost in the political uproar around the Barr memo and the demands for release of the actual report—and counterdemands from the Trump camp and its supporters to, in effect, get over it.

Cindy Otis, a writer and formerly a ten-year CIA analyst, hit on both the substantial policy questions still in play in the days and weeks after Mueller completed his work and the inadequacy of the president's response.

"Any normal U.S. president anticipating the arrival of the Mueller report would have planned a major cybersecurity announcement timed to whenever it landed, to demonstrate seriousness about national security. Even if it was simply to rearrange and merge some cybersecurity offices, form a task force, or create a new special representative position in some federal agency (the government's frequent solutions to show action is being taken)," she wrote in *USA Today*. "After all, special counsel Robert Mueller did confirm that a known foreign adversary conducted a full-scale covert influence operation to undermine American democracy."

She wrote, "Any other administration would also focus on rapidly building our cyber defenses because we are being outpaced by our adversaries' growing offensive capabilities. Agencies like the Department of Homeland Security and others are doing important work, but without the larger policy hand coordinating the process from the White House, capabilities will most likely be built in silos."

The Barr memo confirmed one thing that was already known: "The report outlines the Russian effort to influence the election and documents crimes committed by persons associated with the Russian government in connection with those efforts," Barr wrote.

Barr then moved onto trickier ground: "The report further explains that a primary consideration for the Special Counsel's investigation was whether any Americans—including individuals associated with the Trump campaign—joined the Russian conspiracies to influence the election, which would be a federal crime. The Special Counsel's investigation did not find that the Trump campaign or anyone associated with it conspired or coordinated with Russia in its efforts to influence the 2016 U.S. presidential election. As the report states: '[T]he investigation did not establish that members of the Trump Campaign conspired or coordinated with the Russian government in its election interference activities.'"

The probe found "two main Russian efforts" to influence the election, according to Barr: disinformation and social media campaigns, and the hacking of Democratic offices that provided key raw material for those campaigns.

But lawmakers of both parties knew that and wanted much more information. For one thing, Schiff wanted to know more—much more—about the whole spectrum of investigations related to the 2016 election, including the FBI probe that the *New York Times* had reported on earlier in the year.

"At this point, we don't know whether any of the counterintelligence findings are part of the Mueller report," Schiff told the Daily Beast on March 27. "We have initiated discussions with the intelligence community to make sure that we obtain whatever is found in the counterintelligence investigation, or whether that [inquiry] is still ongoing."

That very day, Nunes joined Schiff on a letter demanding access to this information, a sign of renewed collaboration first reported by CNN on April 15.

"The letter, sent March 27 and obtained by CNN Monday, adds another potential venue where Mueller could testify before Congress about the 22-month investigation that ended last month," CNN reported. "House Judiciary Chairman Jerry Nadler, D-New York, has previously said it's 'inevitable' Mueller will be called in to testify before his panel, too. Like the Judiciary Committee, House Intelligence Chairman Adam Schiff and the panel's ranking Republican Devin Nunes request in the letter all of the underlying materials from the Mueller probe, arguing the material is necessary for the Intelligence Committee to conduct its oversight of intelligence matters."

CNN also noted that Nunes put his name on a March 28 letter calling for Schiff's resignation as Intelligence chairman. So the collaboration was limited. Schiff and Nunes expected different outcomes—Schiff believed there were major unanswered questions about what Russia had done and with whom;

Nunes wanted to probe the roots of what he saw as a biased investigation—but Congress's near-universal demand for the meat in the report was clear.

Finally, Barr announced that he would release a redacted version on April 18.

The redacted Mueller Report on Russia and the 2016 elections contained politically contentious elements on collusion and obstruction of justice, but the aspects directly related to cybersecurity largely had been released and absorbed through earlier reports and indictments.

The document released April 18 by the Justice Department came in an unsearchable format, but there were parts on cyber issues such as botnets, which were heavily redacted, and lengthy discussion of what Russian agents did to hack into computers associated with the presidential campaign of Democrat Hillary Clinton. The basic cybersecurity issues involved were known for some time and were reflected in the Senate Intelligence Committee's election-security recommendations issued in March 2018.

As Barr said in his March 24 memo to Congress on the report, the Russian operation included two facets: the St. Petersburg–based Internet Research Agency's (IRA) social media campaign "to sow discord in the U.S. political system, first through a 'generalized' program" and then through a "targeted operation that by early 2016 favored candidate Trump and disparaged candidate Clinton," as the Mueller Report stated.

"At the same time," the report said, "the Russian government employed a second form of interference: cyber intrusions (hacking) and releases of hacked materials damaging to the Clinton campaign."

The special counsel's office determined that both of these campaigns violated US law, the report said, and in July 2018, the Justice Department announced the indictment against twelve officers in the Russian military's GRU intelligence service for hacking operations aimed at the Democratic National Committee and Hillary Clinton's presidential campaign.

Several pages in the section on indictments and decisions not to issue indictments were redacted.

In fact, extensive portions of the report on both facets of the Russian campaign—social media and hacking—were redacted. But the report said the Russians' social media campaign reached "tens of millions of U.S. persons" and purchased "dozens of advertisements" on Facebook supporting the Trump campaign, for instance.

Further, the report noted that the mainstream media quoted tweets from the IRA-controlled accounts and attributed them to actual people, an example of weaponized social media in action.

On the hacking operation, according to the report, "Two military units of the GRU carried out the computer intrusions into the Clinton campaign," as well as the Democratic National Committee (DNC) and Democratic

Congressional Campaign Committee (DCCC), the campaign arm of House Democrats. One of those units, GRU cyber unit 26165, specialized in developing malware, "spearphishing" campaigns, and bitcoin mining operations.

The unit used spearphishing techniques to access Clinton campaign chairman John Podesta's emails, among other steps. It also planted malware on DNC and DCCC computers.

GRU unit 74455 also conducted hacking operations aimed at state boards of elections, secretaries of state, and election equipment vendors.

A section on the "Trump campaign and the dissemination of hacked materials" was heavily redacted.

Senator Tom Carper (D-DE), a longtime leader on cyber issues and a thoughtful observer of how cybersecurity intersected with the body politic, issued a statement:

> After 23 months, 500 search warrants, 2,300 subpoenas, and 37 indictments, convictions or guilty pleas, the American people can finally see Special Counsel Mueller's unequivocal conclusion: "The Russian government interfered in the 2016 presidential election in a sweeping and systematic fashion." The fact that a foreign adversary successfully interfered in a U.S. election is a serious threat to our democracy that goes far beyond politics. Ensuring that our elections and democratic institutions are protected going forward cannot be a partisan matter. What's more, efforts to ensure that an attack like this never happens again must include the President of the United States, who has repeatedly dismissed and derided our nation's intelligence community and refused to fully acknowledge Russian interference in the 2016 election.

What would come next?

On Easter Sunday, Elijah Cummings (D-MD), the chairman of the House Oversight Committee, discussed next steps with CBS's Bob Schieffer, who asked, "Aren't people tired of this investigation; isn't it time to move on?"

"The Russians are not getting tired," Cummings replied. "They are attacking our democracy every day, if not every hour."

The veteran Democratic lawmaker stared into the camera and beseeched, "I beg you, whistleblowers, call us."

Cummings said he saw a roadmap to further legal action against the president. He wasn't jumping to conclusions, he said, but congressional Democrats would continue to investigate and consider legal steps. (Cummings would pass away in October 2019 after a long battle with health problems.)

Schiff, the House Intelligence leader, said on ABC that obstruction was clearly indicated, but he was cautious on impeachment—not ruling it out, but not jumping in either. Schiff framed this as the first true cybersecurity scandal and tried to relay the importance of this distinction.

"The obstruction of justice in particular in this case is far worse than anything that Richard Nixon did," Schiff told Martha Raddatz. "The break-in by the Russians of Democratic institutions, a foreign adversary far more significant than the plumbers breaking into the Democratic headquarters. So yes, I would say in every way this is more significant than Watergate."

James Lewis of CSIS, a more skeptical voice, said there was a roadmap here for sure, "for the House to chase its tail."

A cybersecurity pro read through the report and said it contained nothing unknown from a security perspective, but that the main takeaway was what a poor job the Obama administration had done, first in failing to deter the Russians and then in failing to counter their moves once it was known they were hacking the US elections.

That was a legitimate argument: For the Obama White House, there was a failure of imagination and a disastrously slow response to the Russian cyber-enabled campaign against the 2016 elections. The Obama team's cyber strategy was focused on critical infrastructure like electricity grids, and it took a while for the Russian campaign to register. The result was out there for all to see, in hacked emails leaked to embarrass Democratic presidential nominee Hillary Clinton, social media uproars churned up by Russian intelligence, and perhaps in the existence of the Trump presidency itself.

But the election hacking of 2016 could be seen as a blessing in disguise, said DHS and private sector cyber leader Mike Echols: "It was the cyber Pearl Harbor, it was the cyber 9/11, and we were blessed, no one was killed."

A Russian assault on US election systems and cyber-enabled manipulation of institutions and public opinion provided all the motivation the nation needed for an all-out cybersecurity campaign, he said, calling it the galvanizing moment that cyber commentators have been forecasting for years.

"What else do you need to get moving?" Echols asked.

"And yet," he said, "it happened and it only caused more division."

The truth of that statement was demonstrated on the Senate floor on May 7, 2019.

Staff for Majority Leader McConnell telegraphed to reporters that a major statement was coming, and the speech would clearly signal the GOP's determination to end the probe into the 2016 election and cast the Trump administration as leading the fight against Russian cyber and other attacks.

McConnell offered a lengthy defense of the Trump administration's response to Russia's cyber-enabled campaign against US elections and other aggression, while asserting that Democrats had been consistently soft on Vladimir Putin.

Senator Charles Schumer of New York, the chamber's top Democrat, would quickly respond, calling McConnell's remarks "an astounding bit of whitewashing."

McConnell said the Mueller Report should end debate over the 2016 election outcome and put the focus on defending American institutions and citizens against "brazen" Russian influence and cyber campaigns.

The Republican leader said the Mueller investigation had "morphed into something else," a partisan effort to reverse President Trump's election, and that it was time to move on. He asserted that Republicans and the administration already had done so in ways such as indicting Russian military officers on hacking charges, use of sanctions, and a "new national security strategy," which he contrasted to the Obama administration's "weak" approach to Russia.

McConnell also pointed to improved cyber information sharing between the Department of Homeland Security and state officials, and expanding the Pentagon's ability to use cyber weapons. He said the Mueller Report and an upcoming report from the Senate Intelligence Committee "will help us" further strengthen US systems.

The Obama administration's failure to stand up to Russia encouraged that country's aggression across a range of domains, McConnell asserted, including the hacking aimed at the Hillary Clinton campaign.

"Maybe stronger leadership would have left the Kremlin less emboldened. Maybe tampering with our democracy wouldn't have seemed so very tempting," McConnell said. "Instead, the previous administration sent the Kremlin the signal they could get away with almost anything, almost anything."

Schumer followed McConnell on the Senate floor and called the Mueller Report "a stunning document," saying it was a "damning appraisal of our election security" but also of "just how willing a major presidential campaign was to accept and amplify the disinformation of a foreign adversary."

"Of course [the majority leader] wants to move on," Schumer said, while noting that additional sanctions against Russia were stalled in the Senate and that McConnell refused to bring election security legislation to the floor.

"It's not done," Schumer said. "If Russia interferes in 2020, it's not done. If this president or future presidents believe that they can avoid the law and even break the law . . . it is not done."

Schumer said McConnell had not responded to his request for a classified all-senators briefing on election security threats, and he reached back to the 2016 election cycle to say the Republican leader delayed sharing with the states—and then watered down—warnings from the Obama administration about Russia's activities.

"So long as this place remains a legislative graveyard," Schumer said, "we're rolling out the welcome mat for foreign adversaries."

There were other impacts on Capitol Hill as well. The bipartisan relationship between the top Democrat and Republican on the House Intelligence Committee was in tatters. Adam Schiff, installed as chairman with the

Democratic takeover of the House, was public enemy number one to Trump aides and allies, the alleged ringleader of the collusion allegation.

Politico quoted Donald Trump Jr. on Twitter: "Has anyone heard from slimy Adam #fullofschiff Schiff today?" he wrote. "I mean it must be embarrassing to have have [*sic*] spent the last 2 years as the leader of the tinfoil hat brigade and have it all come crashing down so quick. I'm legitimately concerned for his mental state."

Politico added, "Top Trump adviser Kellyanne Conway called for Schiff to resign immediately."

That wasn't going to happen. Schiff knew he was in the crosshairs now and didn't have much cover from the Mueller probe. He was pushing ahead with his own investigation of what had happened in 2016 anyway, so the barbs would keep coming and would grow even more pointed.

And what about Devin Nunes, now the ranking member of the Intelligence Committee? He was in the news for filing a lawsuit against a fictional cow. Maybe he would get the last laugh, maybe not. In any case, he would continue as the president's top ally in the small world of intelligence on Capitol Hill.

It was a long drop from the heady days when cybersecurity policy ran through the House Intelligence Committee because it—and its Senate counterpart—was seen as the place that had the most relevant information and could get things done.

Meanwhile, there were no lessons learned at the White House.

"No, Russia did not help me get elected," Trump said on May 30, 2019, stopping to "gaggle" with reporters on the South Lawn on his way to the Marine One helicopter.

Russia and the Mueller Report dominated his tweets that morning: "Russia, Russia, Russia!" Trump tweeted. "That's all you heard at the beginning of this Witch Hunt Hoax. . . . And now Russia has disappeared because *I had nothing to do with Russia helping me to get elected*. It was a crime that didn't exist" (emphasis added).

The "helping me to get elected" line read like an acknowledgment and caught fire on social media. Trump made a beeline toward reporters that morning.

"Russia didn't help me at all. Russia, if anything, I think, helped the other side," the president told reporters.

From the pool report by Todd Gillman of the *Dallas Morning News*: "He asserted that while Russia preferred Hillary Clinton and tried to help her get elected, it also had an 'insurance policy.' 'Guess what, what we're in right now is the insurance policy'—apparently referring to mistrust sown about his own victory."

It would be difficult for the White House and administration to internalize the lessons from 2016 when the president's view was completely at odds with the findings of congressional and independent investigators.

The July 24, 2019, Mueller appearances in back-to-back hearings by the House Judiciary and Intelligence committees would provide one more chance for a public reckoning. Trump had said he wasn't paying any attention, that the issue was finished. But his tweets suggested otherwise.

He tweeted the evening before, "Just got back only to hear of a last minute change allowing a Never Trumper attorney to help Robert Mueller with his testimony before Congress tomorrow. What a disgrace to our system. Never heard of this before. VERY UNFAIR, SHOULD NOT BE ALLOWED. A rigged Witch Hunt!"

More would follow in the morning and throughout the day of the hearings. The opening tweets betrayed prebout nervousness, a boxer batting away self-doubt, as Trump griped with equal intensity over logistical details and matters of cosmic significance.

"So why didn't the highly conflicted Robert Mueller investigate how and why Crooked Hillary Clinton deleted and acid washed 33,000 Emails immediately AFTER getting a SUBPOENA from the United States Congress? She must have GREAT lawyers!"

"NO COLLUSION, NO OBSTRUCTION!"

At the very start of the first hearing, an outraged protester burst past Capitol Police into the hearing room and began shouting about a conspiracy involving presidential son-in-law Jared Kushner and ex-Trump campaign manager Paul Manafort.

Somewhere between those conflicting expressions of outrage and conspiracies, lawmakers were supposed to make sense of a cyberattack on American democracy and where President Trump's responses fell along an arc that ran from reasonable to treasonous.

Trump seemed well aware that his presidency was at stake this day, and when it was over, the president would tweet a stream of testimonials from his supporters in Congress and at Fox News that he had prevailed.

"TRUTH IS A FORCE OF NATURE!" Trump tweeted as the day's hearings came to a close.

But was it true? Did it matter?

Gray and dour, Mueller was carefully led by security and House staffers from a committee room behind the dais to the witness table, professional cameras clicking furiously and dozens of smartphones hoisted up in the audience to immortalize the event. If Mueller was feeling any excitement or nerves in the moment, he didn't betray it. He looked emotionless, more like a man enduring a wait at the airport than a fighter entering a championship ring.

From his weary manner, Mueller might have been answering questions at the airport. His nearly inaudible responses and brief occasional signs of confusion handed media commentators all they needed for a meme about an out-of-touch Mueller who didn't seem to grasp the details of his own investigation. Commentators and headlines blared about poor optics and a failure to capitalize by Mueller and the Democrats.

To Trump, a stumbling performance by Mueller under the lights was all he needed to know to discredit the entire affair. But there was much more to the hearing than that; if it were a boxing match at one of Trump's casinos, Mueller and the Democrats piled up points with jabs and short punches in the clinches, while Republicans hammed it up for the cameras with ridicule and conspiracy theories.

Bipartisanship was in short supply at both committees, but, remarkably, the usually pugnacious atmosphere at the Judiciary panel was more restrained than the bare-knuckled fight at the once-collegial Intelligence panel.

The facts of Russian hacking and "sweeping" cyber-enabled interference in American democratic processes were accepted as givens at House Judiciary, but that consensus fell apart immediately on whether Trump and his 2016 campaign aided and benefited from Russia's sophisticated campaign and then sought to cover up their actions. House Judiciary Democrats and Republicans led Mueller through a granular review of his report, with each side pulling out sharply different conclusions on the legal implications of Trump's actions in the affair.

Judiciary Chairman Nadler said it was about "responsibility, integrity and accountability."

He offered strong praise for Mueller's work—its examination of Russia attacking American democracy in "sweeping fashion," aimed at Hillary Clinton's campaign, and of possible collusion and obstruction of justice in the Trump team's behavior around this massive cyberattack.

"Among the most shocking of these incidents," Nadler said in his opening statement, "President Trump ordered his White House Counsel to have you fired and then to lie and deny that it had happened. He ordered his former campaign manager to convince the recused attorney general to step in and limit your work and he attempted to prevent witnesses from cooperating with your investigation."

"You made clear that he was not exonerated," Nadler said, asserting that anyone else who acted in this way would be charged with a crime, which became the Democrats' main theme.

And Nadler hinted at how Democrats planned to move past the disappointment within their ranks that Mueller's report didn't clearly specify crimes and call for specific actions. "[Y]ou said quote the Constitution requires a process other than the criminal justice system to formally accuse a sitting president of wrongdoing closed quote."

Nadler said, "That process begins with the work of this committee."

That might or might not mean impeachment, but it clearly meant an ongoing, exhaustive dig into the actions of 2016 and afterward. Representative Doug Collins of Georgia, the top Judiciary Republican, was ready with another narrative.

"We were told collusion was in plain sight," Collins said, but the report showed no collusion. Democrats charged obstruction of justice, but Trump never shut down the investigation, even though he had the authority to do so. "He knew he was innocent," Collins said.

A little close scrutiny obliterated all of the charges against the president, Collins told his colleagues and Mueller, and what remained was the question of how this investigation got started in the first place. The probe itself was the problem, and, among other things, it "paralyzed" the work of this and other congressional committees.

And the fight was on.

In his opening statement, Mueller said his investigative team charged more than thirty defendants with crimes, including twelve officers of the Russian military, and that it did not establish that members of the Trump campaign conspired with the Russian government. "First, our investigation found that the Russian government interfered in our election in sweeping and systematic fashion."

"Second," Mueller said, "the investigation did not establish that members of the Trump campaign conspired with the Russian government in its election interference activities. We did not address collusion, which is not a legal term. Rather, we focused on whether the evidence was sufficient to charge any member of the campaign with taking part in a criminal conspiracy, and it was not."

Mueller explained that investigators decided they would not make a determination on whether the president committed a crime, a decision he said they were sticking with.

Further, he cautioned that public testimony could affect ongoing cases and that he was unable to address issues such as the origin of the investigation and related matters, a prime focus of Republican lawmakers. After conducting an extensive investigation over two years, Mueller said, "The report is my testimony."

Mueller repeatedly told lawmakers that his investigation was precluded from filing criminal charges against the president under Department of Justice rules and thus was not organized along those lines. He agreed with Democrats that the report did not "exonerate" the president on allegations of obstruction of justice and that the president was less than fully cooperative in the investigation.

Throughout the hearing, Judiciary Democrats hammered away at their point that anyone other than a sitting president would have been indicted given the evidence at hand, while Republicans said the report revealed no criminal acts by the president and argued that Mueller exceeded his authority and charter through the report's lengthy discussion of possible crimes.

"Did you exonerate the president?" Nadler asked.

"No," Mueller said. He perhaps said that more firmly than any of the other words he spoke in nearly seven hours.

"Did you find that the president exerted undue influence on the investigation?"

"Correct."

When Collins's turn came to question Mueller, he said, "Just—thank you. Isn't it true the evidence did not establish that the president or those close to him were involved in the charged Russian computer hacking or active measures, conspiracies, or that the president otherwise had unlawful relationships with any Russian official, volume 2, page 76, correct?"

Mueller: "I will leave the answer to the report."

Collins: "So that was a yes. Is [it] true, your investigation did not establish that members of the Trump campaign conspired or coordinated with Russian government in the election interference activity, volume 1, page 2, volume 1, page 173?"

Mueller: "Thank you. Yes."

Representative Zoe Lofgren (D-CA), sponsor of House-passed election-security legislation, questioned Mueller on the vast scale of the Russian effort and how its intelligence services used campaign polling data supplied by a Trump campaign official in tandem with material hacked from the Democratic National Committee.

Lofgren said House Democrats "counted 126 contacts" between the Trump campaign and Russia-affiliated individuals, while eliciting from Mueller that Russia's efforts were aimed at benefiting one candidate: Donald Trump.

She sought to connect the dots between Russia-Trump campaign contacts, and how material shared by a Trump official would directly help the Russians in targeting their secret social media activities.

Lofgren said, "So, you wrote in volume 1 that the Russian government interfered in the 2016 presidential election in sweeping and systematic fashion. You also described in your report that the then-Trump campaign chairman, Paul Manafort, shared with the Russian operative, Kilimnik, the campaign strategy for winning democratic votes in Midwestern states and internal polling data of the campaign, isn't that correct?"

"Yes."

"They also discussed the status of the Trump campaign and Manafort's strategy for winning Democratic votes in Midwestern states months before that meeting. Manafort had caused internal data to be shared with Kilimnik and the sharing continued for some period of time after their August meeting. Isn't that correct?"

Mueller agreed.

"In fact, your investigation found that Manafort briefed Kilimnik on the state of the Trump campaign and Manafort's plan to win the election and that briefing encompassed the campaign's messaging, its internal polling data. It also includes discussion of battleground states, which Manafort identified as Michigan, Wisconsin, Pennsylvania and Minnesota. Isn't that correct?"

"Yes," Mueller said.

"Did your investigation determine who requested the polling data to be shared with Kilimnik?"

"Well, I would direct you to the report—what we have in the report in regard to that particular issue."

"We don't have the redacted version—that's maybe another reason why we should get that for Volume 1. Based on your investigation, how would the Russian government have used this campaign polling data to further its sweeping and systematic interference in the 2016 presidential election?"

"It's a little bit out of our path."

But the suggestion was: Here is the tangible value the Russians derived from their Trump contacts and from their hacking efforts, which was funneled into a massive pro-Trump social media campaign illegally financed by Russia. But the Trump official who authorized such activity was shielded by redactions.

She summed up: "So, while the Russians were buying ads and creating propaganda to influence the outcome of the election, they were armed with inside information that they had stolen through hacking from the DNC and that they had been given by the Trump campaign chairman, Mr. Manafort. My colleagues will probe the efforts undertaken to keep this information from becoming public. But I think it's important for the American people to understand the gravity of the underlying problem that your report uncovered."

Representative Sheila Jackson-Lee (D-TX) cited "10 possible acts of obstruction" identified in the report related to efforts to curtail DOJ and special counsel work, including Trump's alleged instructions to fire Mueller.

While Democrats tried to use their questioning to illuminate specific cases of obstruction that they found throughout the report, Republicans treated Mueller as a hostile witness and targeted what they framed as political bias, inconsistencies, omissions, and overreach in the investigation.

GOP lawmakers argued extensively that the investigation was based on false information from the very beginning, that Mueller exceeded his authority as special counsel, and that, in any case, the probe demonstrated no crime had been committed by Trump.

Representative John Ratcliffe (R-TX), who once headed the House Homeland Security cyber panel, said the attorney general's instructions to the special counsel were to write a report on decisions reached in the probe; yet they "wrote 180 pages on decisions not reached" and charges not made. He charged that the entire second volume of the report was not authorized under the special counsel's charter.

"I agree with the chairman, Donald Trump is not above the law," Ratcliffe said, "but he damn sure shouldn't be below the law."

That one went viral and positioned Ratcliffe as one of the president's lead champions on the Hill. Four days after the hearings, DNI Coats announced his long-expected resignation, and Trump swiftly named Ratcliffe as his nominee to be the new director of National Intelligence. Senate Democrats reacted negatively, to say the least, and Ratcliffe later would withdraw from consideration amid intense scrutiny of his credentials.

Meanwhile, Judiciary Democrats emerged confident that the session provided plenty of ammunition for their next steps in the investigation, which had yet to be determined. Republicans charged Mueller with "obfuscating" on issues like political bias within his team and the origins of the investigation. But they felt they'd done their job too.

When the House Intelligence Committee took over the hearing room minutes after the Judiciary members departed, Chairman Schiff and ranking member Nunes immediately clashed over the meaning and implications of Mueller's report. The Democrat argued it provided extensive evidence of misdeeds by the president and his associates, while Nunes said it was the "last gasp" of an elaborate hoax aimed at undermining Trump.

Schiff asked Mueller, "In fact the campaign welcomed the Russian help, did they not?" to which Mueller replied, "I think we report in our report indications that that occurred, yes."

Schiff asked, "When your investigation looked into these matters numerous Trump associates lied to your team, the grand jury and to Congress?"

"A number of persons that we interviewed in our investigation it turns out did lie," Mueller said.

"And when Donald Trump called your investigation a witch hunt that was also false, was it not?"

"I would like to think so, yes," Mueller said.

"When the president said the Russian interference was a hoax that was false wasn't it?"

"True."

Schiff said Russia wanted Trump to win the election, informed Trump associates of that fact, and broke federal laws by hacking in order to help Trump. Mueller agreed.

"The Trump campaign officials built their strategy, their messaging strategy around those stolen documents?" Schiff asked, underscoring the cyber-enabled nature of the alleged crime.

"I—generally that is true."

"And then they lied to cover it up," Schiff said.

"Generally that is true," Mueller replied.

As a TV courtroom drama, that may have been Schiff's best moment, and he punctuated it in clipped, Perry Mason fashion. "Thank you. Mr. Nunes?"

When his turn came, Nunes charged that Mueller failed to interview key Russians about how the allegations came about in the first place, saying it was all based on a rumor provided by a foreign politician with ties to Hillary Clinton.

Ratcliffe pressed Mueller to expand on his earlier clarification that the special counsel's decision not to indict was made because there was no evidence of a crime, not strictly because of DOJ guidelines against indicting a sitting president.

"We did not reach a determination as to whether the president committed a crime," Mueller said. He added, "We did not start a process on culpability."

Representative Mike Quigley (D-IL) asked about Trump's public praise for WikiLeaks publishing hacked material.

"Well it's problem—problematic is an understatement in terms of what it display—displays," Mueller said. "In terms of giving some, I don't know, hope or some boost to what is and should be illegal activity."

The nation's cybersecurity needs finally got a specific mention at the end. In response to a question from Representative Will Hurd (R-TX), a former CIA officer, Mueller told lawmakers the Russians would be back in 2020—that, in fact, they've never left when it comes to a sophisticated, cyber-backed campaign to target and undermine democratic processes in the United States.

"Much more needs to be done" to counter foreign interference in US elections, Mueller said at the end of the Intelligence Committee hearing. He specifically called for more collaboration and info-sharing among campaigns, government agencies, and other entities.

At a press conference that evening, some jubilant Republicans said lawmakers should turn now to election security. With the collusion and obstruction issues disposed of—in their words—perhaps attention could turn to action on securing the ballot box and election systems from Russian hacking.

But when Senate Minority Leader Schumer tried to move election-security bills the next day, Majority Leader McConnell shut him down, signaling how difficult it would be to separate cyber-related election measures from partisan narratives following Mueller's testimony.

"Let's forget the political divisions" and pass election-security measures, Schumer said on the floor. He pressed again for action on bipartisan bills that would set cyber requirements for election vendors and establish new tools for deterring foreign aggressors. But when he and Senator Richard Blumenthal (D-CT) offered motions to proceed, McConnell blocked the moves. The GOP leader said Schumer was pushing "partisan bills" and noted $380 million in election security funding given to states in 2018. That was enough for now. (In September, McConnell would agree to an additional $250 million in election security funding for states.)

"What kind of makes me crazy," Warner would tell MSNBC, "is we're not doing enough to actually make our country better protected. There are—there's commonsense things we can do, simple things. There ought to be an affirmative obligation. If a foreign government intervenes, tell the FBI. . . . [E]very ballot ought to have a paper ballot backup. We ought to make sure that if a country attacks us, we put sanctions on them and they know that ahead of time."

He said, "We ought to make sure that in social media there's a requirement to report if foreigners or others advertise. We need some guard-rails around Facebook and Twitter. These are things that would get [an] overwhelming majority of the votes, but this White House and the majority leader refuse to allow any of these bills to come to the floor, and that to me is not making our country safer."

Warner said, "I think that these votes—these bills would get 70, 75 votes on the floor of the Senate. I like—I think a lot of the reluctance is coming from the White House."

The House Democrats held their own meeting following the Mueller hearings. They were clearly conflicted on what to do next, lacking the big boost they had expected from Mueller for a move toward impeachment, but all in all they were convinced that they had a strong case—on the merits, that is, not necessarily with the public optics.

Speaker Pelosi called Mueller's testimony before the Judiciary and Intelligence committees "a crossing of a threshold, in terms of the public awareness of what happened."

More investigation was warranted, she said, and impeachment was not off the table. "Ten instances of obstruction, yes," she said. "No exoneration. That's some of what we heard today."

On impeachment, Pelosi said, "My position has always been whatever decision we make in that regard would have to be done with our strongest possible hand and we still have some outstanding matters in the courts. It's about the Congress, the Constitution and the courts. And we are fighting the president in the courts."

Nadler, who wanted to get started with impeachment, said, "Mueller found that Trump would and did benefit from Russia's help and that the campaign welcomed that help. Mueller found multiple instances where all three elements for charging criminal obstruction of justice were met. Trying to fire the special counsel in order to stop the investigation, trying to have people lie and cover up for him for the same purpose, trying to limit or impede or constrict the special counsel's investigation, trying to tamper with witnesses, tamper with witnesses cooperating with investigators. All of these were found with evident great evidence."

Democrats might or might not follow through on impeachment, but these charges were going to underlie much of their interaction with Trump on cybersecurity in general and election security in particular. But in the weeks and months after the Mueller hearings, the pressure building within the Democratic Party base and large segments of the House Democratic Caucus never eased off. Tempered analysis about the futility of an impeachment bid based on the Mueller findings bounced off the steely belief that Trump had violated the law, was in contempt of a coequal branch of government, and was wiping his nose on the US Constitution on a daily basis.

In September, reports emerged about a government whistleblower from the intelligence community, a Trump phone call with the leader of Ukraine, and the US president allegedly withholding military aid to an ally in order to further his own political interests.

It had nothing to do with cyber or the 2016 election, but this latest affair would propel the House of Representatives into an actual impeachment inquiry against Donald Trump. And it seemed that every questionable aspect of the Trump approach to cybersecurity—or any other policy area, for that matter—was present in this "case of the Ukrainian phone call."

There were freelancing Trump associates like Rudolph Giuliani operating with little regard for US interests or national security. US allies were bullied or ignored, and the idea of partnership was treated as a joke. A policy with major implications for the US-Russia relationship—assistance to Ukraine in its battle against Russian-backed separatists—was being formulated in a black box, with details known only to Trump and perhaps Giuliani.

The intelligence community and State Department were frozen out of the president's solo Ukraine initiative. There was no coordination—the national security adviser was frozen out too—and no desire for input from stakeholders in the military or diplomatic corps who might have provided valuable advice.

In short, everything that Trump did to undermine himself as a leader on cybersecurity was also present in the Ukraine case that would actually launch an impeachment process.

The day after the Mueller hearings, meanwhile, the Senate Intelligence Committee tried to do its part to offer a way out, at least on securing the upcoming elections.

Senators Warner and Burr released "Russian Efforts against Election Infrastructure," the first in a five-volume set intended to spell out what happened in 2016 and what the country should do about it. It was wonky, practical, and maybe just what the situation called for.

"It is my hope that the Senate Intelligence Committee's bipartisan report will provide the American people with valuable insight into the election security threats still facing our nation and the ways we can address them," Chairman Burr said in a statement. "There is still much work that remains to be done."

Said Warner, "There's still much more we can and must do to protect our elections. I hope the bipartisan findings and recommendations outlined in this report will underscore to the White House and all of our colleagues, regardless of political party, that this threat remains urgent, and we have a responsibility to defend our democracy against it."

The report, extensively redacted by the Office of the Director of National Intelligence, urged more steps on election and critical infrastructure security, and possibly more financial aid to states. It repeatedly cautioned that federal policymakers must pay heed to state officials' primacy over election management. It emphasized the federal government's role in deterring foreign aggressors and implementing a credible cyber doctrine, and called for working with allies to develop international cyber norms of behavior.

More reports were coming on "the Intelligence Community Assessment of Russian interference, the Obama Administration's response to Russian interference, the role of social media disinformation campaigns, and remaining counterintelligence questions."

It was intended to be a canon for policymakers, a guide through a new and extremely dangerous cyber threat with a catalog of recommendations. And it was for the cybersecurity-minded, staying clear of the politics that had subsumed investigative efforts on the House side. It took shots from critics who said its proposed solutions were too soft given the gravity of the threat, that it didn't endorse mandating cybersecurity controls for elections and other critical infrastructure. But a congressional committee, on a bipartisan basis, had managed to formally recognize the cyberattack that occurred in 2016 and propose practical cybersecurity steps for moving forward.

Given the atmosphere on Capitol Hill in the age of Trump, that was a sizable accomplishment.

As stated, impeachment was a political decision to be made by members of Congress and ultimately would be pursued outside of the cybersecurity policy domain. But Russia's cyberattack, meticulously described in the Senate Intelligence Committee report and in Mueller's work, was a tangible fact that still had to be confronted by the cybersecurity community, with or without help from the White House and lawmakers.

12

Disruptor, Enabler, Underminer

"It's really hard to know what's in this president's mind," commented one cyber policy veteran with deep experience working around other presidents. There were positives, this source said, but the inconsistencies, the abrupt changes, the disdain for allies and for policy work and . . . the source trailed off.

Trump's own view of his presidency as expressed on Twitter shaped the narrative around it. As such, cyber was mostly a subset of various running fights with Hillary Clinton, Robert Mueller, and other targets of the day or week. There were a couple of cyber policy statements amid nearly forty thousand tweets, but that wasn't Trump's interest.

After two years in office, the Trump tweets included sixty-seven mentions of "hack" or "hacking" but mostly to describe someone as a "hack" or to discuss Hillary Clinton and the DNC hack or the Mueller probe.

Seven presidential tweets mentioned cyber or cybersecurity between January 2017 and November 2019. One was stock language on the release of his cyber executive order, and one on his move to elevate the status of US Cyber Command, marking two big policy hallmarks of his administration.

One tweet, on April 15, 2019, expressed outrage that "Chinese Telecom Giant Huawei hires former Obama Cyber Security Official as a lobbyist. This is not good, or acceptable!" Unmentioned by the president: Chinese telecom giant ZTE hired about a half dozen Trump campaign veterans, Politico reported.

In advance of the Helsinki summit with Vladimir Putin, Trump posted two tweets on July 9, 2018. He cited an earlier summit with the Russian leader where they discussed a proposal for cyber collaboration that took off like a lead balloon: "The fact that President Putin and I discussed a Cyber Security unit doesn't mean I think it can happen. It can't-but a ceasefire can,& did!" read one.

"Putin & I discussed forming an impenetrable Cyber Security unit so that election hacking, & many other negative things, will be guarded," the president tweeted.

The following week at the Helsinki summit and immediately after, the tweets explained Trump's thinking as many in the United States expressed shock at the outcome:

> A productive dialogue is not only good for the United States and good for Russia, but it is good for the world. I would rather take a political risk in pursuit of peace, than to risk peace in pursuit of politics.
>
> As I said today and many times before, "I have GREAT confidence in MY intelligence people." However, I also recognize that in order to build a brighter future, we cannot exclusively focus on the past—as the world's two largest nuclear powers, we must get along! So many people at the higher ends of intelligence loved my press conference performance in Helsinki. Putin and I discussed many important subjects at our earlier meeting. We got along well which truly bothered many haters who wanted to see a boxing match. Big results will come!

For three years in the age of President Trump, cyber policy was thoughtful and advanced when left to the pros. That was good, but also incomplete under one established maxim: Cybersecurity was such a ubiquitous, confusing, challenging issue that the very top office in the US government had to set the goal posts for government, industry, and citizens. The government told corporate CEOs and boards of directors that they—personally—must take responsibility for the issue, or the demands simply wouldn't be met in every corner of their organizations. Any weakness, any hole in the fence, could doom the whole enterprise. The same rules applied, or should apply, to the vast enterprise that was government: the top officer absolutely needed to be in charge.

Under Trump, the issue wasn't mentioned by the president and was always subject to buffeting political winds and often undermined by competing political needs, impatience with his own staff or department heads or allies, or by the everlasting Russia controversy. The result has been a chaotic organizational and policy environment, with no cyber coordinator to make sense of the whole.

In policy, the Trump administration was putting responsibility—and accountability—into the hands of specific officials to shore up cyber in their government departments, surely a positive step. But agencies like the FCC were also stepping back from exercising meaningful oversight of—and providing any kind of safety net for—the cybersecurity efforts of industry.

The president took bureaucratic steps to empower the powerful US military to more fully engage in cyberspace, using its fearsome arsenal of cyber weapons where necessary, with fewer internal hurdles to clear than back in the Obama days.

"Adversaries toward the end of the Obama administration concluded they had overestimated the U.S. ability to retaliate in cyberspace," said CSIS's Lewis. "Forgive me—Trump has reversed that impression. That's not to be too Jesuitical and say the ends justify the means. But that's been our policy since Dec. 7, 1941."

But Trump never publicly spelled out what this might mean—for allies, foes, or the American public. To crib from the Cold War classic satire *Dr. Strangelove*, what good is a deterrence policy if you don't tell the Russians you have it?

As former White House official Ari Schwartz observed, the Trump administration never explained its process for ensuring that a US cyber strike on an adversary didn't trigger blowback that disproportionately hurt other American stakeholders like tech companies. Senator Mike Rounds (R-SD) assured a reporter in a brief hallway interview in 2019 that this problem was recognized and had been "addressed." But that didn't really get at informing and engaging with the stakeholder community, much less the American public.

John Carlin, the former top cyber cop at the Justice Department, said "we need to think carefully" in this space. "We are more vulnerable . . . because we are moving more quickly than anyone else to digitize." Using a cyber strike as retribution against an adversary could trigger cyberattacks in response that, in the end, might be more costly to the United States.

Trump's White House also moved to address the nation's cyber workforce problem with a well-received executive order in May 2019.

And the president issued the supply-chain executive order, which was motivated by the China trade talks but at least addressed 5G, emerging as one of the most significant cyber issues of the times. However, a cloak of secrecy covered implementation of the supply-chain order, suggesting problems in coordination and even in actual commitment to fulfilling goals that were stuck between competing security and trade policy demands.

Still, those were four important pieces—cyber accountability at government agencies, making greater use of cyber weapons for deterrence and retribution, strengthening the cyber workforce, and shoring up supply-chain security—being addressed by the Trump White House.

At the same time, Trump consistently questioned the value and honesty of his intelligence services—front-line actors in the global cyber war, and increasingly an important source of information for industry.

Here's how the US intelligence community, in its annual assessment released in January 2019, saw the problem:

> Despite growing awareness of cyber threats and improving cyber defenses, nearly all information, communication networks, and systems will be at risk for years to come. Our adversaries are becoming more adept at using cyberspace capabilities to threaten our interests and advance their own strategic and economic objectives. Cyber threats will pose an increasing risk to public health, safety, and prosperity as information technologies are integrated into critical infrastructure, vital national networks, and consumer devices. The IC must continue to grow its intelligence capabilities to meet these evolving cyber threats as a part of a comprehensive cyber posture positioning the Nation for strategic and tactical response.

Innovative new technologies were coming online, and American companies increasingly had access to advanced cybersecurity tools. But there was no comprehensive attempt to close the loop by ensuring companies knew about these tools and were properly motivated to use them. Incentives could be tax breaks or avoiding regulatory hammers, but, in any case, no one at the top of the US government was thinking about such things.

Meantime, the wheels of government turned and cyber pros went to work every day—at least the ones not idled by a government shutdown. The dedicated professionals continued to build on and expand and improve policies developed over the previous fifteen years—pros within and outside government.

The negative effects of the era of Trump were tangible: in frayed trust among allies, broken bipartisanship around cyber on Capitol Hill, damaged institutions such as the intelligence community and DHS, and a demoralized government workforce, for a few examples.

On the positive side, the policy arc continued and was energized—to an extent—in places like the military and in industry leadership. But Trump's was an ad hoc approach that in many ways violated basic tenets of cybersecurity, needlessly challenged consensus and partnerships built over many years, and provided comfort to cyber adversaries. It didn't amount to a cyber strategy.

One well-respected private sector security professional, in an interview on an entirely separate topic, went off the record to say that Trump, a "disruptor," was providing a valuable service across government by forcing stakeholders to rethink basic premises. "He challenges why we are doing it this way," the source said, "and that's good for cyber. Even if it is uncomfortable. I'm glad we're going through this exercise."

Another security industry pro, during an interview at a major cyber conference, also went off the record to say Trump's 2017 executive order was forcing accountability on the federal bureaucracy. "Whatever you think about Trump politically, he was the first president to issue a cybersecurity executive order," the source said. Reminded that Obama issued five cyber EOs, the source said, "Well not like this one. The accountability is key. People who don't like Trump didn't like the E.O., but it did force agencies to finally act."

Trump led a remarkable and possibly dangerous detour in cyber policy for intertwined—and often confounding—reasons. This was set against the work of diligent professionals in government and the private sector, in nothing less than a remarkable test of the resiliency of the American system of governing and confronting challenges.

Cybersecurity was still a baby of a policy area when Trump took office. It was in the midst of developing its own principles and codes of conduct, among the people who were making and implementing the policy. It was different from other areas like energy or health, where old battle lines dictated the terms of engagement and often led to tired answers and debates.

But cyber couldn't remain immune from the Trump effect. And the full implications of that fact will only become clear in the years ahead. Trust in the American system of government had fallen steadily over fifty years, a descent fueled by failures, scandals, and politicians who fanned the flames for their own benefit. Amid many policy failures and disappointments—and little general respect for or recognition of successes—candidate Donald Trump in 2016 capitalized on doubts that "the system" could produce positive results on anything.

The result was utter distrust in "the system" and a demand for faith in one man. A policy approach characterized by a lack of either trust or sustained commitment, as well as a "caudillo" attitude toward leadership in which all sensors responded only to the whims of one man, were antithetical to cybersecurity and ensured growing danger for the digital lives of all Americans.

The discord within the American system was staggering, and yet the president's intentional actions brought even more chaos—which scarcely seemed possible—to relations with US allies overseas. Tighter collaboration among allies was one of the touchstones of cyber policy since the days of Bill Clinton and George W. Bush.

Senate Democratic leader Schumer, on the day of Trump's 2019 State of the Union Address, observed, "The state of the Trump foreign policy is woefully backward, it's inside out. Our allies are alienated and criticized, our adversaries are emboldened and praised. Dictators and strongmen are given license by this administration while our NATO allies receive harsh words."

International cyber relations was a complicated space, and progress could be hard to measure, but cybersecurity professionals were pushing forward on both sides of the Atlantic and the Pacific. Their work was not helped by Donald Trump.

Consider this small episode from the government shutdown of 2018–2019: House Speaker Pelosi said Trump should postpone his State of the Union address, citing security constraints as government employees were furloughed and many Department of Homeland Security employees were working without pay. Politics certainly played a role too, in seeking to deny Trump this stage during the shutdown fight.

Trump retaliated—clearly—by yanking authorization for transportation for the Speaker's planned trip to visit troops in Afghanistan. That trip was to include a stop in Brussels, which the White House portrayed as a holiday.

Referring to the congressional delegation, Pelosi's spokesman tweeted on January 17, 2019, "The CODEL to Afghanistan included a required stop in Brussels for pilot rest. In Brussels, the delegation was scheduled to meet with top NATO commanders, U.S. military leaders and key allies—to affirm the United States' ironclad commitment to the NATO alliance."

The consultation with the European allies would've come amid what John Carlin called an urgent need for "more multilateral action. . . . That's important but it needs leadership, and we're not getting leadership at the presidential level."

Astute observers will recall that DHS Secretary Nielsen's April 2019 firing came after Trump grew incensed that she was meeting with European allies on cyber and other issues, while the president was loudly proclaiming a crisis at the US-Mexico border.

Affirming that commitment to allies was not a priority for the president.

There was also a need for the president to affirm an "ironclad commitment" to his own intelligence services.

As the Foundation for the Defense of Democracies (FDD) noted in an otherwise laudatory report, "One urgent issue to address is the president's refusal to consistently accept the U.S. intelligence community's assessments of Russian cyber operations during the 2016 presidential election. The politicization of the investigation into Russia's cyberattacks and cyber-enabled information operations undermines the bipartisanship necessary to implement effective responses to cyber vulnerabilities not only in U.S. election systems, but across all critical infrastructure."

The very week of the FDD report, Trump got into a spat with the intelligence services again, saying they were wrong about North Korea's ongoing work on nuclear weapons and other issues. The intelligence agency heads raised serious questions about whether North Korea had stopped its nuclear weapons work at all in the aftermath of the first Trump-Kim summit. Trump was incensed at the public suggestions.

Asked by reporters at the White House on January 31, 2019, whether he'd registered his displeasure with intelligence officials directly, the president said, "I did and they said they were totally misquoted and taken out of context. . . . Call them. They said it was Fake News."

The intelligence leaders never said that, and they never retracted their assessments of what North Korea was really doing.

The Trump approach didn't get much better elsewhere on the planet: With China, the strategy was piecemeal and sometimes incoherent, but there were formats and venues for creating a national policy. It was centered on trade, which led to fundamental miscalculations on the potential cybersecurity costs and benefits, but at least there was the semblance of a strategy. With Russia, however, there were investigations that Trump despised, there were sanctions that his government levied on Moscow, but there was no strategy agreed to across the US government.

One lasting cyber impact of the Trump presidency: Perhaps inadvertently, Trump had redefined the concept of cybersecurity to include cyber-aided influence campaigns aimed at Western democracies. The Obama administration looked broadly at cybersecurity as a transformational issue, but it focused on securing the digital highways and lifeline industries like power plants. Election systems weren't designated as critical infrastructure by DHS until the very end of Obama's second term, after the Russians had already completed their mission to wreak havoc in the 2016 campaign and help elect Trump.

A tangible impact was a scramble in 2017 and beyond by state officials, Congress, and the Department of Homeland Security to secure voting machines, computer systems that held voter data, and more, including social media.

Of significance, cybersecurity managed to retain a bipartisan luster in this era of intense partisan strife, said Kiersten Todt, the executive director of President Obama's national cyber commission. In an early 2019 discussion with me, she cited an ongoing commitment to collaboration as key to confronting a range of security challenges.

Todt pointed to the Trump administration's embrace of many elements of the commission's late 2016 report—on the Internet of Things and cyber workforce, for instance—as reflecting a continuous arc from one administration to the next, which helped insulate cybersecurity policy from the political turbulence rattling many other issue areas.

She said Trump's 2017 cyber executive order emphasized priorities similar to those flagged by the Obama administration and noted that former Obama officials served as informal advisers as the Trump executive order was being crafted.

The Obama-appointed Commission on Enhancing National Cybersecurity's December 2016 report was "a foundation to bridge the gap between two administrations—it helped the new administration not waste time and, given the nature of cybersecurity, continuity is very important," Todt said.

And the Trump team didn't waste it, even with fingerprints of former Obama officials all over the product. In fact, the Trump 2017 executive order on cybersecurity was a "terrific transition document," Todt said.

"The workforce piece was very key," she said. "They're defining it very broadly because everybody is part of the cyber workforce. There is a cultural shift that needs to happen, recognizing that everyone has a responsibility."

Todt didn't mention it, but, ironically, the Trump administration was taking a sophisticated view of the cyber workforce at the very time the Trump White House was trashing the morale of the entire federal workforce by making shutdowns—with days, weeks, or even a month-plus of work-without-pay days—the norm for working in the federal government. Well, the sophisticated view of the cyber workforce would end up helping the private sector, which was scooping up government employees fed up with the uncertainty.

The 2016 report also "spelled out how the lines around critical infrastructure are blurred," which ended up looking "prescient in light of Facebook and the 2016 election," Todt said.

"Technologies are impacting our democracy in critical ways," Todt noted. "The commission debated whether we should define 'critical infrastructure'—it was a battle we didn't want to fight given the time demands, but we did say there is a need to think more broadly about what critical infrastructure means."

She noted that the commission report in its introduction said the Internet of Things (IoT) "blurs the lines of critical infrastructure, that was an 'early adapter' statement, no else was saying that yet at the time."

And, Todt said, the report stressed the importance of building security into IoT devices as well as the need to ensure government-industry collaborative structures are in place before an incident takes place.

"The report recognized that security goes beyond physical boundaries, it's more than just transportation infrastructure, for example," she said. "The weak link in a personal device is the weakness" of the whole system.

Todt said the commission's call for a major public education effort "is as relevant now as it was then." There was a concurrent need, she said, "to move security responsibility away from the end user and at the same time educate the end user. You can't entirely remove the consumer from the loop."

But most significantly, for Todt, the first two years of the Trump administration drove home the point that cybersecurity was a nonpartisan issue, noting that Obama officials worked closely with Trump officials on the 2017 executive order.

She questioned the Trump decision to get rid of the White House cybersecurity coordinator post after Rob Joyce left the position in 2018. International participants at the annual 2019 Munich Security Conference were still raising the question of who to contact within the administration in the absence of a coordinator, she said, noting that Michael Daniel was frequently the point of contact for foreign governments.

"It's important to have an individual who is anointed by the president who can deal with other countries on cyber," Todt said.

Todt said strong leadership on cyber from the White House was crucial, even with the "very good" efforts going on across agencies and departments. She cited the Department of Homeland Security's initiatives and leadership on cyber, as well as the cyber work being led at the Department of Energy, as particularly impressive.

"A lot of people are working hard on this issue throughout the administration," Todt said. While the Obama administration decided to have a centralized leadership role at the White House, "the Trump administration is choosing to address cybersecurity through a different vehicle, the leadership of the agencies."

"I'd say you need both," Todt said. "Leadership from the agencies—like what you're seeing with [cyber director Karen] Evans at DOE—combined with leadership from the White House would be very powerful."

The lack of coordination could also be seen in the 2019 executive order on supply chain, she suggested. "We actually don't have a 5G strategy, a strategy that addresses innovation in this digitized world," Todt asserted. "The battle is development of next-generation communications in an open-source environment versus a closed environment. Where is the strategy?"

The supply-chain executive order was a "Band-Aid," she said. "We need a strategy that's based on collaboration with like-minded countries."

That, of course, wasn't a Trump strong suit.

But Todt stressed, "We need a comprehensive global strategy to develop the next generation of telecommunications. It has to go beyond stifling one company like Huawei. Otherwise it's just whack-a-mole."

Ann Beauchesne of the Aspen Institute hit similar notes. "It seems trite to say public-private partnerships are the key to all this, it ebbs and flows, but we have seen some gains," Beauchesne said. "The creation of [the Cybersecurity and Infrastructure Security Agency] is a good step forward—I'm hopeful, because [Director Christopher] Krebs gets it, he's been on the industry and the government side. And I like their supply-chain focus, I think the priorities are right."

Likewise, she said, "looking at national critical functions from a risk perspective is the right way to do it, you have to prioritize." DHS devoted substantial energy to producing a list of national critical functions across industries to inform its infrastructure risk management efforts.

But Beauchesne was worried: The various pieces of an overall cyber strategy still remained to be fashioned into a coherent whole. The Trump administration undermined such an effort by eliminating the White House cyber coordinator position, for instance.

"There was a DOD cybersecurity strategy and a DOE strategy and a DHS strategy, but since [former cyber coordinator Rob] Joyce's departure, how is any of this coordinated?"

Beauchesne added that the coordinator played an important role in reaching out to the private sector. Obama's coordinator "spoke to us all the time and we don't have that right now," she said, referencing Daniel's engagement with industry groups.

Further, she said, "one of the biggest challenges is international coordination, and when the president contradicts the intelligence community, that doesn't help in the relationship with our allies. A year or two ago we were talking about international norms, and what are we talking about now, since they got rid of the White House coordinator and the State Department [cyber] coordinator?"

This administration, like many before it, "focuses on the crisis *du jour*," she said, "which is why it's important to have someone in that role to focus and coordinate on cyber. It needs to come from the White House."

In the absence of presidential vision on the issue, Beauchesne said tensions remained over the fundamental question of whether cybersecurity should be addressed through regulation or collaboration, warning that rules "shouldn't be written in a vacuum."

She said the US Chamber, major trade associations, industry-based information sharing and analysis centers, and others "are all engaging, but you still need somebody to bring all these pieces together. We don't want to go back to silos, we want cross-pollination, but where is that supposed to happen?"

Beauchesne said, "There are all these groups doing good work, but why isn't there more focus on it at the highest level of government? We need a sustained focus, something ongoing that people will pay attention to."

Half jokingly, she suggested Tom Brady and Beyoncé for a cybersecurity public service campaign along the lines of antismoking and auto seatbelt efforts in the past.

"Behaviors need to be encouraged on a sustained basis," she said.

With episodes like the global "NotPetya" attack as a backdrop, Carlin said a cybersecurity initiative on the scale of the World War II "Manhattan Project" would be the appropriate response, given the growing threat in cyberspace and ever-larger potential consequences.

"There was a completely inadequate response to NotPetya," Carlin said of the 2017 cyberattack—attributed to Russia by the CIA—that was aimed at

Ukraine but ended up devastating banking, transportation, and other systems throughout the world.

"They used a weapon of mass destruction and it got no attention from the president," Carlin said. The White House issued a short statement attributing the attack to Russia in February 2018, eight months after it took place.

"A Manhattan-style project would be a good idea," he said in an interview with Inside Cybersecurity.

"The thing that concerns me now," Carlin continued, "is that no, we are not on the right path considering the degree of vulnerability. The issue is not getting the national attention it deserves, in terms of congressional action, executive leadership, strengthening alliances, taking advantage of technological innovation and doing things like building security into 5G" networks.

"I hope this becomes a big issue for the presidential candidates," he offered.

An outsider appointed to lead a very large organization, Donald John Trump shook things up and thus produced forward movement in cyber areas like empowering the military and industry, as well as in holding agencies responsible for patching the holes. Tangible steps were taken and boxes could be checked by the president's people. Many cybersecurity professionals and policy leaders willfully exercised a brand of tunnel vision as they achieved incremental progress in specific cyber areas.

And many of these steps were continuations of President Obama's policies. That made sense, in an incremental way, as did the recommitment to collaboration with partners in industry and states, for example.

But where it came apart began with the lack of an overarching vision for cyber—from the president or vice president. DHS was shaping a pretty good strategic outlook and approach, and the Pentagon was all over the issue too. But where was that focus of leadership?

Was this important? Couldn't the positive steps be tallied to render a verdict of success on the Trump presidency's cyber record?

Consider this piece by the *Washington Post*'s well-informed and insightful cyber writer Joseph Marks on March 12, 2019:

> When President Trump took the oath of office in January 2017, cybersecurity industry officials were anxious—to put it mildly.
>
> They fretted about the possibility of whiplash-inducing policy shifts that would scrap years of progress protecting government and industry from cyberattacks.

Marks and the rest of a small group of cybersecurity reporters in the nation's capital had been following these anxieties through two years of sometimes stomach-jolting political upheavals.

> What a difference two years can make.
>
> Cybersecurity industry leaders and former government officials are now heaping praise on the Trump administration's digital security policies—describing them as smart and measured.
>
> In fact—from how the government protects its own networks and critical infrastructure to how it cooperates with allies—experts at the RSA conference said the best word to describe Trump cybersecurity policy is continuity.
>
> "It's so remarkable I almost don't want to call it out—the consistency you have [in cybersecurity policy]," Ryan Gillis, vice president for cyber strategy at Palo Alto Networks, told me in San Francisco.

The continuity was undeniable. And the willingness to break out of the Obama mold in areas like more fully utilizing military cyber power and in demanding that agencies secure their networks—in essence, putting a sign in the window naming the official in charge—deserved respect.

But.

The success of the Trump cyber policy in most ways was rooted in its continuity with the Obama policies, as Kiersten Todt noted in Marks's story. The main departure was in the deterrence realm, making greater use of cyber weapons in the military's hands and forcefully arresting or indicting bad actors. On the military side, the cyberattack on the Russian Internet Research Agency was the main piece of evidence of this new willingness to "fight," followed by reported actions aimed at Iran. Indictments and sanctions were tools also used by the Obama team. And who's to say the Obama administration's policy evolution wouldn't have ended up, eventually, with steps like ordering Cyber Command to suppress the Internet Research Agency?

But all that policy consistency was matched with all the baggage Donald Trump carried with him into any discussion.

Was it worth it?

For all the positive work on cyber at DHS, the department was under a permanent cloud because of Trump's outsized and perhaps unrealistic demands on immigration. The Defense Department was moving—effectively, by many accounts—into a more pronounced cybersecurity role, but it often seemed to operate permanently under an "acting secretary."

Adam Schiff wasn't exactly a neutral observer, but he nailed something with this tweet on April 9, 2019:

> A quick update on our national security leadership:
>
> Defense Secretary: Vacant. DHS Secretary: Vacant. UN Ambassador: Vacant. FEMA Director: Vacant. Secret Service Director: Vacant. ICE Director: Vacant. DHS Deputy: Vacant.
>
> President: Present, but unaccounted for.

That picked up more than ten thousand likes in a half hour.

The same day, Democratic leader Schumer said on the Senate floor, "Now today the watch word in the executive branch is chaos. This chaos stems from one source and one source only, President Donald Trump, his extreme agenda, and America's paying the price."

It was another partisan voice, to be sure, but at least a few Republicans and industry representatives were fretting about the chaotic environment too, though most were unwilling to publicly articulate their fears.

Chaos was part of the price of admission with President Trump.

Trump's performance was "very disappointing," said one former national security official who was on the front lines of cybersecurity efforts and spoke to the author on background. "He has been affirmatively harmful through his use of the bully pulpit. After incredible work to attribute the election cyber-attacks to Russia, he casts doubt and criticizes his own intelligence services. He downgrades cybersecurity in the White House. He's not leading on cyber either internationally or domestically."

There was "incredible work going on by cybersecurity professionals," the source said, calling this "one good sign."

But overall, "it's not good."

Cybersecurity, meanwhile, as an issue and as a national challenge, kept evolving at its own rate.

Early in 2019, Vikram Phatak of NSS Labs was deep in conversation in a corporate suite on the twentieth floor of a San Francisco hotel. Within a few blocks were about thirty thousand cybersecurity professionals, swarming around the annual RSA Security Conference at the Moscone Center. He was talking about the amazing revolution being delivered by the Internet of Things and gestured toward the tall windows and the panoramic view. It was or would be all connected, within a handful of years—the lighting and heating, the elevators, the streetlights, the refrigerators, TVs, cars . . .

And where was the strategic thought, where was the leadership to inform the public of both the benefits and the challenges and responsibilities that would come with this brave new digital world? Actress Helen Mirren opened the 2019 conference that day with a multimedia presentation in which she hailed the cybersecurity community as heroes. Helen Mirren got it.

Where was the president to expound on that message?

"It seems like we're in an in-between state right now," Phatak said, "and things are about to change dramatically."

He pointed to the utterly unpredicted changes brought by introduction of the iPhone in the summer of 2007—including creation of whole new industries and services—and said 5G would cause a "huge paradigm shift" by enabling a vast expansion of the Internet of Things.

Phatak gestured toward the city skyline and said San Francisco wouldn't manage its own new "smart" system, but would hire contractors and subcontractors. "From a security perspective, you can't do it on your own anymore either. Within three years [businesses and cities] will have to have security services for everything."

A plethora of policy questions quickly rose to the surface, he said, including related security and privacy standards, possible rules around whether foreign interests should manage the digital infrastructure of US cities, and more.

The stakes and dangers would rise exponentially in the next few years.

"It's about cyber having an impact on the physical world—the kind of attacks that are getting through today just won't be acceptable anymore," he said. "The lights going off, the heat going off, these things will be a problem" as connectivity within the IoT grows, he said, "and people's perceptions will change."

And that was going to mean change in the way cybersecurity firms operate, he suggested. "They're going to have to adapt too, the standard they've been held to is going to change—by customer demand!"

He pointed to two converging factors: the impact of cyber failures would move from the digital to the physical space, and as more and more elements of daily life were interconnected, security firms would have to make their services much more user friendly.

"Failure right now is lots of digital things, but what happens when the heat goes out or cars start crashing into each other? The consequences can be really grave."

The Moscone Center next door had over seven hundred thousand square feet of exhibit space, and during RSA week it was filled with the best and the shiniest of what the security industry had to offer, calibrated for what Phatak called "MBLE" (maximum blinking light effect).

But Phatak was deeply troubled about whether the cybersecurity ecosystem was ready for "the switch to get flipped" to this new era.

"Like with the iPhone, with 'Smart Cities' the world is going to be so much better, no one will want to go back," he said. "But it means the solutions that need to be brought to bear don't exist today. A couple of companies see it coming, and a lot of people are selling buggy whips."

Looking in the direction of Washington, DC, he downplayed the Trump administration's efforts to get ahead of this looming transformation. After nixing the White House cyber coordinator position, "who's thinking about these things?" he asked.

"This is the kind of stuff government should be getting ahead of and I just don't see it," Phatak said. "Three years from now, it'll really start to take shape. In five years, it will have happened."

Mike Echols, the former DHS official, was eyeing the big picture too.

"When I left DHS, I had a mission to mature cybersecurity," he said. Echols had the connections in government and industry, and wanted to "bring together communities," raise awareness, and "call out the people and organizations out there that should be taking leadership roles and aren't."

That was no small challenge.

"People in government are afraid to step out and cite problems because they're afraid of being fired," he said. "In the private sector, people are afraid to speak up because they're afraid of regulation. And political people tend to mosey about on cybersecurity—the people they regulate are also funding their campaigns."

What was missing right now was leadership, he said, starting at the presidential level.

Opportunity was out there, a potential "win-win" to strengthen the cyber workforce, heighten awareness throughout the public, get cyber tools into the right hands, and—pulling it all together—create vast new "cybersecurity economy" opportunities in disadvantaged communities and across the country. They would be called "cybersecurity zones," patterned after an existing economic opportunity zone program.

Echols saw a chance to go beyond general outreach and "STEM classes" to "create an ecosystem that actually starts to do economic development, that would involve cyber awareness campaigns and training targeted at kids, seniors, small business and executives. A lot of these things are occurring in pockets, but it all comes back to a lack of leadership," he said. "There's no face of cybersecurity in this country, there are no commercials, public service announcements. Why should anybody care?"

But they should, of course. There's "no central place to seek help" when people and businesses are hacked, he said. There was never a face attached to statistics showing that hacked businesses often go under, he said.

"Where's the list of companies that go out of business?" Echols asked. "Show that this is happening." Echols proposed publishing such a list when he was at DHS, he said, but the idea was shot down over privacy concerns.

That led back to the cybersecurity zones, which would provide a "physical presence" across the country. "My goal is to create cybersecurity zones throughout the country, which would create a value proposition down the line," Echols said.

He created a firm—MAX Cybersecurity—to serve as the vehicle for this ambitious project, in which "I'm trying to show that a public innovation initiative can also be profitable."

At its core, Echols said, "I'm promoting the idea that cybersecurity is risk management—vulnerabilities-threats-consequences—and taking that message to the youngest citizens all the way to senior citizens. We'll format this in a way that people can ingest it—it's like telling people to look both ways before crossing the street so you don't get hit by a car."

But again, Echols stressed, "the biggest problem is a lack of leadership."

He explained, "On Wall Street, they listen to the Fed and every word makes a difference. The public hears so much noise, people prioritize. If there isn't one word on cyber from the White House, in commercials, that makes it harder for me."

Cybersecurity was "more like a public health issue than a criminal or terrorism issue—there's a reason we call them viruses," he said. That was one way to get the public's attention. But again, it took leadership.

"There is currently an opportunity that may not exist again," Echols said.

"It takes leadership to move companies off the block, to pull government agencies in the same direction," Echols went on to say. "That's what the White House cyber czar was meant to do. If you eliminate that position, what message are you sending to the public?"

Further, he said, "You don't have to breach an election system, you just have to create doubt. When the president won't say the breach occurred, he's created doubt that's disruptive."

The Trump effect on cyber, Echols said, was "sowing doubt" and "removing leadership."

"Our security comes from continuously moving forward and he's created a scenario where we don't move forward," Echols asserted. "We're sitting in a vulnerable space."

On May 3, 2019, President Trump spoke with reporters in the Oval Office as he met with the prime minister of the Slovak Republic. The White House had let it be known that Trump held an hour-plus phone conversation with Putin that day.

A reporter asked whether the Mueller Report had come up with Putin.

"We discussed it," Trump said. "He actually sort of smiled when he said something to the effect that it started off as a mountain and it ended up being a mouse. But he knew that because he knew there was no collusion whatsoever. So, pretty much, that's what it was."

Did he ask or warn Putin not to meddle in the 2020 elections?

"We didn't discuss that. Really, we didn't discuss it. We discussed five or six things. We also—we went into detail on various things, especially, I would say, the nuclear. Especially, maybe, Venezuela. We talked about North Korea at great length, and pretty much that's it."

And that was it. Beyond the Oval Office, what was at stake for the United States, and the world, when it came to cyber in the age of Trump?

The fate of digital commerce, with the related questions of the wealth of nations and who would control the twenty-first-century economy, was surely in play.

Rules around privacy in a digital world were a giant question mark.

The United States' preeminent position in global economic and political affairs was on the line.

But the stakes in the global game of cybersecurity were actually much higher than any of that. The 2016 election hack demonstrated that it was really about the fate of democracy in the digitized world.

Allowing cyber chaos to reign actually undermined democracies and empowered the tyrants who tightly controlled what their citizens were allowed to see. In a zero-sum game among nations, the liberal democracies would be the losers. The renegades of the dark internet would chip away at the rules-based society for their own gain, but the Putins of the world would be the real winners. And the tyrants would certainly stamp out these "rebels" whenever they ceased to serve a purpose, just like Xi Jinping squashed China's freelance hackers and then let them reemerge when useful to the regime.

Maybe the tyrants wouldn't be able to control the dark web either, over the long haul, but they could align with it long enough to undermine and perhaps topple a flawed but rules-based society.

America and countries sharing democratic values can still avoid that fate.

It will require the direct attention of the president. It can be framed as a moonshot, a battle for cyberspace or a quest for the digital future—the moniker is irrelevant. The point is that the top officer must imbue the mission with value and importance; there are too many conflicting demands for attention across government and society for the president to simply delegate cyber to the second and third tiers of government. This is the existential issue for democracy in the twenty-first century.

Just as the markets look to the Fed chairman for signals about what's important in the economy, the government and citizenry look to the president for similar signals on the issues that really matter. Is securing cyberspace as important as building a wall on the Mexican border? Is it as important as the US trade balance with China?

It will require a unity of purpose and trust across government, including respect for the workforce. The policy environment must be both stable and creative. A White House coordinator empowered by the president is essential. An entire Department of Cybersecurity would be reasonable.

It will require trustworthy partnerships with allies internationally and collaborations at home where responsibilities are well defined between government and the private sector and each party fulfills its obligations. The times demand a consistent approach to cyber adversaries, as defined by the threat they pose to the freedom and security of an open, digitized society.

Like every other issue in America, it will require respect for different, even conflicting, views and bearing in mind that, when it comes to cyber, we're obviously all in this together. The cyber community has avoided the factionalism that stalls and stagnates policies in other areas. Rather than descending into the mire, cybersecurity can still be a platform for enlightening political engagement and consensus building.

A war has been launched in cyberspace by geopolitical adversaries and a powerful criminal underworld. It's a twilight battle, as John F. Kennedy said of the Cold War, often fought on the margins and in the shadows, often with average citizens unaware they are right in the middle of it.

But make no mistake about it: Cyberspace is burning, even as President Trump spends an amiable hour chatting with his friend Vladimir Putin.

Acknowledgments

THIS WORK WAS MADE POSSIBLE by generous and long-running support from Alan Sosenko, the owner and founder of Inside Washington Publishers (IWP) and one of the great champions of journalistic excellence and independence. Alan has created a news business and atmosphere over four-plus decades that serves readers with nonbiased insights on how government actually works. IWP has been a home and a launching pad for generations of reporters and editors.

I gratefully acknowledge the contributions of colleagues to Inside Cybersecurity, including cofounder Rick Weber and reporter Mariam Baksh, as well as former colleague Maggie Miller, all of whom are cited in the body of this work. But every reporter whose byline has graced the digital pages of @InsideCyber has brought great energy and dedication to exploring the proposition that cybersecurity is a unique space in American politics and policy.

The work of cyber and security reporters Ellen Nakashima, Tim Starks, Joe Marks, and Dustin Voltz, among others, has contributed substantially to the policy discussion and is cited throughout the book.

Likewise, special thanks are due to sources from government, industry, think tanks, public-interest organizations, and others who took time to share their insights and continue to engage on the front lines of the battle for cyberspace.

Bibliographical Essay

Chapter 1

Candidate Donald Trump's views on cyber deterrence were reported by me in October 2016 in Inside Cybersecurity.

Information on the FBI's joint task force on cyber can be found here: https://www.fbi.gov/investigate/cyber/national-cyber-investigative-joint-task-force.

A July 12, 2017, article in *Infosecurity Magazine* discussed data breaches affecting guests at Trump hotels: https://www.infosecurity-magazine.com/news/trump-hotels-hit-with-third-data. Tara Seals, "Trump Hotels Hit with Third Data Breach in Three Years," July 12, 2017.

A *Fortune* article of September 23, 2016, discusses the Trump International Hotels Management settlement with New York State over data breaches: https://fortune.com/2016/09/23/trump-hotels-settles-new-york-data-breaches/. Reuters, "Trump Hotels Settles with N.Y. Attorney General over Data Breaches," September 23, 2016.

Matthew Scholl of the National Institute of Standards and Technology discussed cyber issues on a panel at the 2019 RSA Security Conference in San Francisco in March 2019.

President-elect Donald Trump's comments on cyber in December 2016 were covered by GovTech.com in a story that can be accessed here: http://www.govtech.com/blogs/lohrmann-on-cybersecurity/president-trump-on-cybersecurity.html. Dan Lohrmann, "President Trump on Cybersecurity," January 20, 2017.

Jeremy Batterman of Trustwave discussed cyber issues with me during a February 2019 interview at his Chicago office.

Vikram Phatak, founder of and then-CEO of NSS Labs, was interviewed by me for Inside Cybersecurity at the 2019 RSA Security Conference and separately in 2018: https://insidecybersecurity.com/daily-news/messages-black-hat-cybersecurity-tools-are-better-and-risk-worse. "Messages from Black Hat: Cybersecurity Tools Are Better, and the Risk Is Worse," August 15, 2018.

Politico in May 2018 reported on White House staff concerns about President Trump's use of devices: https://www.politico.com/story/2018/05/21/trump-phone-security-risk-hackers-601903. Eliana Johnson, Emily Stephenson, and Daniel Lippman, "'Too Inconvenient': Trump Goes Rogue on Phone Security," May 21, 2018.

The "NotPetya" attack was discussed extensively on a "cryptographers panel" at RSA on March 5, 2019.

The Seoul Olympics attack was examined in an article by the British newspaper *The Telegraph*: https://www.telegraph.co.uk/news/2018/02/25/russian-hackers-pose-north-koreans-launch-cyberattack-winter/. Harriet Alexander and Julian Ryall, "Russian Hackers Posed as North Koreans to Launch Cyberattack on Winter Olympics, Claims US," February 25, 2018.

The VPNFilter malware was discussed at RSA on March 5, 2019.

A CNET.com article discussed the Exactis hack: https://www.cnet.com/news/exactis-340-million-people-may-have-been-exposed-in-bigger-breach-than-equifax/. Abrar al-Heeti, "Exactis Said to Have Exposed 340 Million Records, More Than Equifax Breach," June 28, 2018.

The blog by security writer David Bisson can be found here: https://www.tripwire.com/state-of-security/security-data-protection/over-4-5-billion-records-breached-in-h1-2018-finds-report/. "Over 4.5 Billion Records Breached in H1 2018, Report Finds," October 9, 2018.

CBS News covered the Tribune Publishing attack here: https://www.cbsnews.com/news/tribune-publishing-company-cyberattack-affects-newspapers-distribution/?ftag=CNM-00-10aac3a. Caroline Linton, "Cyberattack Hits Major U.S. Newspapers and Affects Distribution," December 30, 2018.

A CNET.com article delves into "WannaCry" here: https://www.cnet.com/news/wannacry-wannacrypt-uiwix-ransomware-everything-you-need-to-know/. Ian Sherr, "WannaCry Ransomware: Everything You Need to Know," May 19, 2017.

Vox.com explains the Baltimore City hack here: https://www.vox.com/recode/2019/5/21/18634505/baltimore-ransom-robbinhood-mayor-jack-young-hackers. Emily Stewart, "Hackers Have Been Holding the City of Baltimore's Computers Hostage for 2 Weeks," May 21, 2019.

A wrap-up of 2019 hacks, including the one targeting ASUS computers, is provided here: https://cybersecurityventures.com/cybercrime-diary-q2-2019-whos-hacked-latest-data-breaches-and-cyberattacks/. John P. Mello Jr., "Cybercrime Diary, Q2 2019: Who's Hacked? Latest Data Breaches and Cyberattacks," April 2, 2019.

"The Dark Side of Asia: An Inside Look into Asia's Growing Underground World" was released in August 2018 at Black Hat USA by IntSights, Itay Kozuch's cybersecurity firm, which has offices in Tel Aviv, Singapore, Amsterdam, Dallas, and New York. Kozuch discussed cyber threats in an article published by Inside Cybersecurity on August 15, 2018.

Tim Erlin of Tripwire discussed that firm's 2018 "State of Cyber Hygiene Report" in an article published by Inside Cybersecurity on August 9, 2018.

Darren Guccione, CEO of the security firm Keeper, was interviewed by me at his Chicago office in February 2019.

The *Washington Post* reported on January 11, 2019, on Trump's comments comparing congressional Democratic leaders unfavorably with the leadership of the Chinese Communist Party. The story can be found here: https://www.washingtonpost.com/opinions/trump-doesnt-know-the-meaning-of-the-word-honorable/2019/01/11/288bfa58-15c6-11e9-b6ad-9cfd62dbb0a8_story.html?utm_term=.676ca9b028ed. Dana Milbank, "Trump's Bizarre Statement on China Dishonors Us All," January 11, 2019.

The E&E News story on the incident affecting Western Electric grid operations can be found here: https://www.eenews.net/stories/1060242741. Blake Sobczak, "'Cyber Event' Disrupted U.S. Grid Networks—DOE," April 30, 2019.

Chapter 2

Marine Corps general John Kelly's confirmation process was covered by me on January 11, 2019, in Inside Cybersecurity.

Robert Joyce's experience at the National Security Agency was detailed in a 2017 article by FCW.com, available here: https://fcw.com/articles/2017/03/15/joyce-white-house-cyber.aspx. Sean D. Carberry, "NSA Vet Rob Joyce to Lead Cyber at White House," March 15, 2017.

Homeland Security adviser Tom Bossert's speech on cybersecurity priorities was reported by me in Inside Cybersecurity on March 15, 2017.

President Trump's May 11, 2017, executive order on cybersecurity can be found here: https://www.whitehouse.gov/presidential-actions/presidential-executive-order-strengthening-cybersecurity-federal-networks-critical-infrastructure/.

The cybersecurity implications of the WikiLeaks release of alleged CIA hacking tools were discussed by me in Inside Cybersecurity on March 8, 2017.

Virginia Tech's Charles Clancy shared his observations about the WikiLeaks revelations in a March 2017 email to reporters.

Foreign Policy's May 2017 story on a possible White House investigation of the Department of Homeland Security's "Automated Indicator Sharing" program is available here: https://foreignpolicy.com/2017/05/18/trump-team-planning-possible-retaliation-for-classified-leak-allegations/. Jenna McLaughlin, "Trump Team Planning Possible Retaliation for Classified Leak Allegations," May 18, 2017.

I reported in Inside Cybersecurity on June 9, 2017, regarding possible policy fallout after former FBI director James Comey's Senate testimony.

An article in *Wired* in August 2017 explained the significance of elevating US Cyber Command to the status of unified combat command: https://www.wired.com/story/cyber-command-elevated/. Jim Watson, "The US Gives Cyber Command the Status It Deserves," August 19, 2017.

The White House statement on Cyber Command is available here: https://www.whitehouse.gov/briefings-statements/statement-president-donald-j-trump-elevation-cyber-command/. I covered cyber implications of the 2017 North Korea crisis in Inside Cybersecurity on September 7, 2017.

Representative Patrick McHenry (R-NC) made his comments on the impact of the Equifax hack at a February 26, 2019, House Financial Services Committee hearing. The Equifax CEO's op-ed explaining his company's actions was covered by me in Inside Cybersecurity on September 13, 2017.

CNBC's article on mysteries in the aftermath of the Equifax hack can be found here: https://www.cnbc.com/2019/02/13/equifax-mystery-where-is-the-data.html. Kate Fazzini, "The Great Equifax Mystery: 17 Months Later, the Stolen Data Has Never Been Found, and Experts Are Starting to Suspect a Spy Scheme," February 13, 2019.

CNBC reported on the move to downgrade Equifax's rating here: https://www.cnbc.com/2019/05/22/moodys-downgrades-equifax-outlook-to-negative-cites-cybersecurity.html?__source=twitter%7Cmain. Kate Fazzini, "Equifax Just Became the First Company to Have Its Outlook Downgraded for a Cyber Attack," May 22, 2019.

Chapter 3

The "one-team, one-fight" approach was articulated by former White House cyber adviser Melissa Hathaway and is discussed extensively in *Hacked: The*

Inside Story of America's Struggle to Secure Cyberspace, published in 2016 by Rowman & Littlefield.

Distil Networks's "bad bots" report can be found here: https://resources.distilnetworks.com/white-paper-reports/bad-bot-report-2019. I covered reactions to Tom Bossert's firing as homeland security adviser in an April 12, 2018, article in Inside Cybersecurity, and reactions to eliminating the cyber coordinator position in a May 16 Inside Cybersecurity article.

Mashable.com provided a detailed explanation of the ZTE sanctions in a 2018 article: https://mashable.com/2018/06/07/us-ends-zte-sanctions-trump/. Rachel Kraus, "Welp, the U.S. Is Already Ending Its ZTE Sanctions. Here's How It Happened," June 7, 2018. I interviewed key players on perceptions of a cyber leadership vacuum for an article in Inside Cybersecurity on May 17, 2018.

Chapter 4

The article by David Corn and Dan Friedman on the Mueller report appeared in *Mother Jones* on March 8, 2019: https://www.motherjones.com/politics/2019/03/robert-mueller-has-raised-big-trump-russia-questions-will-his-report-answer-them/. "Robert Mueller Has Raised Big Trump-Russia Questions. Will His Report Answer Them?"

The *Washington Post*'s Michael Birnbaum reported on expectations heading into the NATO summit in a July 8, 2018, article: https://www.washingtonpost.com/world/europe/ahead-of-nato-summit-allies-wonder-will-nato-survive-trump/2018/07/08/3af62604-8134-11e8-b3b5-b61896f90919_story.html?utm_term=.22eb4d2de44b. "Ahead of NATO Summit, Allies Wonder: Will NATO Survive Trump?"

Christopher Painter, Anne Beauchesne, and Bruce McConnell discussed the upcoming Trump-Putin summit in interviews with me for a July 16 article in Inside Cybersecurity.

The text of the Trump-Putin news conference in Helsinki can be accessed here on CNN.com: https://www.cnn.com/2018/07/16/politics/trump-putin-news-conference-transcript/index.html. "READ: The Full Trump-Putin News Conference Transcript."

Reactions to the *New York Times* article on the FBI investigation on whether Trump could be a Russian "asset" are found in this Yahoo News story: https://www.yahoo.com/news/u-house-democrats-eye-reported-fbi-probe-trump-025945223.html. David Morgan and Timothy Gardner, "U.S. House Democrats Eye Reported FBI Probe of Trump," January 13, 2019.

Chapter 5

The August 15, 2018, *Wall Street Journal* article on reversal of Presidential Policy Directive-20 was titled "Trump, Seeking to Relax Rules on U.S. Cyberattacks, Reverses Obama Directive" and was written by Dustin Volz: https://www.wsj.com/articles/trump-seeking-to-relax-rules-on-u-s-cyberattacks-reverses-obama-directive-1534378721?tesla=y&mod=djemalertNEWS.

The Foundation for the Defense of Democracies report discussing Trump administration deterrence efforts is available here: https://www.fdd.org/wp-content/uploads/2019/01/fdd-report-trump-midterm-assessment.pdf. John Hannah and David Adesnik, "Midterm Assessment: The Trump Administration's Foreign and National Security Policies," January 2019.

The CATO Institute study of offensive cyber warfare is available here: https://www.cato.org/publications/policy-analysis/myth-cyber-offense-case-restraint. Brandon Valeriano and Benjamin Jensen, "The Myth of the Cyber Offense: The Case for Restraint," January 15, 2019.

I reported on the release of the Trump administration's national cybersecurity strategy in Inside Cybersecurity on September 20, 2018.

Politico's Tim Starks discussed the Cyber Deterrence Initiative in a March 20, 2019, report: https://www.politico.com/newsletters/morning-cybersecurity/2019/03/20/top-state-cyber-official-talks-huawei-deterrence-552356. "Top State Cyber Official Talks Huawei, Deterrence."

The January 11, 2019, *New York Times* article on the FBI Trump-Russia probe is available here: https://www.nytimes.com/2019/01/11/us/politics/fbi-trump-russia-inquiry.html. Adam Goldman, Michael S. Schmidt, and Nicolas Fandos, "F.B.I. Opened Inquiry into Whether Trump Was Secretly Working on Behalf of Russia."

Washington Post writer Max Boot's January 13, 2019, article on allegations about Trump and Russia is available here: https://www.washingtonpost.com/opinions/here-are-18-reasons-why-trump-could-be-a-russian-asset/2019/01/13/45b1b250-174f-11e9-88fe-f9f77a3bcb6c_story.html?utm_term=.828b90e4bd03. "Here Are 18 Reasons Why Trump Could Be a Russian Asset."

The *Washington Post* February 26, 2019, article on the first-of-its-kind offensive action by US Cyber Command is available here: https://www.washingtonpost.com/world/national-security/us-cyber-command-operation-disrupted-internet-access-of-russian-troll-factory-on-day-of-2018-midterms/2019/02/26/1827fc9e-36d6-11e9-af5bb51b7ff322e9_story.html?utm_term=.4dc8168ac37c. Ellen Nakashima, "U.S. Cyber Command Operation Disrupted Internet Access of Russian Troll Factory on Day of 2018 Midterms."

Paul Rosenzweig and James Lewis discussed offensive action in cyberspace on March 6, 2019, at the RSA Security Conference.

Chapter 6

I covered the Department of Homeland Security's July 31, 2018, cybersecurity summit in New York City for Inside Cybersecurity.

The *Washington Post* article on Homeland Security secretary Kirstjen Nielsen's work on the Hurricane Katrina disaster as a staffer during the George W. Bush administration is available here: https://www.washingtonpost.com/world/national-security/trumps-pick-for-dhs-chief-was-at-center-of-katrina-disaster/2017/10/14/1a8f12a2-b067-11e7-9e58-e6288544af98_story.html?utm_term=.eaf80c79b407. "Trump's Pick for DHS Chief Was at Center of Katrina Disaster," October 14, 2017. I interviewed former DHS attorney Allison Bender, now of the ZwillGen law firm, on the sidelines of the 2018 Black Hat conference in Las Vegas. I interviewed Trustwave's Bill Rucker at the 2019 RSA conference.

Information on current cybersecurity job openings is updated here: https://www.cyberseek.org/heatmap.html.

Politico's article on government shutdown impacts at the Department of Justice is available here: https://www.politico.com/newsletters/morning-cybersecurity. Tim Starks, "Previewing Lawmaker's Rest-of-Year Cyber Agenda," September 5, 2019.

The April 9, 2019, *Washington Post* article on Stephen Miller and the firing of DHS Secretary Nielsen is available here: https://www.washingtonpost.com/politics/twelve-days-of-chaos-inside-the-trump-white-houses-growing-panic-to-contain-the-border-crisis/2019/04/09/8ca5ade2-5a11-11e9-a00e-050dc7b82693_story.html?utm_term=.e1f8da406b15. David Nakamura, Josh Dawsey, and Seung Min Kim, "12 Days of Chaos: Inside the Trump White House's Growing Panic to Contain the Border Crisis."

The May 17, 2019, Daily Beast article on Cybersecurity and Infrastructure Security Agency employees being encouraged to volunteer at the border is available here: https://www.thedailybeast.com/department-of-homeland-security-urges-cybersecurity-staff-to-deploy-to-border-instead. Betsy Woodruff and Sam Brodey, "DHS Urges Cybersecurity Staff to 'Deploy' to Border Instead," May 18, 2019.

Chapter 7

Former Federal Trade Commission member Terrell McSweeny's op-ed in *The Hill* newspaper is available here: https://thehill.com/blogs/pundits-blog/technology/322312-fcc-should-not-leave-broadband-privacy-rules-to-ftc?mkt_tok=eyJpIjoiT1RrNE1XSm1NVE5rWkRJMyIsInQiOiJLbEt6TWM3cTMyTU5cL3dOTzB2ZWJvVW1TY0w4SVR5NUNJckdmSWo4UH

FaUWdPb0RsbStZckJRKzVCRElqTEJSc3llc1hpMmRSV3JLTHJVMzNzQ0pEOUg3cHVMOHJTQlJQUU9TSUpZTVJxREZqcjByMUZBZkdHZWNMY2JqVE1mSmgifQ%3D%3D. "FCC Should Not Leave Broadband Privacy Rules to FTC," March 5, 2017.

An explanation of the US 9th Circuit Court of Appeals' February 2018 "common carrier" decision is available here from the *Harvard Journal of Law and Technology*: https://jolt.law.harvard.edu/digest/ftc-v-at-t-9th-circuit-broadens-ftcs-regulatory-authority-with-regards-to-the-common-carrier-exemption. Nati Hyojin Kim, "FTC v. AT&T: 9th Circuit Broadens FTC's Regulatory Authority with Regards to the Common Carrier Exemption," March 13, 2018.

The Axios article on a National Security Council memo suggesting a nationalized effort to build 5G networks is available here: https://www.axios.com/trump-team-debates-nationalizing-5g-network-f1e92a49-60f2-4e3e-acd4-f3eb03d910ff.html. Jonathan Swan, David McCabe, Ina Fried, and Kim Hart, "Scoop: Trump Team Considers Nationalizing 5G Network," January 28, 2018.

Former FCC chairman Tom Wheeler's blog on the 5G nationalization idea is available here: https://www.brookings.edu/blog/techtank/2018/01/29/building-a-secure-5g-network-without-nationalization/. "Building a Secure 5G Network without Nationalization," January 29, 2018.

A report on David Redl's departure from the Commerce Department is available here: https://www.benton.org/headlines/ntia-director-david-redl-resigns. John McKinnon, "NTIA Director David Redl Resigns," May 10, 2019.

Hacked: The Inside Story of America's Struggle to Secure Cyberspace, published in 2016 by Rowman & Littlefield, offers an extensive account of 2014–2015 efforts to develop a cybersecurity strategy for the telecom sector.

The January 2019 FierceTelecom report article on DDoS attacks is available here: https://www.fiercetelecom.com/telecom/report-two-thirds-ddos-attacks-take-aim-at-communication-service-providers. Mike Robuck, "Report: Two-Thirds of DDoS Attacks Take Aim at Communications Service Providers," January 21, 2019.

Chapter 8

Inside Cybersecurity reported here on the administration's "moonshot" initiative: https://insidecybersecurity.com/daily-news/ideas-moonshot-workshop-focus-message-only-you-can-prevent-cyber-attacks. Mariam Baksh, "Ideas at 'Moonshot' Workshop Focus on Message That 'Only You Can Prevent Cyber Attacks,'" April 18, 2019.

The May 30, 2018, Commerce-DHS "Report to the President on Enhancing the Resilience of the Internet and Communications Ecosystem against

Botnets and Other Automated, Distributed Threats" is available here: https://csrc.nist.gov/publications/detail/white-paper/2018/05/30/enhancing-resilience-against-botnets—report-to-the-president/final.

Retired admiral David Simpson provided Inside Cybersecurity with a detailed assessment of the botnet report, reflected in a May 31, 2018, article.

The November 2018 cyber "moonshot" report by the President's National Security and Telecommunications Advisory Committee is available here: https://insidecybersecurity.com/sites/insidecybersecurity.com/files/documents/2018/nov/cs11012018_NSTAC_Moonshot.pdf.

Inside Cybersecurity's Mariam Baksh reported on the "moonshot" effort on September 7, 2018.

The military's concerns about the cyber vulnerabilities of civilian infrastructure are discussed in *Hacked: The Inside Story of America's Struggle to Secure Cyberspace*, published in 2016 by Rowman & Littlefield.

Chapter 9

Information on the "Paris Call for Trust and Security in Cyberspace" is available here: https://www.diplomatie.gouv.fr/en/french-foreign-policy/digital-diplomacy/france-and-cyber-security/article/cybersecurity-paris-call-of-12-november-2018-for-trust-and-security-in.

Inside Cybersecurity reported in November 2018 on the effort to craft global norms of behavior in cyberspace: https://insidecybersecurity.com/daily-news/us-bucks-business-backed-paris-cyber-call-think-tank-produces-cyber-norms-principles. Charlie Mitchell, "As U.S. Bucks Business-Backed Paris Cyber 'Call,' Think Tank Produces Cyber Norms Principles."

The *Washington Post* reported on January 25, 2019, on Microsoft CEO Brad Smith trying to gin up interest in a global code of conduct around cyber: https://www.washingtonpost.com/news/powerpost/paloma/the-cybersecurity-202/2019/01/25/the-cybersecurity-202-microsoft-chief-urges-trump-administration-to-stand-with-democracies-in-cyberspace/5c4a04791b326b29c3778cb7/?utm_term=.2f1d8918b608. Joseph Marks, "The Cybersecurity 202 Microsoft Chief Urges Trump Administration to Stand with Democracies in Cyberspace."

Chapter 10

The *Washington Post* reported on January 19, 2019, about senators' concerns over Chinese technology on railcars built for the Washington, DC,

Metro system: https://www.washingtonpost.com/local/trafficandcommuting/senators-urge-metro-to-guard-against-chinese-spying-in-new-subway-cars/2019/01/19/bd0f2dca-1b53-11e9-8813-cb9dec761e73_story.html. Robert McCartney, "Senators Urge Metro to Guard against Chinese Spying in New Subway Cars."

China Daily reported on *Fortune*'s 2018 "Global 500": http://www.chinadaily.com.cn/a/201807/20/WS5b518b77a310796df4df7b77.html. Zhang Jie, "Global 500: Chinese Companies Race Ahead," July 20, 2018.

The article about hacking in China by Grady Summers of FireEye ran in *Security Week* and is available here: https://www.securityweek.com/china-target-just-us. "China Is a Target, Just Like Us," February 12, 2019.

The *China Daily* article on a China–European Union agreement on reviews of 5G security is available here: http://www.chinadaily.com.cn/a/201903/27/WS5c9a6768a3104842260b2b57.html. Xinhua, "Huawei Welcomes 'Objective and Appropriate Approach' of Brussels' Recommendation on 5G Security," March 27, 2019.

The head of Germany's Federal Office for Information Security discussed Huawei in a July 2019 interview with *Spiegel*: https://www.spiegel.de/international/business/german-cybersecurity-chief-threats-posed-by-huawei-are-manageable-a-1279009.html. Marcel Rosenbach and Wolf Wiedmann-Schmidt, "'The Only Thing That Can Help Is Definitive Action.'"

The January 26, 2019, TechCrunch.com article on whether Huawei products posed cybersecurity risks is available here: https://techcrunch.com/2019/01/26/is-huawei-a-national-security-threat/. Zack Whittaker, "Without Proof, Is Huawei Still a National Security Threat?"

For an extensive examination of Huawei, see the *Los Angeles Times* article of April 10, 2019, "The Man behind Huawei": https://www.latimes.com/projects/la-fi-tn-huawei-5g-trade-war/, by Norman Pearlstine, David Pierson, Robyn Dixon, David S. Cloud, Alice Su, and Max Hao Lu.

Inside Cybersecurity reported on US indictments aimed at China in a December 20, 2018, article.

The CATO Institute report on "cybersecurity or protectionism" is available here: https://www.cato.org/publications/policy-analysis/cybersecurity-or-protectionism-defusing-most-volatile-issue-us-china. Daniel J. Ikenson, "Cybersecurity or Protectionism: Defusing the Most Volatile Issue in the U.S.-China Relationship," July 13, 2017.

The February 18, 2019, *New York Times* article on advances made by Chinese hackers is available here: https://www.nytimes.com/2019/02/18/technology/hackers-chinese-iran-usa.html. "Chinese and Iranian Hackers Renew Their Attacks on U.S. Companies," February 17, 2019.

The March 15, 2019, Rhodium report on the cost of Trump's tariffs on China to the US tech sector is available here: https://rhg.com/research/assessing-the-costs-of-tariffs-on-the-us-ict-industry/. David H. Rosen, Lauren Gloudeman, and Badri Narayanan Gopalakrishnan, "Assessing the Costs of Tariffs on the US ICT Industry: Modeling US China Tariffs," March 15, 2019.

The March 12, 2019, *Wall Street Journal* article was titled "Navy, Industry Partners Are 'Under Cyber Siege' by Chinese Hackers, Review Asserts," written by Gordon Lubold and Dustin Volz: https://www.wsj.com/articles/navy-industry-partners-are-under-cyber-siege-review-asserts-11552415553.

The *Washington Post* reported on March 13, 2019, on former White House adviser Gary Cohn's criticism over the president's approach to the China trade talks: https://www.washingtonpost.com/business/economy/gary-cohn-says-trump-is-desperate-for-trade-deal-with-china/2019/03/13/56af2396-45c9-11e9-8aab-95b8d80a1e4f_story.html?utm_term=.7b18f345fb77. David J. Lynch, "Gary Cohn Says Trump Is 'Desperate' for Trade Deal with China."

Bloomberg reported on the state of the US-China talks on March 14, 2019, saying a possible Trump-Xi summit had been pushed back: https://www.bloomberg.com/news/articles/2019-03-14/china-u-s-said-to-push-back-trump-xi-meeting-to-at-least-april. Jenny Leonard, Jennifer Jacobs, and Jeff Black, "China and US to Push Back Trump-Xi Meeting to at Least April."

Inside Cybersecurity reported on Senator Mark Warner's Council on Foreign Relations speech in a June 18, 2019, article: https://insidecybersecurity.com/daily-news/warner-stresses-long-term-huawei-risks-part-intensifying-challenge-china. Charlie Mitchell, "Warner Stresses Long-Term Huawai Risks as Part of Intensifying Challenge from China."

The *Times of London* report on US intelligence officials making "the most serious claim" so far linking Huawei to Chinese intelligence is available here: https://www.thetimes.co.uk/edition/news/cia-warning-over-huawei-rz6xc8kzk. Lucy Fisher, "CIA Warning over Huawei," April 20, 2019.

The *Washington Post* March 27, 2019, article on the United Kingdom report on Huawei cyber risks is available here: https://www.washingtonpost.com/world/national-security/britains-spy-agency-delivers-a-scathing-assessment-of-the-security-risks-posed-by-huawei-to-the-countrys-telecom-networks/2019/03/27/ab16d7d2-50fd-11e9-8d28-f5149e5a2fda_story.html?utm_term=.209c79513ffb. Ellen Nakashima, "British Spy Agency Delivers Scathing Assessment of Security Risks Posed by Huawei to UK Telecom Networks."

A CNN report on Huawei's profitability is available here: https://www.cnn.com/2019/03/28/tech/huawei-earnings-china/index.html. Sherisse Pham, "Huawei's Profits Jump by 25% Despite US Efforts to Curtail Its Business," March 29, 2019.

The Justice Department's 2019 indictment related to the Anthem breach can be accessed here: https://www.justice.gov/opa/press-release/file/1161466/download?utm_medium=email&utm_source=govdelivery.

Chapter 11

The relationship between House Intelligence Committee leaders Devin Nunes and Adam Schiff is discussed in *Hacked: The Inside Story of America's Struggle to Secure Cyberspace*, published in 2016 by Rowman & Littlefield.

The Huffington Post provided a detailed account of Nunes's controversial White House visit here: https://www.huffingtonpost.com/entry/nunes-trump-surveillance-white-house-credible_us_58dbd216e4b05463706418e9. Sam Stein and Jessica Shulberg, "Devin Nunes' Story about His White House Grounds Visit Simply Isn't Credible," March 30, 2017.

Reporting by Inside Cybersecurity's Rick Weber on the House Intelligence Committee Russia report is available here: https://insidecybersecurity.com/daily-news/house-intelligence-committee-report-russian-hacking-calls-states-adopt-nist-standards. "House Intelligence Committee Report on Russian Hacking Call for States to Adopt NIST Standards," April 27, 2018.

Nunes's Twitter lawsuit can be seen here: https://www.scribd.com/document/402297422/Nunes-Complaint-3-18-19.

Senate Intelligence Committee–generated reports on the Russia affair: https://www.intelligence.senate.gov/publications/reports.

The January 25, 2019, Reuters report on Russia cyberattacks targeting Ukraine is available here: https://www.reuters.com/article/us-ukraine-cyber-exclusive/exclusive-ukraine-says-it-sees-surge-in-cyber-attacks-targeting-election-idUSKCN1PJ1KX. Pavel Polityuk, "Exclusive: Ukraine Says It Sees Surge in Cyber Attacks Targeting Election."

The *Washington Post* report on reactions in Russia to the Mueller report is available here: https://www.washingtonpost.com/world/europe/russia-joins-trump-in-post-mueller-report-victory-lap/2019/03/25/7a5bc442-4e76-11e9-bdb7-44f948cc0605_story.html?utm_term=.636bb04edb45. Anton Troianovski, "Russia Joins Trump in Post-Mueller Report Victory Lap," March 25, 2019.

Susan Glasser's *New Yorker* piece on Mueller report fallout is available here: https://www.newyorker.com/news/letter-from-trumps-washington/trump-wins-the-president-the-mueller-report-and-our-new-political-normal?utm_source=twitter&utm_brand=tny&mbid=social_twitter&utm_social-type=owned&utm_medium=social. "'Trump Wins!' The President, the Mueller Report, and Our New Political Normal," March 24, 2019.

The *USA Today* op-ed by Cindy Otis is available here: https://www.usatoday.com/story/opinion/2019/03/27/mueller-fallout-trump-should-focus-russian-aggression-not-himself-column/3277738002/. "Mueller Fallout: Trump Should Focus on Russian Aggression, Not His Supposed 'Exoneration,'" March 27, 2019.

The Daily Beast article on Representative Schiff seeking details on the FBI counterintelligence probe is available here: https://www.thedailybeast.com/schiff-wants-to-know-if-fbi-has-continued-counterintelligence-inquiry-into-trumpworld-over-russia.

Sam Brodey and Spencer Ackerman, "Schiff Wants to Know If FBI Has Continued Counterintelligence Inquiry into Trumpworld over Russia," March 27, 2019.

A CNN report on the bipartisan request from the House Intelligence Committee for more materials from the Mueller probe is available here: https://www.wral.com/house-intelligence-panel-requests-mueller-briefing-counterintelligence-materials/18327737/. Jeremy Herb, "House Intelligence Panel Requests Mueller Briefing, Counterintelligence Materials," April 15, 2019.

Here is a link to the redacted Mueller report: https://apps.npr.org/documents/document.html?id=5955997-Muellerreport. Politico's story on Kellyanne Conway demanding Schiff resign is available here: https://www.politico.com/story/2019/03/25/kellyanne-conway-adam-schiff-resign-1234370. Kyle Cheney, Sarah Ferris, and John Bresnahan, "Democrats Rally behind Schiff Amid Withering GOP Assault," March 25, 2019.

The Atlantic's insightful July 25 article on optics trumping substance at the Mueller hearings can be found here: https://www.theatlantic.com/politics/archive/2019/07/mueller-testimony-congress-optics/594676/?utm_source=newsletter&utm_medium=email&utm_campaign=politics-daily-newsletter&utm_content=20190725&silverid-ref=MzEwMTkxNDgyNTMzS0. Todd S. Purdum, "Robert Mueller and the Tyranny of 'Optics.'"

The Senate Intelligence Committee July 2019 election-security report can be accessed here: https://www.intelligence.senate.gov/sites/default/files/documents/Report_Volume1.pdf.

Chapter 12

Kiersten Todt, Anne Beauchesne, Mike Echols, Vikram Phatak, and John Carlin discussed the cyber landscape in exclusive interviews with me in 2018 and 2019.

The article in *Wired* on the "NotPetya" attack is available here: https://www.wired.com/story/notpetya-cyberattack-ukraine-russia-code-crashed

-the-world/. Andy Greenberg, "The Untold Story of NotPetya, the Most Devastating Cyberattack in History," August 22, 2018.

A collection of all of President Trump's tweets is available here: http://www.trumptwitterarchive.com/.

James Lewis of the Center for Strategic and International Studies discussed deterrence policy on a panel at the RSA Security Conference on March 6, 2019.

President Trump's executive order on the cyber workforce can be accessed here: https://www.whitehouse.gov/presidential-actions/executive-order-americas-cybersecurity-workforce/.

The report by the Obama-appointed Commission on Enhancing National Cybersecurity can be accessed here: https://insidecybersecurity.com/document/report-presidential-commission-enhancing-national-cybersecurity.

Index

About the Author

Charlie Mitchell is the author of *Hacked: The Inside Story of America's Struggle to Secure Cyberspace*, published in 2016 by Rowman & Littlefield. *Hacked* examines the emergence of cybersecurity as one of the nation's most pressing challenges during the Obama presidency and how security pros, politicians, industry, privacy advocates, and other stakeholders fought over and fashioned first-time cyber laws and policies.

Mitchell is the editor of Inside Cybersecurity, a premium news service he cofounded at Inside Washington Publishers to cover the cybersecurity community and the political and policy challenges of securing cyberspace.

A veteran journalist, Mitchell previously served as editor in chief of the Capitol Hill newspaper *Roll Call* and as a senior editor and writer at *National Journal's Congress Daily*, services widely respected for probing, nonpartisan coverage of Congress. He wrote a cybersecurity column for the *Washington Examiner*, a Washington, DC–based political column for the *Carroll Daily Times Herald* family of Iowa newspapers, and is a regular speaker on the conference and webcast circuit.